STARLOST
Unauthorized
And the Quest
for Canadian
Identity

By

D.G. Valdron

FOSSIL COVE PRESS

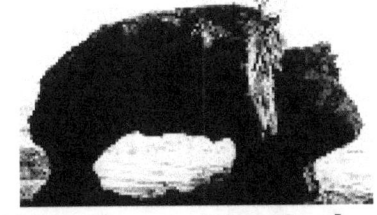

Winnipeg, Manitoba

DEDICATION

My gratitude and thanks to you, my Patrons
on the Starlost Unauthorized Kickstarter
project, who believed in this book.

WARREN FREY

KAT MARTENS

JARED VALDRON

NORMAN JAFFE

PAUL STOCKTON

ANGUS KOHM

ANNA VALDRON

DEEJAY DAYTON

JON JORDAN

FAIR WARNING

The nature of a book like this, divided into
different parts, is that there will be a
certain amount of redundancy and
overlap between sections.
Just letting you know.
No big deal. Don't sweat it.

While the different sections are organized,
the chapters can be read in any order.
Feel free to dive in wherever
it catches your interest,
even ignore what doesn't.

Finally

Thank you for your support

STARLOST Unauthorized
And the Quest for Canadian Identity
By D.G. Valdron

Fossil Cove Publishing, 1301 - 90 Garry Street, Wpg, Man, Can, R3C 4J4
www.denvaldron.com

EBook - ISBN: 978-1-998453 -03-0
IngramSpark Print edition - ISBN: 978-1-998453-17-7

Specific quotations from William Davidson, Ed Richardson, John Colicos and Norman Klenman taken from Science Fiction Television Series: Episode Guides, Histories, and Casts and Credits for 62 Prime-Time Shows, 1959 through 1989 © 2006 [1996] Mark Phillips and Frank Garcia by permission of McFarland & Company, Inc., Box 611, Jefferson NC 28640, pages 382-382 and 387-390. www.mcfarlandbooks.com

Additional specific quotations from interviews with Ben Bova and Gay Rowan, reproduced with permission from Bruce Callow and Peter Kenter.

Quotations from Starlost Series Bible, by Harlan Ellison and Ben Bova, April 10, 1973.

Cover image – NASA, Hubble Telescope

Text set in Garamond

STARLOST Unauthorized
Table of Contents

INTRODUCTION

STARLOST AND FOUND

One night, a few years ago...

I watched a cheesy robot preside over a debate to the death about the future of Canada between a Star Trek guy and the astronaut from 2001: A Space Odyssey.

It wasn't a drug-addled hallucination, or some bizarre comedy sketch. It wasn't even Mystery Science Theatre 3000. It turned out to be an episode of the notorious flop sci-fi series, the Starlost.

It wasn't about the future of Canada, not explicitly. The series was set on a giant space ark carrying the last remains of humanity, drifting out of control and on a collision course with a sun. Walter Koenig, Chekov of Star Trek, was playing an alien named Oro, and he was making an offer our heroes couldn't refuse. Oro was promising to save the Ark, as long as he could park it in orbit around his planet Exar, because they wanted to harvest the wealth of its vast resources. In return for becoming a satellite and its people losing their freedom and identity, the Ark and its inhabitants would be guaranteed safety and security.

Keir Dullea, the astronaut, David Bowman, in Stanley Kubrick's 2001: A Space Odyssey, was Devon, an escapee from a 19th century habitat on a quest to save the ship. He wanted to take a chance with freedom and have the people of the Ark pursue their own course, seek their own destiny, and solve their own problems. Even if that meant taking a risk. He didn't want his world to become a satellite to be plundered by a greedy neighbor.

So, among threadbare sets, with chromakey effects, the fate of humanity would be decided in a debate judged by a crude robot, with the loser electrocuted,

I was stunned. I recognized those arguments, those words and phrases. I'd grown up with them. For anyone in Canada, if you grew up between 1965 and 1985, you recognized the language, the ideas, the issues in play. This was the great Canadian debate, the arguments over Canada's national identity, over our role in the world, our very future: To be a satellite of America, or chart our own destiny.

Here it was, the national dialogue, played out on a stage set centuries in the future, a hundred light years out in space, between an alien and a rustic, judged by a robot. I was stunned.

I had never watched The Starlost when it aired originally. That wasn't a matter of choice. It just didn't air where I was. But I did grow up with science fiction, captivated by stories with rockets on their covers, tales of exotic worlds and remarkable machines. I devoured magazines, read the books, watched whatever I could, and read about what I couldn't watch.

Eventually, I heard about Starlost; mostly bad things. Harlan Ellison's incendiary hatchet job gave it an infamous reputation. It was the great Canadian Star Trek, but instead of going boldly forth, it had fallen disastrously flat on its face to live on in infamy.

Oh well, that was the country we lived in. Canada was a nice place to grow up, but clearly nothing interesting or important happened here. Insignificance was our national vibe.

Still, I was vaguely curious. Curious to see the target of the Great and Powerful Harlan Ellison's invective. Curious to see the great Canadian space opera even if it was a dud. It rattled around in the back of my head for years.

When I finally found some episodes, I was up for watching it, if for no other reason than historical curiosity. I was surprised: The stories were interesting, the ideas more ambitious, the characters more appealing than I expected. The limitations were tolerable and of their era.

But the episode, the Return of Oro, was a revelation. Not only was it well done, but it was actually about something. It was about something that I'd never seen in a story, but had heard and witnessed much of my life. It was about us. Somehow, in the sea of American media, it spoke to me as a Canadian.

That lead me to take another look, to watch all of the episodes and to reassess what I was watching. I was intrigued to discover Canadian issues, Canadian perspectives and sensibilities. This wasn't the show we all thought it was.

Had the show really been a failure?

Or had it simply been something else? A show whose ideas and sensibilities were just slightly alien to an American audience. But a show that nevertheless reflected the issues and concerns of its society. That talked about things I'd grown up with, that were part of my own identity, but that I'd never seen in this form.

I thought that was fascinating and perhaps I can convince you.

So please, join me on this journey.

PART ONE- GOING DOWN THE ROAD

STARLOST TO CANADA

The Starlost: A group of regions, self-contained and oblivious to each other, yet bound together, hurtling aimlessly into the future, struggling to find themselves and come together, before they are swallowed up or fall into destruction.

We can't think of a better description of Canada in the 1970s.

And yet, this concept which described us so well, was founded elsewhere. Like so much in Canada, The Starlost didn't start out as a Canadian production. It's an immigrant we adopted. All the original businessmen and creatives, Robert Kline, Douglas Trumbull, Keir Dullea and Harlan Ellison, the people who put the show together, they were all Americans.

But somehow, shortly after birth, by March or April, 1973, Starlost became a Canadian production and all the big American names eventually went away, leaving it to a cast and crew of mainly Canadians.

Only Keir Dullea, the most Canadian of the Americans remained to star, joined on the cast by co-stars Gay Rowan, Robin Ward and regular William Osler.

The actual production of the series was in the hands of Canadians – William Davidson, Ed Richardson. Norman Klenman and a host mainly Canadian writers, directors, actors and crew.

These people, perhaps deliberately, perhaps incidentally, created a show that uniquely reflected Canadian sensibilities and values and spoke to Canadian issues.

The genesis of the show was rapid – in February, 1973, Robert Kline invited Harlan Ellison to pitch a television series. There was talk of shooting in England. Then suddenly it's in Canada, picked up by CTV's production arm, Glen Warren. According to Ellison, movie star Keir Dullea, and special effects wizard Doug Trumbull were attached shortly after. All before Ellison's even written the series bible on April 10, 1973.

In fact, because Hollywood was in a writer's strike at the time, Ellison wouldn't even work on the bible until he was guaranteed that it was a Canadian production, and therefore exempt from the strike.

We don't actually know how or why the project ends up in Canada with CTV. We know it happens very early on, sometime in March, a month or so after Ellison's original meeting. Perhaps CTV was simply on Kline's radar. Or CTV was actively looking for a project.

The most likely possibility that it ended up here because of the Writer's Strike in Hollywood.

According to Ben Bova, the series science consultant, interviewed by Peter Kenter for TV North, *"The series was being developed by 20th Century Fox when a writers strike hit Hollywood and the production was moved to Toronto."*

This is less conclusive than it sounds, Bova appears to have come into the project relatively late, through Harlan Ellison, and he wasn't privy to Robert Kline's or 20th Century Fox's decision making process.

But the timing is suggestive. The strike began on March 6, 1973, only a few weeks after Ellison had made his pitch to Kline. The key deals to put the package together with Dullea and Trumbull, as well as the syndication sales were all being struck literally on the threshold, or at the beginning, of the strike. It's likely that even in January and February, people were seeing the possibility of a strike and perhaps making contingencies. Once it was on, nothing was going to move in Hollywood, so they'd have to look elsewhere.

Despite the strike, a designated Canadian production would be under a different union and wouldn't be affected. Writers could still work, the production could still go ahead, and it could sell in the U.S. So it's possible Kline and others were already looking north. Or up in the north, CTV was already putting out feelers in the south.

The uncertainty and disruption produced by the strike may have made it attractive to syndicators and television markets. No matter how long the strike lasted, or how it turned out, or how it disrupted American programming, a Canadian syndicated program could be counted on to deliver its episodes on schedule.

Another possibility is that it was because of Keir Dullea. Although born in New Jersey, Dullea was an idiosyncratic actor who seemed reluctant to work in the Hollywood system. He did a lot of stage work and international work instead. In 1973 he was living in England, but he'd worked in Canada on The Fox, in 1967, and immediately prior to Starlost, had featured in the independent Canadian production, Paperback Hero from 1972.

After Starlost, he'd go on to appear in a number of Canadian productions, Black Christmas, the Haunting of Julia, and Welcome to Blood City. Dullea actually came to be so identified with Canadian film when I was young, that I was shocked to discover he was actually an American. So the theory is that it ended up in Canada because Dullea preferred to work here, instead of in the United States.

We've heard of stranger things. As a bankable movie star with 2001, A Space Odyssey on his resume, Dullea was probably the single big make or break for the project. Harlan Ellison was mainly a big name in science fiction. Doug Trumbull was a technician, but not on the public radar. Dullea was a star, and he was associated with the project literally from the beginning. Without him, there might not be a project. He could swing a lot of weight, if he wanted to. If he favoured Canada, that might have been a factor.

"Keir Dullea was intended as the lead from the beginning," Ben Bova remarked in the interview with Peter Kenter for TV North. Again, this should be taken carefully, but the implication is that Dullea's connection with the

project may precede Ellison's and he may have had a great deal of influence over the early production decisions.

It's tempting, for instance, to wonder if Dullea had any role in bringing special effects wizard, Doug Trumbull on board, given that both of them had worked together on 2001: A Space Odyssey.

There may have been any number of other reasons for producing in Canada. It was literally a short plane ride to either New York or Los Angeles, Proximity seemed to offer advantages in terms of access to studio executives, markets, technical crew, actors and writers. For the American backers to commit to Toronto, this may have been a factor.

Arthur Weinthal of CTV and Ted Delaney of CFTO-Glen Warren were involved as Kline's counterparts in Canada, and appear to have been central to making the deal. The Canadians may have been actively angling or searching for a deal on their own. Or they could have already been in Kline's rolodex waiting for a match.

The final possibility is that Canada was just cheap. William Davidson, the producer, appears to suggest that there might have been some kind of bidding or at least price negotiations. In an interview with Phillips and Garcia, Davidson noted *"CFTO / Glen Warren studios agreed to mount the production at a fraction of the budget estimates."*

There were Budget estimates at this early point? Apparently so.

Our most vocal source of information is Harlan Ellison, who might not be entirely reliable or fully informed about certain aspects. Most of the business arrangements would have been opaque to him. But this all suggests that the business plan came together quickly. A lot of the pieces may have already been in place, or ready to come together before Ellison walked into Kline's office.

But there was one thing that neither Harlan Ellison nor Robert Kline anticipated, something unknown to Doug Trumbull and Howard Zeitman, to Ben Bova, or to Preston Fischer or the other Americans involved.

Canada was in the process of building its identity.

Robert Kline and Harlan Ellison, to their respective shock and dismay, found Starlost was going to be subject to Canadian Content requirements imposed by the government.

Ellison claimed it was 98%. He exaggerates, but it was there. To be a Canadian production, to avoid the strike, the show would require a majority of Canadian actors, writers and directors. It's likely that this wasn't something planned for, or even anticipated, but there it was.

Ellison records it only as yet another example of Robert Kline's endless treachery and perfidy. From Ellison's point of view, its Kline calling up and going *"Whoops! Change of plans. We're in Canada. No explanations!"* And then *"Whoops again!"* and then *"One more time!"*

All these were restrictions and conditions that Ellison didn't understand and didn't care about. From his point of view it was all clearly a conspiracy of Robert Kline, the Canadian Government, and literally everyone else, to screw Harlan Ellison over in the most sleazy, underhanded way possible.

But the truth is that no one involved in the project, except perhaps Keir Dullea himself, saw it coming. They were all Americans, with the typical American self-absorption. Canada was just a place to move a production. It might have been as simple as getting around a strike.

They probably didn't understand what they were getting into: A country in the throes of self-definition; uncertain, aggressive, questing. Both raw and oddly pugnacious

It may have come as a bit of a shock.

THE GREAT CANADIAN IDENTITY CRISIS

"The thing that really surprised me was that whenever I was called up for a problem there was a great deal of national chauvinism on the set. I was a 'Yankee.' For the first time in my life, I heard phrases like 'the flea knows how to live with the elephant.'"

Ben Bova, quoted from the book TV North.

Bova was the Scientific Consultant on Starlost, brought in by Harlan Ellison. He was also, one of the premiere science fiction writers of the era, and during this time, the Editor of Analog magazine, the foremost hard science fiction magazine.

Canada must have been a strange experience for Bova, akin to a story from Bradbury's Martian Chronicles. He'd come to Canada, was surrounded by people who looked and sounded just like Americans and acted like Americans. He could step out doors and find himself in a city indistinguishable from any other American city. By any metric, it was just... America.

And yet it wasn't.

For all the familiarity, he might as well have been among Bradbury's Martians. Despite being identical to Americans, they weren't, they had attitude, this weird chip on their shoulders. For every bit of familiarity, there was something alien beneath it all. They thought different, acted different, spoke different, had different preoccupations.

Canadians were like Bradbury's Martians, on the surface they were normal and completely familiar, but somewhere beneath, they were unpredictably alien.

Let's back up a bit, because we need to explain how and why the Canadian government was suddenly imposing all these restrictions, and why Canadians were so suddenly up in arms, in ways that were entirely inscrutable to the American cousins.

There's some history here.

What makes Canada unique is that it gradually evolved into nationhood. There arguably isn't one single defining moment that established Canada as a country – there was no Revolutionary War or Civil War. There was no specific point where we were one thing, and then after that, we were something else.

Canada started out a series of British colonies strung out along the American border. Following the American Civil War these unified into the Dominion of Canada in 1867. But even then, it was almost more an administrative arrangement than some profound transformation.

Canada remained largely a confederation of regions, still more a series of colonies than a nation. The individual provinces all largely went their own ways often interacting with Britain or the U.S. more than with each other, or in the case of Quebec, drifting along in splendid isolation.

There were nation building events – the Red River and Northwest Rebellions, projects like the National Railway. But for a lot of that early history, Canada wasn't so much a country as a subdivision of the British Empire, and that was how Canadians saw themselves.

Canada didn't even have a navy until 1910. In 1914, when Britain declared war on Germany, that meant Canada was automatically at war with Germany. It didn't occur to anyone that Canadians as a whole would have an opinion or a right to an opinion on that decision. Britain declared, and we were automatically in. As it turns out, people had pretty strong opinions both ways.

It wasn't until 1939 that Canada had evolved to the point that it made its own declaration of war on Germany, symbolically asserting its identity.

Events like the Great Depression, World War II, the militarisation and rapid industrialization that came with and followed the war and the nascent Cold War of the 1950s, these were all shared national experiences which pushed Canada's drift from being a subdivision of the British Empire to being its own nation.

But alongside this emerging separation from Britain, another dominating presence was challenging the idea of a Canadian nation: America.

The reasons were obvious. Canada looks big on a map, but for all practical purposes, Canada is a ribbon a couple of hundred miles thick, spreading for three thousand six hundred miles along the American border. Strung out like that, it's hard to really develop a cohesive identity, Canadian cities are a string of pearls from east to west. Away from Toronto and southern Ontario, even the idea of Canada having a center was hotly contested.

Against that there is this huge country to the south, with ten times the population, much more unified and centralized, exerting immense gravity. Simple geography has its own force.

I grew up in New Brunswick, Canada. I visited Maine long before I ever saw Toronto or Vancouver. For a populace strung out along the border, that's probably the experience for the majority of Canadians.

That American presence, and trying to cope with it, had always been part of Canada's reasons for existing. It was a major motivating force for Confederation in 1867. It had driven the national railroad project through the 19th century. In 1929, concerns about American influence and domination of emerging radio lead to the creation of the Canadian Broadcasting Corporation. The existence and the gravity exerted by the United States always meant that Canada had to build national institutions to counter it.

But again and again, there's no one moment that redefines the landscape for us. There's no single moment in our history where we go *"Before this, we are something else, after this, we are Canadian."*

It's just a series of milestones. Yes, Confederation was in 1867. But the British North America act wasn't repatriated until 1982. Canadians didn't officially take legal control of their Constitution, until a hundred and fifteen years later.

The Canadian cultural journey is similar, there's not truly a defining moment where we go from one to the other. There's no clear signpost to mark the emergence of a national identity.

There were definitely regional cultures all across Canada, from the century's old Atlantic with its deep rooted communities and sailing traditions, to French Quebec with its English aristocracy, to the old empire loyalist in Ontario, and the freshly settled prairies brimming with new immigrants. There were regional songs, stories, writers and politics, and from that, some national sensibility began to slowly form.

Canada was far from united. French Canada, particularly Quebec, was in a unique situation, having existed for centuries before Confederation, with its own language, its own culture and identity, with a unique nationalism and distinctiveness that would support both vibrant cultural industries and a movement towards political autonomy and even independence.

In the 1960s, Quebec had spawned the FLQ, its own terrorist movement seeking independence. This eventually culminated in the October crisis of 1970. In 1976, the separatist Parti Quebecois won the Provincial election. Literally alone in the western world, Canada was dealing with an actual separatist movement that wanted to break up the country.

Ontario, the largest, richest and most industrialized province was the center of Confederation. But nobody liked Ontario. Out west, British Colombia stood behind the Rockies, apart from the rest of Canada. On the prairies, Alberta, perennially frustrated with central Canada, suddenly rich with oil wealth found more in common with Texas than Ontario. In the 1970s Alberta launched an economic war and literally an oil blockade against the Federal government and central Canada. The Maritimes had their own distinctive history and traditions, while Newfoundland had only joined Confederation a couple of decades earlier. Canadians couldn't seem to get along with each other.

All of which meant that Canadians stumbled into the 1960s and 1970s with a certain amount of ambiguity. An identity of sorts had emerged or was emerging in English Canada, but it was a tentative and uncertain one. It was time to start figuring out who we were.

The 1960s were a tumultuous time for everyone – the West was in the throes of the baby boom. Youth movements were shaking the world. The US had its Vietnam War and Civil Rights movement. China had its cultural revolution. The old Colonial Empires fell apart and new nations were sprouting all over Africa and Asia.

Canada was caught up in these new waves of change. Canada in the 60s had undergone a demographic shift, with population and political and cultural centers of gravity moving from towns and rural areas to cities and urban regions. The baby boom was flowering. The post-World War II industrialization and economic boom was in full swing. New national institutions were forming, from a national highway system, to agricultural monopoly boards, to national commitments to health care and education.

The youth movement was revolting against the old order. Feminism was in, racism was out and a cultural rebellion threatened to overturn art and politics.

Outside of Quebec, economic, demographic and institutional shifts challenged regionalism, and fostered a more national outlook. Canadians struggled with being two nations, and struggled with the tensions between regionalism and centralisation.

During this period, one of the greatest challenges to a national identity, was the presence the United States. This was probably inevitable. Having an American border was literally the one thing that almost every Canadian province had in common. English Canada and the United States spoke the same language and shared history, values and fashions.

The United States was the biggest customer for Canadian products, and biggest seller in the Canadian market. America poured across the borders in every possible way. The Americans came north to buy everything from cottages, to farmland to factories.

American television, American movies, American music, American money and American pollution all flooded over the border like an unending tidal wave. American television constituted 90% of the prime time television watched. American movies featured in 99% of Canadian movie theatres.

For many Canadians seeking their fortune, America beckoned. It was the place to go to make a living or find success, and in turn, that meant a brain drain, a flow of talent and ability south.

And for many Canadians who remained at home, this overwhelming American presence, economic, cultural and political, posed a challenge. Who were we? Were we a real country? Or had we just traded the experience of being a British Colony for being an American colony? Did we have our own destiny? Or were we doomed to be a satellite in eternal orbit around the United States?

Despite this, although Canada was next to the United States, its experiences were not identical. Like America, we had our youth movement. But we weren't in the Vietnam War, instead we sat it out, observing from the periphery and hosting draft dodgers.

Along with sitting out the Vietnam War, came an effort to stake out a different foreign policy based on international cooperation and consensus and an effort to avoid or undermine the Cold War and cold warrior sensibility.

Lester B. Pearson, as a diplomat in the 1950s, had pioneered international peacekeeping and multilateralism as an alternative to the standoff between the US and USSR. In the 1960s he became Prime Minister in a series of minority governments, trying to lead the way forward. Pearson moved leftward and struggled to promote a national identity and a centrist foreign policy as Canada celebrated its centennial.

Despite proximity, American issues were sometimes alien to Canadian sensibilities. The US had segregation, Jim Crow and lynching, none of which had been substantial elements in Canada, and now faced the backlash of the Civil Rights movement. This was something observed from the sidelines while we ignored the indigenous skeletons in our own closet.

Instead, there were unique concerns created by proximity. Pollution was a common issue, for instance. But the US was far more industrialized, so for Canadians, a major issue with pollution related to it crossing the shared border, filling the air with smog, poisoning waterways, and producing acid rain.

American money flooded into Canada buying land and businesses. American businesses competed in Canada with the advantage of economies of scale, establishing branch plants and excluding Canadians from management. Canadians wondered if they would be second class citizens in their own country.

Beginning in the 1960s and 1970s, Canadians began to ask these questions and began to struggle with these issues. The question: We're not Americans, so who are we?

Sometimes that answer was simply 'We're not Americans!' That can be seen as Anti-Americanism, this defiance, this insistence on taking a negative identity. It reflected a feeling of being threatened and assaulted by America, we were defined by it. It's not that Americans were or are actively the enemy, they're not stealing or deliberately suppressing Canadian culture. But they're so large and loud, that trying to establish who we are often involves the struggle of saying 'we aren't you!'

Which leads to people befuddling Ben Bova with inscrutable talk about 'fleas in bed with elephants.' We're sure he must have thought it was insane, all these people, utterly indistinguishable from the folks back home, with these gigantic chips on their shoulders.

That's what Kline and Ellison and all the rest were stepping into, an emerging pugnaciousness in the face of the monolith, and a determination to find ourselves.

DEFINING A NATIONAL CULTURE

Against these two poles - massive internal divisions and the awesome gravity of a giant neighbor, Canadians were forced to ask who they were and what they stood for?

Did they have a future? And if so, what did that mean? Was there value in a united Canada? How centralized should it be?

Was there room for an independent Canada that made its own decisions and followed its own path? Or were all its decisions going to be made south of the border?

Who are we? And what do we want? This was the great national debate of the late 1960s and early 1970s. It was the great national identity crisis.

These were not questions that Americans asked themselves. They had different issues. They weren't going to be anyone's colony, they'd ditched that long ago. But they confronted their own internal divisions within their society, between right and left, rich and poor, black and white, men and women. Internationally, they confronted the Soviet Union in the Cold War. But the one thing Americans didn't need to ask was who they were.

The questions and concerns that occupied Canadians and Americans were very different.

What Canadians had instead was a unique period of national soul searching, of debate and dialogue. This was a genuine debate. We all read about it in the newspapers and magazines of the day, it was discussed on television on news and current affairs shows. People talked about it in high school and university classes, in sidewalk cafes and at cocktail parties. The debate filtered across the country, through different regions, in big cities and small towns, and the practicalities of daily existence.

There was an immediacy to it, foreign investment and foreign ownership mattered for jobs and business decisions, it affected promotions and career paths. Foreigners buying land or businesses affected communities. Foreign pollution poisoned our waters and forests.

Beyond the impact of America, the question of identity persisted. Balances between regions and local aspirations warred with national concerns. Issues of language were real and visceral and played out on bilingual Corn Flakes boxes at the breakfast table. Identity was a discussion that permeated all levels of Canadian society, in one way or another.

This was the era when people like Mel Hurtig or Gordon White became powerful advocates for a national outlook, part of this search for identity. Margaret Atwood pondered whether Canada could be said to have a distinctive literature. There were opposing sides as to what the country should even look like. Quebec nationalists, or Alberta malcontents, Maritimers and Indigenous people were all struggling to be heard.

It was a dialogue going on throughout the country, and particularly in arts and literature.

In 1972, Margaret Atwood published 'Survival: A Thematic Survey of Canadian Literature.' A semi-academic, popular analysis that was practically a manifesto.

Atwood argued that every country had their national narrative – the Americans had their frontier, the British their identity as an Island and so forth. For Canada, she claimed, our national narrative, our identity, was survivors.

According to Atwood, we lived in a country that was so vast and implacable, it could never really be conquered or tamed, not the way the Americans had tamed their frontier. The best we could do was inhabit it, coexisting with it. But it was a harsh landscape, our positions were precarious, so our literature, our heroes and victims, our stories, were really about hanging on, enduring and surviving.

There's something to that. If you look at Canadian history: Whether it's the Acadians being expelled and digging in, the Quebecois learning to live under conquest, the Newfoundlanders huddling on their barren shores in fishing Outports, the Empire Loyalists kicked out of the revolutionary thirteen colonies and resettling in the dregs of British North America, Icelanders forced to relocate by a volcano, First Nations fleeing the Indian Wars in the south, Metis displaced by Settlers, Eastern Europeans leaving famine and tyranny for western Canada, it's all about people getting kicked around and hanging on despite it all, enduring and surviving.

We're not bold settlers conquering and taming the wilderness. We're survivors, dispossessed, refugees and castaways, battered enduring a harsh world and holding on. It's not about winning, but one way or the other, getting through it so that we're still standing.

There are things that come with that. A sense of fragility. When you have to endure forty degree below zero winters, or evacuate from forest fires, or lose an entire village's fishing fleet, you come to understand how very willing nature is to kill you and yours, and how delicate and vulnerable existence can be.

There's a different sense of community, again when nature is so very willing to kill you, and what may keep you alive are your neighbors, even if you don't like each other.

There is less certainty, more ambiguity. The qualities that lead to heroism are also the qualities that lead to blundering off a cliff. You may not survive or recover from a bad choice, so make choices carefully. A more uncertain world produces more ambiguity.

In America, a gunfighter is a hero or a villain, in Canada, he's a fool with pretensions, likely to get someone, including himself, killed. A hero is regarded with caution rather than worship, he's someone that can get other people killed.

A sense of fragility feeds a concern with things like pollution and clearcutting, damaging the environment, intruders and foreign ownership. The environment provides, but when it's damaged, that damage doesn't go away. We may need those trees we're cutting down and shipping off. We have to drink the water those factories discharge into.

Atwood's book, aimed at a general rather than academic audience, was extremely influential in 1972, only a year before Starlost, and it was read and discussed widely. The book and its ideas have remained in circulation ever since. Atwood's ideas would have been fresh and influential, in first bloom, when the show was being produced.

She wasn't alone with these ideas. Canadian academics Northrop Frye and D.F. Jones wrote about similar themes in 1970 and 1971. So definitely, these notions were floating around then, and continue to float around today.

Admittedly, there are criticism of these ideas, even rebuttals. It is literature, you're always going to get arguments. But academic debates aside, this was a book and these were ideas that were being widely read and discussed in Canada, particularly in the arts and entertainment communities that included Starlost's creative and production staff. The fact that they were part of national discussions meant inevitably that these ideas and sensibilities would find their way into cultural productions now and then.

The debate about identity stretched out in every direction from literature to politics and beyond. It was a discussion that would pervade anyone actually living here. Anyone working in the arts, particularly anyone working in Canada in film or television production, was literally at ground zero for the national discussion.

There were real consequences to this. Again, we'll repeat that this wasn't just an abstract discussion. It affected people's lives, and significantly, there were efforts to actually do something, to put these ideas and impulses into practice.

There was a concerted attempt at Provincial and Federal levels, not just to find that Canadian identity, but to build it.

Canada established a principle of universal levels of social services, the poor provinces and regions would not be left behind in health care or education. Bilingualism and the respect for two languages and identities became a national policy. Infrastructure was constructed all across the country. All in the service of nation building, and a sense that being a Canadian had to mean something.

On the economic front, there was a concerted effort to develop a national economic policy and to create national economic institutions; such as Petro-Canada, which was both a national oil company and a public brand. There was an effort establish international trading relationships with other countries besides America. The Foreign Investment Review Agency was established to ensure that the nation's assets and businesses would be guarded and not be sold away completely to foreigners (Americans).

On the cultural front, there was an aggressive push for Canadian content, as the Federal government looked for ways to encourage homegrown film and television production.

This took the form of tax credits or direct funding for Canadian productions, and the establishment of criteria to determine whether or how much Canadian content was in a production. It wasn't just enough to shoot in Canada, or to have Canadian extras or grips, they were looking for Canadian writers, Canadian Directors, people in creative or management positions.

Organizations like Canada Council for the Arts, Telefilm and the Canadian Film and Television Fund emerged to support local television, film and publishing. The intention was to not just support cultural activities, but to create cultural industries. There were attempts to restrict foreign content, attempts to promote Canadian production instead.

As they debated the nature of their identities and the future of their country, Canadians were also struggling to build that identity.

CREATING A CULTURAL INDUSTRY

The reality was that American culture was sweeping across the border in a tidal wave. It was simple geography and population.

At ten times the population, and centralized in New York and Los Angeles, American film and television, books and magazines could achieve massive economies of scale. Basically there was almost no extra cost to sell into the Canadian market. By the time it got here, it was all paid for and cheap to buy.

On the other hand, because of geography, Canada was broken up into a string of regions, so our economies of scale were local and very bad, and it was difficult and expensive to even market across our regions. It was easier for a Nova Scotia publisher in the east to sell to New England, than it was for them to sell books to Alberta in the west.

So all the films in movie theatres were American, all the prime-time television, the books in the bookstores, the magazines on the racks... all American or nearly so.

There were Canadian films, magazines, books, television shows but they were mostly forced into obscure corners, operating on the margins, or simply drowned out. Occasional flashes in the pan.

To offer an example, in 1973, the year Starlost was produced, there were over eighty movies released from Hollywood, and only three from Canada. Box office revenues were even more lopsided with Canadian film relegated to a fraction of a per cent.

There were Canadian writers, artists, film makers, actors... and to make a living, many or most of them had to go down to the United States where they told American stories to Americans.

So in the 1960s, when the question was what our identity was going to be... Maybe the answer was, that there wasn't?

To be fair, this issue had been around for a while: The CBC had been created back in 1929, and the National Film Board in 1939. So obviously, there was concern even then. But the sheer volume of the cultural tidal wave wasn't nearly as great, nor was concern so deep in those early days.

But in the 1960s, this American tidal wave, accelerated by television and consolidation, induced something like a national panic. We needed to get an Identity, and quick, or we wouldn't have one at all! We needed to do something!

The result was a flurry of initiatives and actions to build or support institutions of culture. A lot of things started to happen very quickly.

The Canada Council for the Arts was established in 1958, to support Canadian creators. This was followed in 1963 by the Ontario Arts Council, and through the rest of the 1960s, literally every other Province established its own arts funding body.

Legislation was introduced in 1961, which allowed for the establishment of CTV, a second, privately owned Canadian television network alongside the CBC. Over the next decade it slowly took form.

1967 saw the Montreal Expo, a national showcase, and the establishment of the red maple leaf flag. After a hundred years, Canada was finally getting its own flag. That had to count for something?

For visual media, the Canadian Radio and Television Commission was only established in 1968, it only formally became the CRTC in 1976 when it was reworked. The Canadian Film Development Corporation, what would become Telefilm and the Canadian Film and Television Development Fund only dates to 1967, and it was barely doing anything the first few years.

It was incredibly difficult to get Canadian movies made, and typically, they were made with far less money than their American counterparts, and faced immense challenges in getting distribution in theatre or television. Most efforts sank without a trace.

As an example, of two thousand films broadcast out of CBC Toronto television station between 1967 and 1974, only two were Canadian. That's one tenth of a percent. The overwhelming majority were American, but you had better chances of seeing a British, Australian, Italian, French even a Swedish film on CBC in this period, than a Canadian film.

In 1968, Keir Dullea had come to Canada to star in The Fox. But despite being shot in Canada, the book it was adapted from, the script-writer, the director, the composer, the editor, literally everyone involved was American or British. It was the epitome of branch plant culture. It was only Canadian by virtue of being shot here.

The first notable English language Canadian film - Going Down the Road was from 1970. The next, Paperback Hero, starring Keir Dullea, was 1972. The Apprenticeship of Duddy Kravitz was 1974. There were films before then, sometimes simply shot in Canada by outsiders, sometimes home grown, but none of them had had a national impact.

We should acknowledge that Quebec, by virtue of a different language and historical tradition, had the opportunity to develop its own homegrown cultural industries. But English Canada, without any cultural or language barrier had no protection and faced the tidal wave head on.

It was in the 1970s that the Federal Government initiated tax credit schemes to encourage Canadian film and television. Basically tax credits amounted to backdoor funding, allowing private investors to get their money back by investing in film. This accompanied other forms of direct government investing such as subsidies and other incentives.

And of course, provinces like Ontario had their own incentive and support programs for film and television. The point was to make film and television production economically viable, even profitable, in Canada. But the challenge was that it had to actually be Canadian.

But if Federal and Provincial governments were looking for ways to pump money and support into cultural industries, these governments were also unwilling to stand by and simply allow an embryonic film and television industry to be immediately co-opted and colonized like so many other industries. Why put so much money and effort into building it, if the Americans were only going to buy it up, take it over, and leave us back where we started?

To guard against that, Canadian content rules were established in the late 60s and early 70s. To count as a 'Canadian film' at least one of the producers and two-thirds of the key creative personnel (actors, writers, directors) had to be Canadian, and at least 75% of production and post production had to take place in Canada. There were similar rules for television.

One effect of this was a frantic search for 'stealth Canadians.' There weren't a lot of Canadians in Canada working in the cultural field. But there were a lot of Canadians who had gone south to work in Hollywood who could be brought back or recruited in order to meet Canadian content requirements. They were often crucial to the critical mission of accessing the Canadian public funding and tax credits that were vital to production. Lorne Greene, William Shatner, John Colicos, Margot Kidder, as examples, were all Canadians who had found success south of the border.

This worked, sort of. By 1976, there were sixty Canadian films in production. By 1979, there were seventy Canadian films in production, compared to ninety-five from Hollywood. A lot of them were unwatchable, and funding and support models eventually shifted and continued to shift to encourage better quality productions.

But the point here is to illustrate the immense amount of money and effort to literally create an entire cultural industry from almost nothing, to go from three to seventy productions in barely six years. To illustrate the concerted effort ranging from Arts Councils, to funding bodies all across the country, to content requirements and tax breaks across the spectrum, all of it to create national cultural productions and institutions.

We've talked about movies. But on television, the situation was only a little better. Television was an insatiable maw for content, and in those days, local stations in Canada and the US produced some of their own material, often the cheap content to fill the off hours – sports were cheap, children's programming were cheap (then), local news and talk shows were cheap. This low-cost local fodder was most of Canadian television production.

The CBC had a mandate to produce, and tried to do a little more, but it was hard to find a niche in the midst of the avalanche of expensive programming from the south. Canadian drama productions were almost invariably targeted to youth – shows like Adventures in Rainbow Country, disparaged by Harlan Ellison, or The Littlest Hobo about a wandering german shepherd dog who solved crimes.

But Canadian television drama or prime time was all but nonexistent. Prime time was almost completely dominated by Hollywood.

As with film, there was a major push to create or incentivize Canadian production. The long running Canadian series, The Beachcombers only started the year before, in October 1972, and would go on to be an institution, running until 1990. Another iconic Canadian series, The King of Kensington wasn't until 1975. The Canadian comedy series, SCTV began in 1976.

The perception, voiced by Harlan Ellison, is that Starlost went up to Canada, and Canadians were very nice but didn't know what they were doing. There is an element of truth there. But that's the wrong way to look at it.

The reality was that Starlost was part of the ground zero of an explosion. Canadian film and television, Canadian production, an entire cultural industry, the nuts and bolts of an identity, these things were literally being built from almost nothing, being built from the ground up overnight.

One of these things they were trying to build from the ground up was an actual competitive television industry, one that would stand up to the tidal wave of product coming from America, and maybe even sell product to that market.

Which brings us to...

CTV AND GLEN WARREN PRODUCTIONS

In Canada, back in 1973, there were two television networks.

The first is the CBC (Canadian Broadcasting Corporation). Created originally as a national radio network, when television came a few decades later it simply branched out. It's loosely equivalent to the BBC in England.

The second was CTV, established in 1961, as a private television network formed from a patchwork of independent regional or local television stations across the country. In comparison with the American networks, it was a small shoestring operation. This was the Canadian equivalent of Britain's ITV, a private television network operating alongside the public Broadcasting Corporation.

CTV's flagship was the CFTO television station in Toronto. As the largest station in the largest market, it had the most developed studio and video production facilities.

Glen Warren Productions was a sister-corporation to CFTO and basically the production house for CFTO. For purposes of convenience, I'll treat Glen Warren and CTV as interchangeable, and just refer to CTV.

Television production is generally an expensive proposition, even a modest program requires a considerable outlay. And for private commercial stations, that production had to be supported by advertising revenues.

So limited advertising revenues meant limited money for production. Generally local stations opted for the cheapest in house production possible – children's shows, talk shows, sports and news. Or they bought pre-produced shows for much, much less than it would cost to produce themselves.

That's where syndication comes in. If you could sell a program to fifty local stations, you'd only need to charge them a relatively small amount, a fraction of the production costs each. But you could, with that money, mount an ambitious, expensive production, and still turn a profit. The problem is that even with syndication in Canada, it's still not a big market.

CTV as a network, had something of a catch 22. Even as a network of Canadian stations, it was dwarfed by the big American networks, NBC, ABC and CBS, and the big film studios like Paramount and Fox. Its internal advertising revenue, even across the country, was limited, so it was handicapped in its ability to produce content.

South of the border, American networks and studios had access to greater populations, more affiliates and therefore had deeper pockets. They could spend a lot more money to produce shows with much greater production values, and produce many more of them. That's hard to compete with.

CTV was also competing with the CBC, a government established national network, with deeper pockets. But even the CBC was overwhelmed by the sheer volume and production value of American programs spilling over the border.

The inevitable outcome was that a lot of the television shows and movies, particularly primetime, were being imported from the United States.

And in an era of Canadian Nationalism, CTV was running up against Canadian content requirements. The government wasn't going to support CTV with tax breaks or funding if all it did was run cheap but glossy American content. In the era of Canadian nationalism, something more was required. In order to remain competitive it had to generate programming, and it had to find a way to do that effectively, despite its lack of economies of scale.

One way to do this would be to try to syndicate programs into the American market. But to access this market, an American partner was required.

To CTV, Starlost must have seemed like a dream. A project partly/provisionally funded/distributed already by 20th Century Fox, a marketing plan ready to go, big names like Dullea, Trumbull and Ellison attached, one of whom was suddenly a big name in Canadian cinema, the closest thing we had to a Canadian movie star. It was practically a turnkey project. Of course, they would jump right in. All they had to do was produce and deliver.

Fundamentally, for CTV, it was just a business deal. But even so, it was a business deal which would take place in a country obsessed with the question of its own identity, aggressively struggling to build a nation.

This was literally the air they were breathing, the water they were swimming in. It was inevitable that some of this would permeate the Starlost.

CASTING CANADIAN CONTENT

In the end, only the star, Keir Dullea himself, remained as the series established itself in Canada.

He saw the departure of Trumbull, Ellison, Kline and Bova, It must have been strange to be the last man standing as the production turns around you.

Dullea's star power during this time derived mainly from Kubrick's 2001, A Space Odyssey. But we don't think he ever really bought into being a star. Our impression is that first and foremost he considered himself an 'actor.'

Intellectual and liberal, everyone who knew him at the time found him to be a gentle, thoughtful, careful professional. He was described as soft spoken, friendly, without attitude or arrogance.

Due to Canadian content requirements, the other two stars would have to be Canadian.

Gay Rowan was the next cast. Rowan, twenty-five at the time, had wanted to be an actress since she was nine years old.

"I was recommended and then had to audition by preparing 3 different scenes. They provided an actor for me to rehearse with. (Can't remember his name at the moment)," she told interviewer Bruce Callow.

"I had already been in films, Race Home to Die, and The Girl in Blue. They were both fun movies to do," Rowan recalled in another interview. *"I had to confess, I loved working as an actor. It was a pretty wonderful thing to be able to do. I felt very privileged."*

Playing Rachel, Devon's love interest, was sometimes a thankless task. Her character had grown up in a repressive society, and through the course of their adventures, Rachel often didn't have much to do.

Her most prominent roles in the Goddess Calabra and Children of Methuselah placed her character as an object of desire or maternal figure. Although Rachel was supposed to be in love with Devon, the two actors didn't seem to share a lot of chemistry, and Canadian prudishness kept any sign of romance to an absolute minimum.

"To be perfectly honest with you," Rowan told interviewer Bruce Callow, *"I was always agitating to do more, say more, be more dominant in the show but got accused of being "one of those woman libbers"! But I did grow up in the country myself so I had a sense of what it was like to grow up like that. I approached everything with a sense of wonder and adventure."*

This wasn't inevitable, there are many signs of a more competent, and more emotionally developed character in Rachel. But it wasn't followed up all that much. Rowan herself remembers pushing for better lines and more meat in her role.

Other cast and crew members concurred, and both William Davidson and Norman Klenman admitted this in interviews, trying to cover themselves by claiming that if the series had continued, her role would have expanded.

Rowan's acting career began in theatre, and spanned over a decade, from the early 1970s to 1984, before she left the trade and decided to do other things with her life. We have the sense that she may have ultimately found it frustrating.

Canada had initiated the Royal Commission on the Status of Women from 1967 to 1970, and the National Film Board had established Studio D for feminist film makers. But feminism was still unfolding slowly in both Canada and the United States.

There was a tendency in Starlost to make female characters sidekicks to the main guest star. Women were there to give the men someone to talk to: McBride to Farthing in Farthing's Comet, Trent to Mr. Smith, in Mr. Smith of Manchester, Teal to Garoway in Pisces, Tabor to Asgard in In Only Man is Vile.

Robin Ward would play Garth. The character wasn't part of Ellison's original concept. Originally, Ellison had written the lead with Walter Koenig in mind. When Keir Dullea was cast in the lead, Ellison felt the actor was 'wrapped in plastic' and inaccessible.

Ellison decided to create a sidekick character who would be an 'everyman,' a more practical, working class, down to Earth type to balance Dullea. Once again, Harlan Ellison had Walter Koenig in mind. Despite this, it doesn't feel like Ellison had a strong handle on the character.

The 'everyman' sidekick idea was eventually abandoned. Instead, when writing the series bible in April, 1973, Ellison shifted Garth's role, from 'everyman sidekick' to an 'Inspector Javert' from Les Miserables, a sort of duty-driven lawman,' who would be ceaselessly pursuing Devon and Rachel, always one step behind, always nipping at their heels.

Luckily, that was abandoned, and a more complex approach was taken to the character's deceptive simplicity, one that Robin Ward himself liked to describe as a *'Mennonite with a Crossbow.'*

As it turned out Garth proved the most difficult role to cast.

"Keir Dullea and Gay Rowan had already been cast and they had auditioned every actor in town for Garth except me. I think I was an afterthought. Of course their desperation to cast this role worked in my favour. I went in with my enormous hair and nothing to lose and nailed it." Ward recalls.

"I didn't exactly have a reputation as a budding Laurence Olivier in those days and many were appalled at my being cast. (Mainly disgruntled actors who had themselves auditioned for the role).

"I was unfamiliar with Gay Rowan at the time but was thrilled that I would be working with Keir, an actor I greatly admired."

Robin Ward brought rugged good looks and muscles to his role. Indeed, Ward looked like he could fold Dullea up like a lawn chair. By the usual standards of American television, he seemed more likely the hero and Dullea, the slender, intense loner, the sidekick.

"He had a great time," Gay Rowan remembers. *"He was the Lothario of the set. A lot of women found their way to his dressing room. He was quite a guy. He*

was like a big brother. He and Keir. They were wonderful. It gave me a sense of security knowing I had these guys at my back."

Twenty-nine years old at the time of Starlost, Ward came from an entertainment family. His sister had been one of the co-creators of the Beachcombers: "'Zorba on the beach,' was her flash of inspiration."

"I started as a member of a folk music group, the Allen-Ward trio. We made an album in New York on the Vanguard label and hung out with Joni Mitchell, Neil Young and Gordon Lightfoot. (we were the first to record a Lightfoot song even before he did)," Ward recalls.

As the sixties moved along, Ward shifted into acting, notable early roles were as Viktor Frankenstein in Frankenstein on Campus, and Prince Arthur Charming in Hey Cinderella!

After Starlost, "I eventually took a broadcasting job with the same 'Suits' that we had come to dislike so much, something I don't think Keir ever quite forgave me for. But a guy's got to live and it took years working onstage in regional theatres across the country before I was able to re-establish myself as an actor.

Following his role as Garth, Ward went on to have a long and eclectic career that took him across North America.

"In addition to the myriad TV shows over many years I've also acted on stages all over place. Including the U.S. and Mexico and many regional theatres in Canada performing in everything from musicals to Shakespeare to comedies to dramas. I've hosted cooking shows, game shows, panel shows and movie review shows and many more and have generally spread myself very thin over the years.

"It was fun, except when it wasn't," he notes.

William Osler was the overlooked cast member, a gray eminence, he supplied the opening monologue and played the image in the Sphere Projector – a role that basically involved sitting down and looking straight into the camera while blinking and intoning in a dry professional manner. He had a knack for giving a very restricted role a subtle sense of wit.

William Davidson, as reported by Phillips and Garcia in Science Fiction Television, commented, "William Osler was for many years one of the finest character actors on the Toronto scene. He worked for me many times."

Beyond these four, there was a long list of Canadian guest stars and supporting actors across the series. Most supporting parts were local, mainly due to 'low hanging fruit' syndrome, these were the people who were around. But the list also included some prominent Canadian guest stars like John Colicos, Lloyd Bochner, Donnelly Rhodes, and Percy Rodrigues, often expatriates who made their names in America, and likely were selected for Canadian content requirements.

THE NEW GUARD, THE CANADIAN CREW

Behind the scenes, as Americans departed, a new creative team took shape...

Heading up the project at CTV were a small handful of men. Gerry Rochon was listed as Executive Producer, but doesn't seem to have been directly involved in production. He was more a 'make the deal and authorize the budget' sort.

Arthur Weinthal from CTV and Ted Delaney of CFTO/Glen Warren were more involved in bringing the show to Canada, but don't seem to have been all that directly involved afterwards in any creative sense. For the ongoing production, they seemed mainly supportive, perhaps involved in money and scheduling.

Foremost among the actual key creatives was Executive Producer / Producer William Davidson, who made most of the major decisions on a day to day basis. Forty-five years old at the time of Starlost, Davidson was born in Toronto, Ontario. After studying at the University of Western Ontario and the Lorne Greene Academy of Radio Arts, he dabbled in theatre, radio and journalism before joining the National Film Board in 1948, working on documentaries.

Davidson moved to the Canadian Broadcasting Corporation in 1955. In 1957 he went independent, forming his own production company, working with Ontario Educational Television and. by 1973, for CTV. Like all artists who made their living in Canada, there wasn't enough work to really specialize, so he wrote, produced and directed, prolifically. Basically, in that environment you took whatever gig you could get.

Associate Producer, Edward Richardson, worked under William Davidson. He had been the senior production staff man at the CFTO-Glen Warren's video facility and was recruited to the project by Davidson. His internet movie database credits start with Starlost where he was Associate producer for the series and directed the original promo video and four episodes and the original promo video. His last listed credit was 1989.

Davidson and Richardson were the key production people on the CTV side.

Next up was Norman Klenman, the story consultant for the series. He's also credited with writing four episodes and conducting heavy uncredited rewrites of four more, making him directly responsible for half the series. In addition, he admits to minor rewrites on another four. From a story and arc point of view, Klenman's influence as a writer is huge.

Klenman had been born in Brandon, Manitoba, in 1923, and as a young man had knocked around the world for a bit, working as a journalist and sports reporter, doing radio plays for the CBC and children's television scripts for the BBC. In 1952 he was recruited by the National Film Board, and then moved on to the CBC. In 1964, Klenman moved to Hollywood to pursue a career as a free-lancer, working on various television series. Which was where he was when Davidson called.

Davidson and Klenman actually had prior history together. In 1958, they had partnered in Klenman-Davidson Productions Ltd., and produced two feature films: The Fast Ones, and Now That April's Here, based on Canadian literary writer Morley Callaghan's short stories.

Interestingly, after I'd written the original essay that eventually morphed into this book, it wound up with Norman Klenman and he looked me up. He was kind enough to chat with me, back in January 2010, offering these comments.

"I recall getting a call in Los Angeles to come help old friend Bill Davidson (producer), but felt it only right to check first with Harlan, whom I had heard of. Was met with a tirade. He was boiling.

"When I got to Toronto, I found Bill Davidson and his assistant Ed Richardson in a panic. Sked about to begin and they hadn't a script to shoot.

"Harlan had written the bible of Starlost and skedaddled. There was not a script completed nor even in halfway form. Not a trained writer anywhere nearby. Bill handed me the pilot that Harlan had pasted together, incomplete of course. Embarrassed. I read it and saw why. It's unshootable, said Bill. I agreed.

"The worst sin of Harlan: he wrote a strange plan of separate distinct "pods" of the Starlost space ship, rural 19th Century religious in style. And boring as hell. There was no character, no development in the bible, no screen action. No linkage. No jeopardy. No notional line."

To put it mildly, Ellison and Klenman didn't get along. Ellison, saw Klenman as a generic Hollywood hack, brought in with great enthusiasm because of the accident of Canadian citizenship. He tells a story where Klenman calls him up and obsequiously admits that he doesn't know much about writing science fiction, which did nothing but anger Ellison.

Klenman tells a very similar story, which begins with him being polite and self-effacing and ends with him telling Harlan Ellison to go to hell.

Klenman has spoken very critically of Ellison's original script on other occasions. And he did substantially rewrite it. That said, the original version did win an award.

But it's entirely possible to have a great script that is an unshootable mess by production standards. It's one of those things. There are a hundred reasons why a script that might look good on paper can be unusable when it comes to production. The Production process is all about compromise.

"You write a scene where your hero comes bounding out of the jungle,"Jeff Hirschfield, one of the creators and writers of LEXX said once. "But then it goes into production, and a hundred things happen, and in the end your scene ends up as a guy rubbing up against a couple of ferns."

As Mike Tyson famously said, "Everyone has a plan, until they get punched in the face."

Harlan Ellison was famously difficult to work with, and the history of his work, and other people's difficulties with him were well documented, particularly on his work on Star Trek and the Outer Limits.

David Schow's Outer Limits Companion goes into great deal on some of the difficulties of dealing with Ellison on the episode Demon With a Glass Hand.

"Harlan was a fellow member of the Writers Guild of America (West)." Klenman recalled. *"I was also a member of the Hollywood Screenwriters' Guild, which was absorbed by the WGA. Many of the greatest old screenwriters were still members in the seventies. I felt like an idiot with my half dozen credits. Some had thirty, forty, fifty or even sixty major credits from the 20s to the 70s! Fine mentors too."*

"Harlan did have some talent, but was also so self-aggrandising even fellow members could barely suppress their laughter. Anyway it was quite an adventure with the cantankerous Harlan Ellison," Klenman noted.

If Klenman said that there were problems with the script, we would accept that.

The conflict between Ellison and Bova on one side and Klenman on the other was sometimes comical. Ellison was outraged that the protagonists find the Bridge in the first episode, he wanted it to be the season end. Following up on that, Ben Bova was so upset at the idea of a steering wheel on the Bridge he included it in his novel, Starcrossed.

On the other hand, Klenman tells Philips and Garcia about his idea for a fifty foot high, three floor set with a steering wheel straight out of an old sailing ship on top of it all. In production terms, that was simply impossible. It was beyond impossible. Klenman's clearly taking the piss on both Ellison and Bova.

"Much later, maybe two decades later (1990's), Harlan wrote me a poison pen letter, which found me retired on Salt Spring Island off the coast here. Things must still have rankled. I just folded the thing up and mailed it back to him," Klenman recalls.

"Harlan, I said, life is short. You wouldn't want this kind of thing to turn up after your time runs out. And thought that the end of it. So darn it, I got another letter from Harlan, still miffed, only slightly mollified, but still pissed. He included the poison pen letter I had just returned him!"

So... twenty years later, Ellison was still nursing his grudges, and writing hateful ranting letters. I don't think that speaks well of him.

Acknowledging that Harlan Ellison had framed the basic concepts and format, and acknowledging the efforts and contributions of Trumbull and Kline, the final form of the show would be shaped by the people who came after.

Klenman, Davidson and Richardson were really the creative drivers of the series and stamped it with a Canadian soul. Behind them were a host of creatives and crew that were predominantly Canadians – Martin Lager, wrote four more episodes, and has an ambiguous directing credit. Canadians Helen French Marian Waldman, Mort Forer and Alf Harris all wrote episodes. Local directors Leo Orenstein, did two episodes, Francis Chapman another episode.

Klenman, who had been working in Hollywood and had contacts in the scriptwriters community was also able to identify and recruit other expatriate Canadian writers down there to fill out the roster. These included writers and directors like Harvey Hart, Jonah Royston, George McGowan and Bill Davis.

There were American writers and directors, like Joseph L. Scanlon or Shimon Wincelberg. Some of them did solo work. Some split credits with Canadians, which may have suggested that at least some of the Canadian work wasn't up to par. But that's fair, they came in, they did their jobs. In the end, the series had to sell in America, so if some episodes had a Canadian imprint, some didn't – as I said, fair enough.

But on the whole, with Producers, Script Editor, Writers, Directors, with two of the stars, and a much of the cast and production crew being Canadian, inevitably Canadian sensibilities, and themes were going to insert themselves.

These issues were literally floating in the air, particularly in the entertainment field, cast and crew, writers and producers would see them on the news, in magazines and newspapers, in books and documentaries, on television, there was a ferment in universities and public forums. Canadian television and television production was ground zero, and this included Starlost.

"Most of the people involved were accustomed to making documentaries," Ben Bova observed to Peter Kenter for TV North. This was Davidson and Klenman of course, but likely included many in production staff. If you were in film or television in Canada, you'd probably worked with the NFB. Documentary producers and crews were probably even more sensitized to national issues and questions, simply by the nature of their work.

Who were we? What did it mean to be Canadian? Where were we going? Where did we want to go? This is the sort of thing that would be talked about on lunch breaks, discussed at cocktail parties. People were living in this national dialogue, they were swimming in it.

Inevitably, even if it wasn't intentional or deliberate, these ideas would filter in.

They were just what was there.

PART TWO – SEARCHING FOR A FUTURE

STARLOST AND THE CANADIAN SENSIBILITY

"The ratings in Canada were never a problem. It had only been Canadian audiences, The Starlost could have run indefinitely,"

Norman Klenman, in an interview with Phillips and Garcia, for Science Fiction Television, 1996.

As it turned out, Canadians watched Starlost. It was one of the highest rated dramas in English Canada during its run. For CTV it was their second highest rated primetime drama.

It did well enough in the United States. For the first four episodes, it was a leading program in its time slot in the New York and Los Angeles markets. In the following weeks, the ratings fluctuated up and down with no consistent trend. But even in America, it was never a bomb.

It was, though, measurably more successful in Canada, than the U.S. For whatever reason, ratings were higher, the audiences were more loyal. So maybe it was saying something meaningful to Canadians.

The Canadian overtones of the series pose a challenging problem: Obviously, the concepts weren't originally created by Canadians, or created in Canada, or even created with Canada in mind. Yet, despite this, the series does seem to have resonances to the Canadian experience. Why?

Perhaps the resonance, on some level, lead to the series being adopted by Canadians. On the one hand, this seems ridiculous. CTV was looking for a programming opportunity, if the Starlost package had arrived as a celebrity golf sitcom rather than a Sci-Fi series, they would have gone with it. And they'd have gone with any kind of Sci-Fi or adventure premise, if that had been offered. The series more or less fell into their laps after being largely passed on in both the US and Britain.

But, on the other hand, it wasn't picked up for production in the United States. The British turned it down, and while the Americans were willing to distribute and syndicate it, they weren't really wild on producing it.

I'd speculate that one of the reasons the Starlost wasn't produced in these countries was that really, it was alien to their national mythologies. It didn't 'grab.'

The pivotal American space operas of the sixties and seventies were about their mythology as a frontier. Star Trek said it explicitly when it called space 'the final frontier,' and when Gene Roddenberry called it 'wagon train to the stars.' Lost in Space is simply a pioneer drama, Little House on the Prairie done stupid.

Even the quest-format series that bore a resemblance to Starlost, like Logan's Run, Planet of the Apes or Roddenberry's failed Genesis II/Planet Earth pilots were more about the frontier. Unlike Starlost, these unknown communities and strange new worlds weren't visibly seen as tied together but existed as separate continents, waiting to be discovered, and just as easily abandoned and forgotten.

On the other side of the ocean, Britain's principal Sci-Fi of the day reflected its perception of itself as an Island nation, apart and solitary, whether in Doctor Who or the Gerry Anderson productions. The perspectives shifted subtly over time. The early Gerry Anderson puppet shows were optimistic excursions, the island nation dealing with a variety of foreigners, but confident of its place in the world. In Anderson's Space 1999 the protagonists are isolated and alone in hostile seas reflecting the bleakness of the 1970s England. But even in

Space 1999, the British theme shows through - Moonbase Alpha was still an island.

Starlost doesn't relate to either of these national themes. It wound up in Canada, arguably as a result of a series of coincidences and opportunities. But maybe it was also partly because the premise and themes on some levels resonated with Canadians.

Canadians could look at the basic premise, and it said something to them. Perhaps it reflected themes that Margaret Atwood talked about in Survivor. Perhaps the ship of isolated domes, vast yet delicate drifting out of control, reminded Canadians of their own regionalism and uncertainty. The challenges, the issues, the sorts of decisions that the protagonists embraced seemed more authentic.

Starlost was meaningful for Canadians in a way that it wasn't for Britain or the US or other nations. Sitting here in our collection of autonomous provinces, loosely bound, oblivious and hostile to each other, drifting along without apparent direction or leadership, on a possible course to destruction, in danger of becoming an American satellite, we'd look at the Starlost and for some reason, we could relate.

For instance, our trio leaving their homes and seeking the wider world, one which they were poorly equipped for, was a little like Going Down the Road, Canada's first major film.

Ellison's notion of Devon and Rachel being pursued by Garth was abandoned almost immediately, that's a very American thing. Instead, Garth joined them. Canadian film and literature is not replete with hunters and the hunted. Our internal conflicts, our struggles are often messy ones, filled with compromise. Occasional decisive victory is unsatisfying and results in lingering grievances. In the end, the winners and losers have to somehow live together. Our mythology lacks gunslingers and lone wolfs, but rather seems filled with people who cling together, sometimes resentfully, as they struggle through the wilderness. Canadians try to get along, even if we're not happy with the situation, rather than fight or hunt or flee each other. These premises and ideas felt authentic to us.

CANADIAN NATIONALISM IN THE STORIES

Some stories spoke directly to Canadian issues...

For whatever reasons, Canada is a distinctly 'greener' and 'gentler' place than the United States. The United States has defined itself and its mythology as wide open spaces and frontiers to be explored and tamed. As we've already noted, in Star Trek, space is the final frontier, and it's treated like that, with prospectors, settlers, explorers, backward natives, swarthy hostiles and even barroom brawls in frontier saloons.

Canada's self-image and concerns seems to express itself in more timid terms. Our environment, like space itself, is conceived as immeasurably vast, implacable, almost overwhelming. It is something that defies conquest. Rather, existence is hard won, the result of conservation and hard work, delicate networks of contact and communication, farms, homesteads. Even towns and cities are literally built as shelters against an empty nature which ruled once and may rule again, much as the vast Ark is actually a delicate construct in the empty vastnesses of space.

Boris Bohuslawsky, a correspondent on the subject of Starlost pointed out, *"the sense of vast, desolate space which was so effectively communicated by the visuals of unending deserted tubes, and of the exterior of the ark itself — the camera often getting beneath the domes and in between the tubes to capture the model's extraordinary detail. Ultimately, what was unsettling about the show was the sense of loneliness it created. Whether or not this was deliberate is impossible to say, but this characteristic would certainly be of a piece with other expressions of Canadian culture and identity."*

The oddly schizophrenic view of Canadians, of nature as being both vast and implacable on one side and delicate and in need of conservation on the other finds an odd synthesis in The Starlost. Literally, the Ark is vast, it's a series of immense domes, each a world of its own. But it's also finite, made of little islands where people live, its parts in delicate balance. In the end, it's all the inhabitants have.

Or maybe it's not schizophrenic, maybe the Canadian sense of nature being delicate and needing conservation, is simply recognising our own place, our own survival in it. Requiring cooperation and mutual support rather than conquest and personal success. These ideas – the Ark as both vast and delicate - show up again and again in the show.

For example, an oddly Canadian aspect of Starlost might be described as 'fear of America.' Like it or not, the United States will always be a dominating force in Canadian life and thought.

At least a few of Starlost episodes deal explicitly with this theme. Mr. Smith of Manchester represents a first portrait of American society obsessed with production, growth and guns. It's a militaristic society despite having no one to fight. Manchester is all alone in the dome. It's worried about the nonexistent threats of other domes, to the point where it's a totally militarized, totally industrial society. It's a society wrapped up in paranoia, planning a defensive conquest of the Ark, and literally drowning in its own pollution.

Is this really the United States? Consider the time: 1973. The United States was up to its elbows in the Vietnam War (a war that Canadian governments were pressured to join). The illegal bombing of Cambodia and Laos was an open secret. The CIA was exposed overthrowing governments and plotting assassinations in South America and Africa. The FBI was wiretapping its citizens. The White House was keeping a list of enemies and Richard Nixon was slowly being exposed as the psychopathic liar he was.

From north of the border we were looking at a society whose cities were visibly decaying into sprawling slums of poverty and misery while the well to do fled to suburbs. Rivers were catching fire from pollution and Love Canal was only a few years away. It was a society opening fire on its own University students. It was a relentlessly aggressive militaristic society, obsessed with enemies who were at least half imaginary (communists under the bed, anyone?), and consumed with the idea of growth at all costs.

Smith's Manchester was a dead on outsider's portrait of Nixon's America and all its jingoism, militarism and paranoia. Manchester is obsessed with growth, obsessed with production, Smith boasts of breaking records – even while the dome is becoming uninhabitable from its own pollution.

Smith's optimism and drive speak to Manifest Destiny, they're ready to expand, to take over, and they believe that they're entitled to do it.

More clues come from its presentation. If Manchester had been intended as a parable about the Russians, for instance, it would have been easy enough to make it clear. The characters don't have funny foreign sounding names, as Roloff does in 'The Implant People' but good old North American names like Smith and Trent. They don't have foreign accents.

The lead, Ed Ames, playing Mr. Smith, was best known previously as an actor in westerns. He speaks with a down home American twang. There's no effort at all to come across as foreign or alien. Rather, the horror of Manchester is in its down home quality.

And of course, the fear of Manchester getting out, is not simply that it would take over, but also that its pollution might contaminate the entire Ark, which distinctly encapsulates Canadian fears. Manchester and its runaway industrialization, its production and pollution taking over the Ark reflects a Canadian nervousness, not just of American cross-border pollution, but of Americans taking over the whole country.

In hindsight, Mr. Smith of Manchester seems such a blatant and subversive piece of anti-American propaganda that one wonders how it got made at all, much less presented to an American marketplace. Certainly if the Americans had perceived that they were being skewered, many of them probably wouldn't have liked it at all.

Themes of conservation show up several times. If space was the final frontier in Star Trek, the Ark in Starlost is a place of finite wealth. In Mr. Smith of Manchester, unrestrained industrialization has made the environment all but unliveable. In Circuit of Death the scientist,

Sakharov is fleeing the environmental deterioration of his dome abetted by a repressive government. In The Implant People, a similar degradation of the environment, an expansion of poverty and misery, is hinted at. In The Alien Oro, Oro's companion, Idona, comes from a contaminated dome.

There's something very Canadian there. Both Canada and the US are huge countries with vast spaces, but their attitude is very different. Americans saw a massive open frontier to explore, to conquer, and to settle.

Canada, being further north, its climate much more punishing, had a different view of its open spaces. For Canada, the open spaces were implacable and indifferent. You didn't conquer them, you survived or endured them. You built enclaves or shelters, carved niches to survive within that endless expanse. Survival, not conquest, was about fragility and delicate balances. If you messed around, you might not survive the winter. This was space in Starlost, vast and hostile. This was the Ark in Starlost, an immense, but fragile shelter.

Themes like pollution or the Orwellian state were not unique to Canada. They are common to any industrialized society. Whether you are in England or Germany, the United States or Canada, sooner or later you're going to come up against these issues. Each state, each population, has concerns over pollution and the degradation of its environment. Each people have potential concerns over state oversight and infringement of liberty.

But each nation also expresses its concerns differently. Even in the case of pollution, for instance, the issues differ with each nations particular physical concerns. Canadians focused on acid rain, we focused on foreign contamination seeping over our borders, we worried about our lands and resources being taken up or polluted by invaders who had no stake in our country. The Japanese tended to focus on water quality because of their dependence on the fishery. Smog prone London and L.A. were concerned about air. Nations where farmland and industrial lands were cheek to cheek worried about contamination of foodstuffs.

Even the degree of emphasis changed from culture to culture and over periods of time. The United States, for instance, has never accorded industrial pollution anywhere near the level of concern that Canada has. Nor for that matter has it ever questioned seriously the limits to growth. In contrast, American anti-government paranoia has always reached much deeper into the fabric of their society than ours.

Consider the fear in Mr. Smith of Manchester, that the pollution will simply spread across the border and poison or contaminate the whole Ark, as a reflection of the Canadian perspectives on pollution like acid rain as being a cross border phenomenon back then.

Generally, Canadian sensibilities tended to be more focused on environmentalism than Americans. This may be due to the fact that many Canadians live in close proximity to American industrial development, we see pollution first hand sweeping across the border as acid rain, smog, toxic seepage and polluted waters. It may also be that our environment is comparatively harsher than the Americans, and thus we are more concerned with long term survival, with preserving our resources rather than spending it.

Alternately, this may be a defensive reaction to the fact that ours is primarily a resource economy, Canada's wealth is built on the extraction and sale of our finite natural resources, which raises a subliminal concern about what happens to us when it's all gone.

Two key episodes seem particularly drenched in Canadian Nationalism: The Alien Oro and The Return of Oro. In the first, Devon, Rachel and Garth discover a stranded alien: Oro from Exar (XR) played by Walter Koenig.

The symbolism is telegraphed: Oro is Spanish for 'Gold.' His costume is bright gold. And Oro is all about the money. He continuously refers to the Ark in terms of wealth or resources.

Oro's world is pronounced Exar, the phonetic rendering of XR, We've seen it spelled as Xar or Ixar, but in the absence of a script, we don't believe there is a definitive spelling. But XR, feels very much like a simple transposition of letters from U.S.

There's a very strong hint that Oro's nation or culture and his attitude is an analogue for America.

Oro's ship has crashed on the Ark, and he's been playing Robinson Crusoe. In particular, he's been cannibalizing parts of the Ark to fix his ship. Normally, this is a pretty standard adventure scenario. But Devon and his friends are appalled. For Oro, the Ark is just resources, he's just here to take what he needs and leave. But they're living there, they have to live there, they're upset with him plundering. How does anyone know that he won't take something vital to life support, or steering?

Eventually, Oro is allowed to leave, and he promises to try and send help back. But there's a deep disquiet in the episode that seemed to reflect the national disquiet and tension around American investment and ownership in Canadian resources. And this disquiet joined up quite neatly with the Canadian environmental movement.

Environmental movements were universal of course, you saw them in the U.S., and Europe – people everywhere were coming to grips with pollution. But in Canada, because of the effects and proximity to the United States, environmentalism merges neatly with nationalism.

In The Alien Oro, Devon reacts with horror to Oro's dismantling of pieces of the Ark to repair his ship. To Oro the Ark is resources, to Devon, it's a finite home.

This is a theme that repeats in 'The Return of Oro' and is expanded upon, where Oro continually refers to the Ark as a resource to be acquired for his people. 'Wealth' and 'resources' are the terms Oro keeps coming back to.

The images that Oro shows of his world in that episode are of pristine wilderness, itself an environmental message, which contains its own subtext. These images turn out to be archive footage of earth, a lost wilderness, a historical record rather than a live place. Nature is fragile, and in the episode, it's long lost. We could lose our own.

Our raw materials were being harvested, cut down, dug up, and shipped south. Our land is bought out. How do we feel about that? Back in the early 70s, for instance, the Province of Prince Edward Island was so concerned about foreigners (Americans) buying up the cottage land, they actually passed laws restricting it.

But the issue was larger than that, there was the sense that America looked to Canada as a place of resources and raw materials. Canadians were concerned about being plundered, about forests being cut, mines despoiling the land, rivers poisoned and factories and jobs being shipped south. It was all very well for Americans to look north and see vast resources, but Canadians had to live here, and we weren't thrilled with our country carted away, or the contamination left behind.

So what we see in Mr. Smith of Manchester is that fear and disquiet over pollution escaping across the border, poisoning our landscapes. And in The Alien Oro, there's the mercenary plundering of the Ark's resources, without thought to consequence, despite the fact that people had to live there.

Canadian nationalism looms largest though in 'The Return of Oro.' Here, instead of going to the U.S. as in Manchester, the U.S., in the form of Oro of XR comes to our heroes. This was the only sequel episode, so it seems reasonable to assume that there's something very important about the character of Oro and his society. Someone was trying to say something.

It's got Walter Koenig from Star Trek as Oro, of course. But Koenig wasn't a particularly big name, compared to some of the other guest stars, Colicos, Bochner, Converse or Morse were all much better known. Having two Oro episodes, was less about Koenig's minimal star power and more about key issues and concerns being expressed.

Oro shows up again in the sequel but this time he's not a castaway. When he left, he'd suggested that he may bring help. Instead, he comes back with an offer. The Ark is an incalculable bounty of resources, XR wants to own it. So his offer is: Hand it over.

He presents it as a rescue. If Devon and the inhabitants are prepared to surrender it, then XR will tow it into orbit to become their satellite. The inhabitants can become citizens, losing their old identities, and the XR get rich.

Say no, and take the chance of falling into a sun. This sets up the terms of a debate, judged by the ships artificial intelligences, as to whether to sacrifice their independence and become a satellite, or continue their own way and risk destruction.

Oro comes as a saviour, in marked contrast to his previous appearance, he smiles, he's friendly, and he makes a sales pitch for the Ark. He even shows home movies of his planet to prove his good intentions. But in the end, he basically wants the wealth of the Ark. The climax of the episode is a debate to the death where Oro offers survival and security as a satellite and colony of XR and Devon speaks on behalf of freedom and charting their own course, even if the risk is disaster.

This was actually a very Canadian debate. Arguably it was 'The Debate' especially in the early seventies when Canadian economic nationalism, advocated by Walter Gordon and Mel Hurtig, was at its height. Canada faced a kind of crossroads very much like the question in The Return of Oro. The language used in Return of Oro, the terms in the debate is identical to what was playing out in Canada on television, in coffee shops and at universities.

Canadians were basically looking at their future and trying to decide if they had one. Was it possible to have an independent Canada, a nation that charted its own course, sought its own destiny? Could we control our own economy, have our own businesses and policies? Could we survive that way?

Or should we embrace the security, the easier path of falling into the American orbit. Of just being an American satellite? Would Canada's resources be owned by Canadians or by Americans? Should we join up and sell out?

In the end, Devon wins the debate, not necessarily because his argument is more logical, but because it represents the values of the Ark and its creators. Which is a particularly, peculiarly Canadian reasoning. We weren't sure that Canada made sense from a strictly logical point of view, but we still believed in our country anyway.

It was a uniquely Canadian debate. The Americans weren't sitting around asking themselves if they wanted Canada for a satellite or not. The Americans had never ever doubted that they were the masters of their own destiny. They were no one's satellite, in no one's orbit, they acknowledged no gravity but their own.

In short, this sort of debate was absolutely foreign to them. Nothing quite like it ever comes up in Star Trek, for instance. Captain Kirk might occasionally encounter gods or superior beings, but they were almost invariably frauds or crippled with weaknesses, or at the very worst, they were the real thing but told to mind their own damned business. Even the Organians who prevented a war had no further influence on the hearts and minds of the Federation. Kirk never needed to worry about the Federation being drawn into Organia's orbit and becoming a satellite society.

Internationally, many countries, including France, Britain and Australia found themselves complaining of the weight of American power, the omnipresence of Coca Cola and Mickey Mouse.

But these complaints were a distant echo of the situation where Canadians lived literally cheek to jowl with the American behemoth. No major nation in the industrialized world quite confronted the sort of colonial issue with the United States in quite the same way or quite as profoundly as Canada did.

This was one of the most popular and crucial debates of that time period. From it arose a real movement to try and preserve or take back Canadian society and our economy. That was the basis for the concerted effort to lay foundations for a viable Canadian film and television industry. The same television industry that was making the show.

It's absolutely impossible that the people making Starlost in Canada, those writing it, acting in it, producing it, could be unaware of this national debate. As Ben Bova notes, they were definitely talking about it. They were carrying it like a massive chip on their shoulders.

In a very real sense, these people, and the infant film and television industry they represented, even had a personal stake in this national debate. They were inevitably in the center of the cultural storm. It's not a coincidence.

The language of the national debate, ironically inspired by an American space program that was still putting people on the moon, was laced with the space age. Canadians talked in terms of being an American 'satellite,' of Canada being in the American 'orbit,' of the 'gravity' or 'gravitational force' of the American society and economy. It's a small step rather than a giant leap to transpose the whole thing into a Sci-Fi palette.

The Return of Oro wasn't just about XR taking the Ark for its own purposes. It was really about the debate over the heart and soul of the

Canadian nation. The show's debate as to whether be drawn into the XR orbit, become a satellite and abandon their identity or to try to be masters of their own destiny even if that does not seem viable, is clearly drawn from Canadian national debates.

There is, frankly, no comparable parallel in American culture, or even in British or European cultures. This is unique. One of the final episodes of Starlost, and arguably its most important, is about identity and remarkably, this debate over identity is framed in uniquely Canadian terms.

A MORE SUBTLE PERSPECTIVE

Not every episode waved a flag, but a Canadian sensibility slipped in anyway.

Not every episode has to reflect back on issues of Canadian identity. The writers and producers were simply trying to make a science fiction series for an American market, not make statements about Canadian-American relations.

Several of the episodes, of course, are decidedly generic. Take Only Man is Vile where our trio runs afoul of a pair of mad scientists pursuing some debate over the nature of inherent good and evil. It could be a Star Trek or a Lost in Space episode. Hardly surprising, since the writer, Shimon Wincelberg, had written for both Star Trek and Lost in Space.

There's Children of Methuselah, about five hundred year old children, artificially retarded from aging, who have been piloting a fake control room. The Goddess Calabra is about a male only society. There are Sci-Fi cliché episodes – The Circuits of Death features our heroes being miniaturized for a mission. The Beehive is about killer bees, of all things.

This isn't too surprising. Let's face it, this is science fiction, and the genre had a great deal to do with shaping the stories that were chosen and told. Even without Shimon Wincelberg for a writer, Starlost was going to be as heavily influenced by Star Trek or Doctor Who as it would be by W.O. Mitchell or Morley Callaghan.

But even this is a sort of clue. A lot of the episodes really seem to be part of their time – Farthing's Comet features a spacewalk mission.

The Astro Medics has an exterior tour of the Ark. Episodes have space suits and 'spacy' tropes. Why? Because in 1973, we were still in the first bloom of the Space Age. America had progressed from the Mercury to the Gemini Missions to the Apollo Moon launches, the Soviets had a space station, and space probes were flying past the planets. All of this was brand new and wild and literally happening on television nightly news and daily newspapers.

So of course it shows up in The Starlost. The point was, that in doing space tours, and spacewalks, these sorts of stories and images... they were literally scooping off the surface of popular culture.

The Beehive was another story scooped off the surface of pop culture – a reflection of the news stories of Africanized 'Killer Bees' circulating back in the 1970's, and the zeitgeist that lead to a whole series of 'Nature Strikes Back' movies like Frogs, the Swarm, the Bees, Phase IV, Kingdom of the Spiders, and Empire of the Ants.

Circuit of Death might be about miniaturized people, but the protagonist/antagonist is named Sakharov. Why is that significant? Because in real life, Andrei Sakharov was a Russian physicist and peace activist, who won the Nobel prize, speaking out about nuclear disarmament and who was eventually punished for his idealism. If you know the story of the real Sakharov, then Circuit of Death and the struggles of the fictional Sakharov become a completely different episode. In the 1970's when this episode aired, almost everyone knew the story of Sakharov.

In Farthing's Comet, the character of Doctor Linus Farthing seems loosely inspired by two-time Nobel Prize winner Doctor Linus Pauling, and by Sci-Fi writer Isaac Asimov, both famous around this time. It's not deep, but it's there.

Episodes like Farthing's Comet, The Pisces, The Beehive and Circuits of Death are just scooping off the surface of popular culture of the time. They were inspired by the news programs and magazine article.

But if that's true, then inevitably, we have to admit that a number of episodes of the Starlost are explicitly about Canadian nationalism, and Canadian national obsessions.

These things too were part of popular consciousness. Popular ideas and images floating around found their way into the show through osmosis, and this inevitably included Canadian nationalism.

Even the Canadian writers who lived and worked in LA, when they came home, or talked to family and friends from home, were going to be engaged. The fact that they needed to go to America to work brought the issues home to them. It was inescapable.

Manchester, the Oro stories, the Implant People, these episodes were deliberately nationalistic, wearing their politics on their sleeves.

But even when it wasn't explicit and conscious, a Canadian sensibility and perspective tended to encroach on and colour the episodes. Canadians simply thought differently, they had different perspectives, and this made the stories different.

The Sci-Fi genre has its own conventions and its own themes and ideas. In a sense, there's an argument to be made that science fiction is a vocabulary for industrial societies. In a world that changes every time we turn around, in a world where our grandparents grew up with horses and lived to see men walking on the moon; where we've literally made the sum total of human knowledge, art and literature available to anyone at the tap of a screen and have achieved instantaneous communication worldwide, the idea of the present, of time and space, has ceased to exist in many meaningful ways.

We are all literally living in our own future. Hence, Science Fiction, the territory of the future, is a useful canvas for modern industrialized societies to tell its stories, a countryside at once familiar and removed.

While it has its own language, it is not a uniquely American offering, but rather, we see science fiction in literally every industrialized or semi-industrialized nation. There is no reason that something cannot be science fiction and uniquely Canadian, or that exploring one set of themes disqualifies it from exploring the other.

A typical episode, like The Implant People, deals with themes like the usurpation of democracy, of government control over our lives. These were not issues that one would have to research literature and culture to come across.

Back in the 1970s one could find them on the covers of magazines and in the pages of newspapers. These were things that Canadians were actually talking about like everyone else and were concerned with.

The writers were arguably skimming their inspiration off the froth of pop culture, which is hardly elegant, but is sometimes a much more accurate measure of what a culture is about than its allegedly 'significant' works.

In The Implant People, the villain Roloff is a bureaucrat who's become the real ruler of the state, a reflection of the Canadian Mandarins – the unelected institutional bureaucracy that apparently really ran thing despite the elected leaders?

In modern times, the Americans worry about the 'deep state' but arguably, Canadian unease goes back much further. Perhaps because of the British colonial legacy, we have always been uneasy about who really runs things, the elected officials or the bureaucrats.

The Implant People touches on universal themes, found in many western societies, but arguably interprets them in Canadian ways and in light of Canadian experiences, institutions and prejudices.

Or in a more subtle way, consider the sorts of choices that would get made in otherwise typical 'neutral' episodes.

Take Lazarus from the Mist as an example: Very close to the end, there's a scene where Devon and Garth are struggling with the main villain. The villain's henchman fires a crossbow and accidentally hits his boss. In an American series, the heroes would leap to the advantage, dispatch the henchman, and confirm the villain died tragically.

Here it's played differently: The henchman displays a look of absolute horror at what he's done and the fight goes out of him. Suddenly, the conflict ends, and Devon and Garth are rendering first aid to a frightened, wounded man, Garth gently cradling his head as they help him. That feels very Canadian, its' the actions of people living in such a hostile environment, that even if it's your enemy, when someone is hurt everyone tries to help. Where the landscape is so harsh that when necessary, people set aside conflicts for common humanity.

Consider Gallery of Fear. This was an episode where our trio are played with by an artificial intelligence which may be malevolent or insane. In the end, Devon, obviously flashing back to HAL in 2001: A Space Odyssey decides to destroy it. No big deal, Captain Kirk was terminating AI's left and right back in his day.

Strangely, The Starlost here lacks Star Trek's moral certainty. In Star Trek, destroying a governing artificial intelligence was almost mandatory, it was an obstacle to progress, an intolerable relic of past civilizations, now existing without point or purpose.

In Starlost there's more ambiguity, Devon and Rachel must debate with each other over what to do about the AI Magnus, and it's a moral debate which considers Magnus' right to exist. In the end, Devon slowly makes the decision Kirk would have leapt to. But maddeningly, even in the end, though we've given decisive action, we don't get a moral resolution. We're left uncertain as to whether Devon's decision was the right one or whether he is now a murderer.

This ambiguity may represent a distinctly Canadian approach. There's a refusal or unwillingness to accept that a good sock to the jaw solves all the world's problems, or that intractable natives need to be gotten rid of for the sake of progress, which seems practically un-American.

The end of the episode has our hero being accused by the Ark's community of Artificial Intelligences of murder, which clearly rebuts the 'rightness' of the resolution that Devon reached. Kirk walked away having taken swift decisive action, and certain that he'd done the right thing. Devon's action is not taken swiftly but after much debate and there's no certainty for him in the end.

Faced with a rogue AI an American sees a problem and kills or fixes it, he's got certainty. The Canadian lacks certainty, they might do the right thing, but they have to wonder and struggle with the morality of their actions, the consequences of their choices. A Canadian writer, writing the story, automatically defaults to this uncertainty, it's not necessarily a conscious decision.

Or consider Circuit of Death. The plot revolves around the character of Sakharov, an idealist scientist now embittered. When we see him, he's disgraced and literally fleeing arrest, he tried to make a difference, but now he's lost all faith in his dome and in the Ark. As far as he's concerned, it's doomed and not worth saving. He just wants to leave, and he doesn't care if he triggers the self-destruct doing it. Devon and friends come along, and they force him to help them save the Ark by miniaturizing to repair the circuits. Sakharov eventually has a change of heart and dies.

Now, wacky Sci-Fi miniaturizing tropes aside, it's probably a pretty standard Sci-Fi story. But in terms of Canadian cultural perspective, there's arguably a little more going on. Sakharov was a flash point in the Cold War between the US and the USSR. It's difficult to see an American version of the Sakharov story not focusing on the Cold War nexus. But Canada and Canadians weren't as engaged in the Cold War – Canada attempted a foreign policy of multilateralism, it was about peacekeeping missions, detente, de-escalation and building bridges to the non-aligned. So the Starlost version of Sakharov is divorced from Cold War politics, it's about alienation, despair and redemption. The Starlost Sakharov is a black man from an African dome, which places the politics of the episode in Non-Aligned framework. The fulcrum of his story is a personal one of his idealism and disillusionment with his own society, there's no Cold War element, no east/juxtaposition.

But the story may function as a Canadian commentary on racism in the United States, which was at a boiling point. During this time the civil rights movement was in full swing, Jim Crow and segregation had been pushed back, the busing issue was live, black leaders like King and Malcolm X in America, and Lumumba in Africa had been murdered. The black community saw both optimism, but also frustration and despair. At times, racial issues seemed unsolvable, even apocalyptic, as per Charles Manson's 'Helter Skelter' fantasies.

Sakharov is a black man after all, on an Ark which has up to this time been lily white. Does Sakharov's disenchantment with his society, the desire to just blow it up and leave, reflect a Canadian perspective on race relations in America? His redemption is personal, but his judgment that his society is beyond saving isn't really challenged.

Sakharov's story was handled and went a fundamentally different way, because it was written in a Canadian perspective, rather than it if had been written from an American point of view.

It's unlikely that the creators of these episodes were being self-consciously Canadian, not in the way that Manchester or the Return of Oro were. Those episodes are wearing their politics on their sleeves.

What's going on these other episodes, in those moments, or choices, is a bit more subtle. We're seeing a difference in 'natural reactions' or perhaps 'cultural defaults.' These decisions in productions and scripts may have reflected the instinctive way that Canadians thought or reacted. When characters faced situations, they responded in ways that made sense to the actors or writers, or directors or producers, ways that just 'felt' authentic to the culture.

Ways that weren't necessarily the way Americans would see as authentic, or that American film or television would tend to default to. It's possible American audiences may have found such moment's odd and foreign, things not going the way they expected or were used to.

Given that the Canadians were trying to sell this show in the United States, that's an interesting gap.

Ultimately, the producers and creatives of Starlost were trying to cater to an American market. Everything depended on making that American market happy. That's still the quest today, it's easy to name literally dozens of programs made in Canada set in American locations and waving the American flag. So, injecting Canadian-ness is sort of at cross purposes to that goal.

Yet it's there. How? Why? Were the creatives deliberately thumbing their nose? Trying to tell stories they thought were important, or taking inspirations locally? This was an era of Canadian chauvinism, as Ben Bova found, so it's possible.

More likely it was simply there, a kind of unconscious cultural default that they didn't even necessarily recognize. They were doing their best to fake it and tell stories like Americans after all. But they sometimes failed and defaulted to writing as Canadians. They told these stories, they made these choices, simply because that's what felt right and authentic.

Of course, not every episode or every choice reflected Canadian identity. That would be hard to do, and we believe it's an unnecessary requirement.

But over and over, we have episodes that seem to speak to genuinely Canadian concerns and perspectives, or which express universal issues filtered through a Canadian lens, or just seem to manifest Canadian attitudes and choices.

CONSTRAINTS AND STYLE, CREATING A LOOK AND FEEL

A source of the Canadian-ness of the series was its limitations.

Down in Los Angeles in 1967, Captain Kirk got into rousing fist fights, crew men died, beautiful women flounced around half-naked and someone got laid in every episode. In contrast, The Starlost, five years later in Toronto was much tamer.

Sex? There's very little of that. Star Trek rolled out the cheesecake, but in Starlost, there was only the secretary in 'Mr. Smith of Manchester,' and the hostess in 'Gallery of Fear.' After the first episode, the romantic chemistry between Keir Dullea's Devon and Gay Rowan's Rachel faded away. Beyond that, the occasional star crossed romance that was suggested, as in Pisces or the Alien Oro was so tepid as to make no impact at all.

Violence? That did a little better. There were brief awkwardly staged fights in 'The Goddess Calabra; and 'The Implant People.' In 'Mr. Smith of Manchester' a gun is actually fired. Threats were made in both Oro episodes, but compared to American or even British programming of the time, The Starlost was remarkably tame.

Why? Part of this was that the Starlost was coming from a different technical culture than Star Trek. Look at it this way. Where did American television get its ideas? Where did they get their writers, their directors, the cinematographers, stuntmen, fight choreographers, cameramen, and technical people of every sort?

They got them from the movies. This is hardly rocket science. American television emerged mostly in LA the same place that American film had grown up. They drew on that legacy of decades of film production and the accumulated technical skills. They literally had this available on the shelf.

When American television was taking root, producing its own dramas and comedies, it was drawing on the collective technical skill, people, visual and aesthetic traditions developed over some forty years of movie making at every level on a massive scale. In many ways, American television simply tried to be American movies on a smaller screen.

Mostly a Canadian film or Television industry didn't exist, or barely existed, back in 1972 and 1973, whereas in the United States, the studios and networks were basically entertainment factories.

Back in 1973, as I mentioned, the feature film production for the entirety of English Canada consisted of three feature films. That's three low budget minor films, compared to eighty out of the United States studio system.

One of these Canadian films, The Neptune Factor, was the most expensive and for many years, the highest grossing Canadian film. I saw it when it played at the Drive-In where I worked while growing up. Basically, a bathysphere is lost on the sea bottom, there is a rescue expedition that encounters 'monsters' - optically enlarged tropical fish molesting tiny props. It really was sad compared to what was coming south of the border.

Harlan Ellison writes, and Norman Klenman, confirms, that they had no scriptwriters in Canada. That's a little bit of an exaggeration. There were a lot of good Canadian script people, Klenman among them. But many were down in Los Angeles or New York, alongside Canadian actors such as William Shatner and James Doohan.

Why? Because there wasn't enough of a film or television industry in Canada to support them.

Well, think about that for a second. If there wasn't enough of a film/television industry, if there wasn't a solid base of sitcoms and dramas to support writers, then probably there wasn't enough going on to support directors, cinematographers, effects technicians, the whole infrastructure of skilled technical people that you need to pull off a polished action/adventure show like Star Trek or even a generic program like Mannix.

There were skilled people in Canada, of course, but let's face it. Being a cameraman on a game show like Front Page Challenge or a sports broadcast like Hockey Night in Canada was a very different thing than being a cameraman on The Starlost.

So, if the Starlost wasn't drawing on the same kinds of technical and talent bedrock as Star Trek, where were its traditions coming from? If anywhere?

Documentaries and theatre. As noted, many of the production crew came from documentaries, and this probably influenced both political and technical issues on the show.

If Canada didn't have much of a feature film tradition, it did have a very well established stage tradition. Starting with the Vaudeville circuit Canada maintained a small but lively theatrical community. Every major city had a theatre, and even small towns had performing halls for live entertainment. There was a major Shakespearean festival at Stratford.

It was a theatrical tradition which was hardly large by any means, we suspect most Canadians were too busy watching hockey to even notice it. But it was there, an integral part of the Country's culture, and integrated enough into Canadian society that it would perform the works of Canadian writers.

The bottom line, is that if you were in Canada and hiring actors, a lot of what you would get was going to be theatrically trained, rather than cinema trained. Same thing with local directors, writers, lighting people, set designers, prop-masters, make-up artists, etc.

This actually shows in what was appearing on contemporary Canadian television of the era. Most of the CBC's dramatic specials were adaptations of stage plays, often shot as if they were on stage, with minimal sets, basic lighting, few changes and so forth. There wasn't a lot of money in the CBC budget for drama in the first place and not a lot of experience with the format, so adopting a theatrical style with its built in limitations was both cheaper and easier than a more cinematic style.

At least some of this carried over into Starlost.

"The show's distinct quality was due not simply to a starved budget or inferior production techniques, but to a creative sensibility that was perhaps not readily understandable by run-of-the-mill (American) science fiction fans.

"The theatrical orientation of the writing could be seen in the way the dramatic crisis of each episode was structured — not as an "action scene", but as a dialogue, or perhaps monologue, setting out a conflict of ideas. "The Return of Oro" is an obvious example, but I am thinking also of the interesting speeches in "Gallery of Fear", "Circuit of Death" and "Mr. Smith of Manchester".

"The use of theatrically trained supporting cast was often quite evident, with bit-parts being executed with surprising panache (i.e. the spokesman for the fearful citizens in "And Only Man is Vile", and the council leader in "The Implant People"). Contrary to an oft-repeated criticism, the acting was generally of a high calibre; the difficulty, rather, was that the minimal number of cast members in any given episode put a lot of pressure on the regulars and guest stars, making it harder for them to realize the story's dramatic potential," Boris Bohuslawsky wrote in correspondence. We believe he was on the mark enough to reproduce his comments here, to credit him for his thoughts and insights.

The show had to work within the limitations of what was available. The Starlost couldn't afford its own composer, so it borrowed its musical score and cues from another local production from 1970 - Strange Paradise, an occult /supernatural soap opera inspired by Dark Shadows. This may have been serendipitous, the Ark was vast and unknowable and the characters were lost within it. The haunting scoring from Strange Paradise often seemed to fit that sensibility perfectly. Much more so than a more bombastic or conventionally dramatic score.

American cinematographers and stuntmen had over fifty years of westerns under their belts in creating visually effective fights and stunts. The Canadian production crew, being basically stage and non-dramatic television simply didn't have that experience. Allegedly in The Goddess Calabra, they worked without a stunt coordinator, and John Colicos was knocked unconscious during a fight scene.

Inexperience showed in other ways, there's a recurrent story that the production crew, used to lighting hockey games, poured so much light on Doug Trumbull's models that they started to melt.

The result, however, is that British or Canadian drama, like the Starlost, tended to be more formal than its looser and more natural American counterparts.

They tended to be talkier, more thoughtful and slow paced, with more emphasis on acting and characters, more focus on ideas, less on action. Some of the most gripping scenes in Starlost are simply framed as debates.

Characters tended to be more interesting, more unique and less stereotyped. On the other hand, they tended to be less active. The staging tended to be simple and economical, with minimal special effects or action scenes.

The acting tended to be more deliberate and less spontaneous. Even the rhythms of interplay were different.

Does this make British or Canadian television naturally inferior to its American counterpart? Not necessarily. Many British series are recognized as classics.

But, if the Canadian style tended to resemble the British in being more theatrical rather than cinematic, it was clearly genuinely less sophisticated. At the approximate time that the Canadians were trying to syndicate The Starlost to American markets, the British were doing the same thing much more successfully with Space: 1999, by far the more polished and cinematic of the two.

Unfortunately for The Starlost, it was being marketed primarily to an American audience that had grown up and was used to the cinematic Hollywood style. It's more sedate and cerebral theatrical origins and influence was viewed by an audience acclimated to the thrills and chills of Star Trek.

Another factor we have to consider is that the standards existing at the time for Canadian television were much more restrictive.

Ontario, the Canadian Province where the Starlost was shot, was so conservative that it became one of the last jurisdictions to maintain a film censor board. Ontario was, and still is, famous for its prudish and pedantic censors. There is a deeply conservative, perhaps even timid, thread within Toronto's cultural mainstream.

This is a place that banned internationally acclaimed films like 'The Tin Drum' well into the 1980s, and in the 1990s was seizing paintings from art galleries and putting them on trial in the Eli Langer case.

So right from the starting gate, the community standards of 1973 were profoundly prudish with regard to sex, and only a little less so when it came to violence.

Television content, and standards of acceptability were defined by the CRTC (Canadian Radio and Telecommunications Commission, the Canadian equivalent of the FTC), and were guided or further defined by the CBC.

CTV at the time was still a fledgling network, barely a decade old, and struggling to establish a voice. This was literally one of its first major attempts at a dramatic series. In a climate as conservative as Canada's, it probably had no intention of taking risks. This was a major effort and a lot was riding on it, there was little incentive to rock the boat.

So, we weren't going to see a lot of adult sexual content or situations, or if that was present, it was going to be played in a very subdued fashion. Violence was going to be used sparingly.

Part of this, of course, may have been a hidden sensibility that Sci-Fi was actually children's programming. In a sense, perhaps they were taking a leaf from Doctor Who, rather than Star Trek.

The creators of Starlost were trying to create something for the American market. Their goal was a kind of simulated 'Americana.' Later productions, like Night Heat or Street Legal would come much closer, and be much more successful in creating a product indistinguishable from its American peers.

By the 1990's, Sci-Fi programs such as Highlander, Stargate, Earth-Final Conflict and X-Files were ubiquitous in Canada. These were branch plant productions, conceived in the US and owned by US companies, shot in Canada, and pretending to take place in the United States. Any trace of Canada was carefully laundered out.

The Starlost was a cruder production, less American in look and feel, and even style of storytelling. That was a combination of limited resources, different production traditions and genuine inexperience with a show of this kind.

Does this suggest it was more naturally or inherently Canadian because of these limitation?

I don't know that amateurishness, if I want to be cruel, is distinctly Canadian.

But there is a case to be made that that environment contributes to identity.

It's definitely true that there wasn't a lot of money or resources for production design. By modern standards the show feels threadbare. Quite often the music, the lighting, the cinematography seems... basic.

But was it all simple crudity based on lack of experience, or lack of time and resources? Or was it the traces, however young and poorly developed, of a distinctive style and sensibility? W

I suggest that at least some of it, beyond the threadbare qualities, was actually an expression of a different style, perhaps a raw and developing style, but still an inherently different set of choices in terms of production and storytelling. Different but legitimate.

Which gives one pause to think. Obviously, if the Producers of Starlost could have emulated the American model perfectly, they would have. There's no question about that. They were trying to create a product for the American market, not create an artifact of Canadian culture.

But, culture, inherently, is an expression of who you are. The creative personnel and decision makers of Starlost weren't quite sophisticated enough to perfectly fake being Americans.

They could only be themselves.

CULTURE AND IDENTITY

"We all had a sense of Canadian pride that we were part of this big thing that was going on. I didn't have a sense of it in a political sense, but I had this sense of being part of this thing that was Canadian. And there was a lot of Canadian talent in this."

Gay Rowan, who played Rachel.

"I don't think that the people were making this series were that focused on Canada's identity per se. We all felt it was something very different. We all felt enlivened that there was a show like we'd never had in Canada. And a sense of pride that it was a Canadian American co-production. I don't think we had any sense that it was a political consciousness." Rowan concludes.

Gay Rowan's perspective contrasts strongly with Ben Bova's own experience of an almost obnoxious 'in your face' Canadian chauvinism. Rowan's perception was a general sense of pride, while Bova experienced something much more pugnacious and political. Of course, Rowan was born and lived there, while Bova was an interloper. They'd see things differently.

Perhaps culture is something that should happen naturally, as opposed to simply being a deliberate construct. Nobody should sit at a desk and say 'this is Canada,' any more than they say 'this is America' or 'this is Britain.' You can't create culture like that, you can merely try to define it. You create culture by creating, and you recognize it when different creators keep coming up with the same themes and ideas. That definition comes about, as creators look at these themes and ideas and say 'this is who we are!'

Davidson, Richardson Klenman and many of the other ground floor creators, other writers, directors, actors and production crew were Canadians, coming from Canadian sensibilities, Canadian history, Canadian traditions, the same forces that shaped them, in turn shaped the Starlost.

We are defined as much by our limitations, our boundaries, as by our accomplishments and aspirations. The Starlost, for better or worse, was defined in turn by those same boundaries and limitations.

But it was more than just those limits and constraints. Key episodes like Manchester, like the Oro stories, or the Implant People are very deliberately about Canadian issues, they were about fundamental debates and discussions that Canadians were having: Who were we? Where were we going? What was our relationship with the giant to our south? Themes of identity, of conservation, of environmentalism ring clearly.

Even in episodes that aren't so obviously drawn from local issues and controversies, a Canadian sensibility and perspective rings through. We simply don't approach things like Americans, we don't think that way.

We're less certain, more personal, not as grand. And this shows up in episodes like Circuits of Death or Gallery of Fear.

The presence of generic 'off the shelf' episodes, or the reality that often the show scooped off the cultural surface with spacewalks and characters like Sakharov and Farthing, doesn't undermine the argument for Canadianness in Starlost.

Rather, they reinforce it by showing how porous the show was, how easily it picked up on ideas and themes around it, how it was a creature of its time and place, which very much included the country it was produced in and the outlooks of the people producing it.

Many of the stories it told resonated to Canadian sensibilities in ways that were completely inscrutable if not outright repellent to American audiences, and overall, the premise and sensibility betrays a strangely Canadian outlook.

The series is infamous as the worst Sci-Fi series ever, perhaps because the Americans who judged it, never really understood it.

It came here, and if it didn't start out as ours, it certainly finished as a legendary if dis-respected piece of Canadian culture.

And what is more Canadian than getting no respect or recognition?

Or being an immigrant washed up on our cold shores to make our way?

When it first played, I never had a chance to watch it. For years, I heard about it, and heard about how terrible it was. That made me vaguely ashamed as a Canadian. We produced a Sci-Fi series and it was trash.

But then, I finally got the chance to see episodes here and there, on VHS and DVD and online, and I was genuinely pleased. It wasn't perfect, it was definitely slow and threadbare. But it was good.

And astonishingly, I recognized myself in it. I recognized my country in it. Who we were, what we worried about, how we thought.

No one had mentioned that, but there it was.

I am proud of it.

PART THREE – THE EPISODES

PRELUDE -THE PROMOTIONAL VIDEO

Introducing a bold new concept...

Sometime probably around March or early April, 1973, a seven minute video was released to promote the series, hosted by Keir Dullea and Doug Trumbull.

The project is already in Canada at this point, CTV and Glen Warren are mentioned. Ed Richardson, the Associate Producer for Starlost is the director of the segment.

It's not clear who the audience was being produced for. Presumably it's for marketing to affiliates. But Dullea reveals that 20th Century Fox is a distributor and Westinghouse Network, the CTV network and NBC affiliates have already picked it up. Ultimately 48 NBC affiliates picked up the show. Which suggests that the syndication sales were already advanced at the time it was made.

Within the video Dullea and Trumbull, talk about the Starlost concept, and especially about the magicam effects system.

We see some random test footage of the magicam system, featuring a toy monkey and other children's toys blown up to giant size, as a sort of child's fantasyland, while a stuntman dodges among them.

However, at this point, the Ark props and models aren't built yet, or at least aren't camera ready. So instead, spacecraft footage from Doug Trumbull's 1971 film, Silent Running, is used instead.

Silent Running is a film starring Bruce Dern, about Earth's last forests being sent into space, on an immense spaceship called the Valley Forge, composed of a cluster of domes. When the program is cancelled, Dern rebels against the order to jettison the domes and takes the ship into deep space.

The Valley Forge looks and feels a lot like an early version of the Ark. It's tempting to see the ship from Silent Running as conceptual predecessor to the Ark in Starlost. It's possible, Trumbull's effects house built both models, and the resemblance is definitely there.

To confuse matters further, in the video, however, Dullea describes the Ark as a giant ship with a hundred levels three hundred years in the future. This is a concept that Ellison mocked in interviews. So that verbal description may not be his, but an interpolation, based loosely on his twelve minute audio recording, and before his bible from April 10.

Harlan Ellison himself, is mentioned prominently, but doesn't make a personal appearance. Notably, neither Gay Rowan as Rachel nor Robin Ward as Garth are mentioned. But their names appear in the April 10 bible. Keir Dullea's reveals his character is named Victor Enn, rather than Devon, contrary to the April 10 bible. All of this implies that the promo was shot before the bible was written or distributed, again possibly March or early April.

Either that or the Bible hadn't circulated and Dullea, Trumbull and Richardson were simply working from obsolete materials, but this seems less likely. Ellison's name is featured prominently, not just as creator, but as author of six episodes.

Ultimately, it's a curiosity. A seven minute video from very early in the series development. A sales pitch for a show that's already sold to all its markets.

All the pieces are in place, but the production hasn't begun, the disasters have yet to happen.

Creators and Cast

Directed by Ed Richardson
&&&
Keir Dullea

Douglas Trumbull
&&&
Original Airdate: March (?) 1973

VOYAGE OF DISCOVERY – EPISODE ONE

Devon rebels against his rustic community, only to discover the world is not what they believed.

This is the hardest episode to review because it's such a lightning rod.

This was the episode that broke Harlan Ellison. It was the first and only script he delivered to the show. The script whose treatment so outraged him that he broke entirely with the production and took his name off. It was the script that Norman Klenman described as an unshootable mess, but later won an award and was turned into a book.

This was the episode where Douglas Trumbull's Magicam system was weighed, tested and failed. Everything was riding on it, and ultimately it couldn't deliver, and so Trumbull departed.

This was the episode where William Davidson, Ed Richardson and Norman Klenman inherited the mess, a visual effects system that didn't work, a prima donna writer melting down, no other completed scripts in the pipeline, inadequate studio space, no time and Ben Bova wittering around trying to be a science advisor.

It's the episode where behind the scenes, everyone in the production was literally freaking out and going 'Oh man, oh man, game over, we're all going to die!'

There's so much baggage here, it's hard to wrestle with.

We'll be blunt, we're sure the original script is out there to be tracked down. We're not going to. We do have Phoenix Without Ashes somewhere and read it many years ago. We even met and talked with Ed Bryant, who wrote the novel based on that script, also many years ago, though we have very little recollection of that conversation.

Instead, we're just going to ignore all that, and try and deal with the episode on its own terms, without the baggage.

There's something peculiar about trying to review a pilot. We all live in this mediated world without surprise. Personally, I've seen all the episode a half dozen times now over the years. Normally, with television series you are familiar with, you turn on, go in, and right from the start you know what you're getting into – the premise, the characters, the relationships are all there, you know them before the screen flickers. The only new thing is the particular story for that episode.

It's different for a pilot. For the pilot, you go in blind, there are no established characters, no relationships and even the premise is almost unknown. Watching a pilot is different from any other television series experience. It's the one moment, where we as an audience are definitely working without a net.

And for any show, it's a moment that can only happen once for each viewer. Because after you watch a pilot, or your particular first episode of a series, if you enter somewhere later on... after that, it's just another episode. Once you're past the first episode experience, then every episode is a 'just another episode' experience.

So in reviewing, we'll to try and put ourselves in the position of a first time watcher, to see and assess it fresh, without expectations, and see how it works.

With that in mind, Voyage of Discovery, kind of stumbles out the starting gate with it's opening montage. This is standard in television – opening visual montage, clips, titles, perhaps a voice over. In this case, we have a pan of the Ark in space, and William Osler, who plays the computer projection throughout the series, providing a sonorous description which gives the entire story away: Earth is dead, the Ark is humanity's last and final creation, now drifting to destruction unless three young people can save it.

Awkward. So any kind of measured revelation, any opportunity to tease and parse out the mystery, that's just down the drain with that opening monologue.

Oh well.

The episode opens with an interesting choice, Devon, Garth and Rachel, quivering in something like awe or religious ecstasy, as they venture onto the wrecked Bridge to look out over the Ark. For a moment, they're just speechless, astonished, terrified. It's well done, it's a genuinely stunning and effective scene, not least because they allow it enough silence to breathe.

Cut to flashback and a pseudo-Amish community called Cypress Corners. Sterling Hayden, playing the community leader, Jeremiah, is giving a sermon to a humble congregation, dressed in 19th century duds.

It's authentically archaic, and Hayden rocks that 'Old Testament' sensibility so well that you don't quite realize he's wearing a coat with a zipper. What's cool about the scene is the cognitive dissonance. These are clearly pseudo-Amish in look, dress, speech and manner and they're very much stuck in the 19th century. But they're surrounded behind the trees and natural elements, by metal panels and electric lights. The archaic dialogue is peppered by modern terms.

It's a fusion of the primitive, mixed with the advanced, and that's effective. Not particularly novel, Doctor Who did this kind of thing all the time, notably in Mind of Evil. You saw it on Star Trek and other films and television shows. We've seen it endlessly in stories and novels going back to the thirties.

In particular, we've seen it in Brian Aldiss's 'Non-Stop' published in 1958, yet another story of a generation ship whose inhabitants have gone primitive and regressed to the point they've forgotten they're on a ship.

Primitive societies living in the trappings of advanced forbears, or generation ships gone wrong are two well established staples of science fiction. But tropes reoccur because they work, the cognitive dissonance is effective. They dangle haunting mysteries in front of us.

As Jeremiah speaks, we initially see Rachel and Garth in the crowd. But there's a serpent in the garden, young Devon, the malcontent, played by Keir Dullea. Devon attracts attention by showing up to the services late, obviously resentful and challenging.

Noting this, Jeremiah give Devon a verbal smackdown. Although he loves Rachel, he's also a landless orphan and a bit of a troublemaker. A disembodied voice of God announces that Devon's genes are unsuitable and Rachel must marry his best friend Garth, and that's that. Devon is not well liked.

After the service Devon goes off to see his best friend, Garth, the blacksmith, about this romantic triangle. Garth isn't happy about the situation, he doesn't want Rachel, but he doesn't see what can be done.

Moping, Devon goes to hang out with old Abraham, one of his few friends. Old Abraham isn't part of Ellison's script, he's an interpolation by Klenman. But the character works in the story. Abraham is essentially an old version of Devon, once rebellious, now beaten down and burned out but still hanging on as a free thinker. His presence reinforces the sense of the community's long stagnation as well as Devon's frustration and restlessness. Abraham isn't popular with the elders either, and so the friendship, despite being generations apart, is believable.

Then there's a romantic clinch with Rachel, who clearly teeters on the edge or rebellion from her traditional parents.

Later, while wandering about, Devon catches Jeremiah in a 'Wizard of Oz' moment, programming the voice of God. This starts the ball rolling with Devon in full rebellion. It seems not everyone has forgotten they're on a spaceship, and people like Jeremiah use that knowledge to keep the rest of the people in line. Jeremiah can't tolerate the threat that Devon presents. Soon there's a lynch mob.

A word about the effects up to this point – we see several scenes of Devon, Rachel and the lynch mob wandering the countryside. It's not clear if this was just a regular blue-screen composition, or if this is Trumbull's famed Magicam.

Regardless, it's unimpressive. It's clear that the landscape that they're in is a tabletop model, the texture of the image feels odd, there's no depth of field. Everything is in the same focus and a little off, it looks unearthly and alien – not the effect they were looking for, and the compositing is awkward.

It may be that the whole tabletop miniature sets thing was a bad idea, it's hard to get the texture of miniatures just right. Mind you, first time viewers in 1973 would have been seeing it on black & white or color cathode tube television sets made of scan lines with poor resolution, and it would have been for the first time. So it probably would have worked for them. Here in this era of high resolution and jaded sophistication, we're more finicky and flaws are more obvious.

Old Abraham helps Devon escape the mob. Suddenly, he finds himself outside the world he knew, in an Ark corridor.

It's a nice scene, without a word Dullea conveys the terror and wonder of finding himself in an utterly alien environment, and the visuals of these endless corridors are impressive. Quite often, television is narrow and focused on people in confined space. To simply us show an endless corridor or vast landscape works.

What we're saying is, dammit, we like those corridor shots. Not necessarily the zero-G floating, of the bounce tubes, that's kind of stupid and is only used a few times in the first episode, and banished forever after. But the corridors, as both a set and a visual effect signifying empty immensity works well.

Canada, particularly the prairies is often a place of wide open, almost desolate spaces. You get away from the cities and the populated areas, and often you come face to face with unending empty wilderness, stark plains or endless rolling hills and forests. Canadian literature, and Canadian film and television often dwells on that stark, endless emptiness of nature, and whether it was conscious or unconscious, this feels very much a part of that.

Devon blunders across a Sphere Projector, in which a distinguished but cantankerous looking William Osler appears.

The Projector feeds us the backstory, which repeats the opening montage, but Dullea does a decent job of conveying the sort of confusion that an audience might feel, and the information is parceled out effectively. Devon learns his way around pretty quickly, although he struggles to grasp utterly alien concepts like space and stars.

There's also something fascinating in the conversation with the Sphere Projector, a sense that the machine is desperately trying to tell him things, frustrated and struggling with the restrictions of its programming, and with Devon's own thickness. In later episodes, Gallery of Fear and The Return of Oro, we'll find that there is actually a community of Artificial Intelligences on the ship, and this conversation takes on new significance.

Then it's back to Cypress Corners, where Devon walks in on his own funeral. That's a little homage to Mark Twain's Tom Sawyer there, although here done absolutely straight. And it's rather unwelcome, old Jeremiah was looking forward to being rid of Devon, but here he is, back and more heretical than ever, full of outlandish stories, challenging the order of things.

It doesn't go well. Devon is sentenced to death and imprisoned. Rachel visits, but her father pulls her away. Later that night, Garth sneaks by and frees him from jail. In Ellison's treatment, it's Rachel that frees Devon, so this is an interesting departure that goes back to their complex relationships.

But instead of escaping directly Devon runs off with Rachel. Garth is sent off with his trusty crossbow to retrieve Rachel and possibly kill Devon, the friend he rescued, thinking he is out to rescue Rachel, a woman he doesn't want to marry, but he's obliged to follow his elders.

You can tell he's just kicking himself over the whole thing. Try and do a good deed for your best friend, and the next thing you know, he's kidnapped your unwanted fiancé and now you've got to hunt them both down. Awkward.

They all end up outside the wrecked Bridge when Garth catches up to them. Rachel shows strength and confidence, refusing to go back to a life she found claustrophobic. Garth struggles with his conscience, before he finally refuses to shoot and accompanies them onto the Bridge.

The Bridge, it turns out, is literally the neatest wreckage you've ever seen: One skeleton neatly dressed in a clean Ark uniform and a lot of Styrofoam blocks strewn around.

Finally, we come full circle to the silent, awestruck moment where they gaze out over the Ark. We realize now that these three characters have spent their entire lives in a backwards community in a fifty mile dome.

Now we're with them looking out the length of a starship several hundred miles in length, looking at a star, looking at a nigh infinite universe beyond their imagination. It's mind blowing.

It's a powerful image, when we see it at the beginning, and the story arc only builds that power by giving the audience context. This time we know where they are and what they're looking at. We understand what's happening and what the threat is. Full circle. The loop is completed.

As the trio stares out across the domes, a bright blazing light comes into view, illuminating their faces as they stare, awestruck. We understand how naïve and lost they are, looking out over something so beyond anything they've known, it's unimaginable.

The Ark is rotating, and so it appears that the one particular bright star is rising, its harsh blinding light flooding the Bridge.

Rachel asks *"What is it?"*

Devon replies, *"I don't know."*

Of course, we in the audience know that is clearly the death star. The star that the Ark is on a collision course with. The protagonists are staring death in the face, and while we the audience realize it, they are so innocent that they don't even understand what they're looking it. It's a powerful conclusion.

And again, we have an allusion to this recurring Canadian motif of humanity, of the human characters, being small and insignificant, in the face of an immense and unforgiving starkness.

Overall, not a bad episode. Sterling Hayden plays the Patriarch Jeremiah and was vividly remembered. Hayden had been, and still was a highly respected actor, but by this time, he'd drifted into alcoholism and a bohemian lifestyle.

One of the stories about Hayden, who was living in France at the time, was that the production had trouble getting him over to Canada. They sent him a first class airline ticket, and he'd tried to change it to economy, so he could pocket the difference. When he couldn't, he refused to travel, until CTV paid him the difference.

Petty scams aside, Gay Rowan found him thrilling.

"Sterling Hayden was our first guest star and he was an amazing raconteur. He had lots of stories to tell and I loved hearing them all. He told me when I came to Paris to look him up which I did. He lived on a barge on the River Seine. However, he wasn't there. So sad!" she told Bruce Callow.

Robin Ward also had vivid memories of Hayden, "One of the first guest stars to appear on the show was Sterling Haydn a rugged movie star who brilliantly played a corrupt cop in The Godfather."

"Haydn had discovered the joys of cannabis late in life and he became a kind of late in the day hippy. He carried a staff and, invited to stay at Keir's rental house, he insisted on sleeping in the garden with a blanket. He proclaimed his disdain for the acting profession and accordingly never learned his lines and resorted to cue cards."

"He was pleasant and friendly although contemptuous of the proceedings. Hard to understand how he could have given such a rich, nuanced performance in the Godfather which was filmed shortly before his turn on our show."

Gillie Fenwick, was a Lancashire born actor who seems to have moved to and worked almost exclusively in Canada. As Abraham he gave a particularly effective performances, both as a sort of mentor to Devon and a foil to Hayden's Jeremiah. Both Hayden and Fenwick are fun to watch, regardless of who they're bouncing off of.

Keir Dullea's performance as Devon is particularly effective, without his saying a word, you can literally feel the smoldering resentment rolling off him during the sermon. He establishes a distinctive character, his Devon is not a typical action hero or leading man, but a brooding loner continually challenging the world around him.

Later, outside Cypress Corners and in a new world, he does an amazing job with little more than body language and expression, standing still expressing terror and wonder as he explores the Ark.

Robin Ward puts a surprising amount of nuance into his role as Garth, an everyman. Garth isn't a crusader or malcontent like Devon, he just wants to get along in life, even if parts of it are crap. He's constantly trying to navigate his web of relationships and obligations. He'll marry Rachel, because that's what the elders want. He doesn't love her, and he knows that Devon and Rachel love each other, but he sees no way around it.

He saves Devon from execution, because they're friends. But then he's sent to hunt them down. You can almost feel his frustrated tension, the way he's caught between conflicting loyalties. Then when he catches them, Rachel doesn't want to go back. Garth's a simple man struggling with the frustration of complexity.

This is also one of the better performances allowed to Gay Rowan. Rachel's rebellion against her parents, her conversations with Devon and her off-screen running off with him speak to a fearless character. When she first uses the bounce tube, she laughs joyfully. She's nowhere near as intimidated by the Ark as Devon was. There's real steel in her spine when she refuses to go back with Garth. Rowan doesn't get much screen time, but she makes the most of it.

The visuals run the gamut, the actual sets are surprisingly effective, the special effects are wobbly, except when they're trying for big spectacular 'sense of wonder' shots, in which case they carry them off, particularly for 1970s television.

The story structure, that looping flashback, was only used once in the series, within this episode. Its effective, and within Cypress Corners, the arc of Devon's inevitable fall from malcontent to almost-lynching victim, and his complex relationships with the other characters works.

The final moment, 'what is it' as they uncomprehendingly stare death in the face has a genuine punch.

I'll accept that it's not the story that Harlan Ellison wanted to tell, and not told the way he wanted to tell it. But it works, it's a good story.

In production terms, the pilot episode ends with teaser shots of the next two episodes. So it' likely that these episodes were already in production with footage available, while the episode was in post-production.

Given that they were trying to make Magicam work and then having to compensate for it not working, the post-production on this episode almost certainly went longer than planned.

Ultimately, this episode went at least fifty-percent over budget.

Creatives

The creative background is inevitably tangled up, with Harlan Ellison doing his version, and Norman Klenman literally re-writing on the fly. Klenman, as we've noted, would go on to be a key creative person, acting as Story Consultant/Script Editor for the entire series, recruiting other writers and officially or unofficially writing eight of the sixteen stories.

Klenman was a close associate of producer William Davidson, the two had once formed a production company together and had produced two feature films, and so they likely had a close working relationship on the series.

Ed Richardson, associate producer under Williamson would also go on to direct episodes. We've discussed Klenman, Williamson and Richardson and their roles in the series as the creative core.

Harvey Hart, forty-five years old at the time of production, was a Toronto-born writer, director and producer. Starting out with the Canadian Broadcasting Corporation in 1952, he relocated to Hollywood in 1965 and became a prolific television director. He accumulated over eighty director credits, mainly television series and television movies, and fifteen producer credits before retiring in 1990. Hart was credited as Director for two Starlost episodes, Voyage of Discovery and the Goddess Calabra.

He seems to have been particularly well liked, and was noted for his friendly approach to actors. William Davidson, the series producer, told Phillips and Garcia *"I regretted that the late Harvey Hart was unable to direct more than two episodes because of prior commitments. Keir Dullea, Gay Rowan and Robin Ward felt comfortable working with Harvey, who had a marvellous way with performers and a knack for getting the very best of them."*

Backstory and Continuity

With the entire series in context, Devon's conversation with the Sphere Projector, offers a different perspective. The tendency, and certainly Devon's and the viewer's tendency, is to see the Projector as simply an exposition device – something to passively, if unreliably, answer questions.

But watching that initial conversation with the benefit of hindsight, we're struck by how manipulative Osler's Sphere Projector is: It asks him questions; it tells him things he hasn't asked to know; it avoids or evades some questions; it repeats and emphasizes the danger to the Ark, almost visibly frustrated with trying to get it through Devon's thick head. Underneath this apparently passive, allegedly non-sentient device, there's signs of an intelligence with purpose.

On its own, this probably wouldn't amount to much. But in the context of Gallery of Fear and The Return of Oro, where we learn that the Ark is also host to a community of artificial intelligences watching over everyone, with limited ability to affect matters directly, it raises the possibility that the AI's were actively interacting with Devon from the first time he sat down at a projector.

Was this intentional? Probably not, Klenman needed to get some exposition out to the audience in certain ways. It had to be a halfway interesting dialogue. So it's likely not more than that – the desperate attempt to deliver exposition in an interesting way while writing under a deadline.

But often there's a subconscious or subliminal intent, or casual choices early on inspire more developed choices further. Food for thought.

Creators and Cast

Directed by Harvey Hart
Written by Harlan Ellison and Norman Klenman
&&&
Devon: Keir Dullea
Rachel: Gay Rowan
Garth: Robin Ward
Sphere Projection: William Osler
Jeremiah: Sterling Hayden
Old Abraham: Gillie Fenwick
Jubal: George Sperdakos
Rachel's Father: Sean Sullivan
Rachel's Mother: Aileen Seaton
Garth's Father: Jim Barron
Garth's Mother: Kay Hawtrey
Small Village Boy: Scott Fisher

&&&
Original Airdate – September 22, 1973

LAZARUS FROM THE MISTS - EPISODE TWO

Searching for help, our heroes revive a man from suspended animation.

Lazarus literally starts where Voyage of Discovery leaves off. The protagonists are still on the wrecked Bridge, and they find an old recording that sends them off to the crew's medical bay and their next adventure. There are some interesting things going on in this episode.

Not necessarily the plot, or either one of the plots. Don't get us wrong. They're perfectly fine story plots. But they're just not terribly new.

Plot A involves the formerly civilised inhabitants having regressed to brutal savagery, practically cavemen. That's only been done dozens of times in just about every Sci-Fi series ever. It was the main idea in the series of Logan's Run, Planet of the Apes, was utilized regularly in Star Trek and in Roddenberry's Earth 2 pilots, in Doctor Who, in movies like the Time Machine or the Road Warrior, Teenage Caveman. In short stories. In novels. I'm just saying: It's just been done to death.

Plot B involves a man being woken from suspended animation into the strange new world of the post-disaster Ark. That particular idea dates back to pulp stories of the 30s, back to Rip Van Winkle in the 19th century, and even further, if you care to follow the thread. It's been trotted out regularly in almost every series of Star Trek. In this case, the Sleeper wakes up, discovers the world sucks. He tries to help a little and goes back to sleep. Not original, not original at all.

But then, there aren't really any new ideas in the world are there? Someone once said that there are seven basic stories, and everything is just a variation. It's what you do with it that matters.

What's interesting about the second episode, is how closely it follows on the pilot. Typically in television in those days, you did the pilot, established the premise, and after that every episode was supposed to be entirely self-contained. The idea was that the audience could or should be able to drop in anywhere along the way, and stations could or would run them out of order anyway. So continuity, progress from one episode to the next was just a bad idea. You wanted as little of that as possible.

This episode breaks that mold, and suggests that maybe there will be an over-arching continuity, despite stand-alone episodes. That in fact, there may be a larger story in the whole series, something with a beginning, middle and end. Actually, we suggest there is, although it's imperfectly handled. We'll delve more deeply into the idea in the review of the Return of Oro.

Getting back to the story: We start with Devon and his friends at loose ends on the Bridge. They've just escaped Cypress Corners, and they have absolutely no clue. They have no idea what to do or where to go. They have no idea, period.

An old recording directs them to the medical bay. They enter darkened creepy corridors, where shadowy figures flit around just out of their sight. It's actually quite effective, one of the rare moments in the series where they do anything interesting with lighting.

Then they're assaulted by the shadowy dwellers, who we'll call 'cavemen' descendants of security guards regressed to savagery, wearing rags of old uniforms. Garth is captured. Devon and Rachel flee into the cryogenics center. There they wake one of the frosties in the hope that he'll fix the Ark for them.

The bad news is that the man they wake up can't. Doctor Gerald Aaron turns out to be just a communications technician. Also, more bad news, he's only got a couple of hours before he dies of 'radiation virus.'

The good news is that he's not an idiot. Which is vital, because Devon, Garth and Rachel are beyond clueless.

"The Computer keeps saying that the Ark is on a collision course with a sun, but we don't understand what those words mean," Devon tells him. Dr. Aaron mentions travelling through space. *"I don't know what that is."* Devon replies.

There's something deeply affecting about that naïve innocence. It's like a chimp staring innocently down the barrel of a gun, with no idea what's going to come out of it.

Anyway, Aaron knows what he's doing, even if he can't fix the Ark. He's trained, he's competent and he improvises well. He helps Devon and Rachel rescue Garth, and teaches them barely enough to let them start figuring out how to function. He explains the handle on the flush toilet, that sort of thing. That little crash course largely sets our trio up for the rest of the series.

As with this sort of plot, there's the obligatory 'Oh no, what have I lost.' Basically, the sleeper, having woken, has the tragic moment where they come face to face with the fact that their old life, their loved ones, their favourite espresso bar are gone forever.

We sound cynical about it, and perhaps that's cruel. Loss is a poignant emotion, and the sleeper's tragic sense of things gone forever is at the heart of why this kind of story sort of story is so popular.

In this story the emotional fixture is Aaron's wife. Her name's literally the first thing on his lips when he wakes, and even after he realizes how much time has passed, he still hopes to find her in cryogenic suspension.

Aaron's search ultimately leads him to her final video recording. She got to live a few years longer. For some reason, she wasn't eligible for cryogenics, so she recorded a good-bye to her husband for whenever he woke. Aaron is listening to a love letter and a farewell from a woman centuries dead. It's genuinely sad.

Unfortunately, while Aaron is really competent, he doesn't do tragedy so well. It falls a little flat, and that's disappointing. There's a serious missed opportunity for genuine pathos here.

Maybe we're seeing too much Canadian restraint. After all, the love of your life is dead, everyone and everything you've ever known is gone and the glorious project to save humanity has fallen apart, reduced to hicks and cave men on a derelict heading into the sun. But let's not make too big a deal out of it or get too emotional.

This sort of emotional stoicism, this 'cautious restraint' becomes a running feature of the series. It can be mistaken for bad acting, but really it may be more the product of a culture whose middle and upper classes simply weren't demonstrative. And in a sense, this is reflected in the Canadian cinematic and television culture of the era.

Or there may be a more practical reason. It could be bad acting after all. Or bad directing. Or just circumstance.

Late scripts and short timelines can really cripple a production. A script comes in at the last minute, the Director doesn't have time to fully read it or absorb it, doesn't have time to find the emotional core of the story or prepare for it. They don't have time to plan their shots to serve that emotional core. The actors don't have time to read through or rehearse, to find their characters. Shooting days are limited, and so without any opportunity to think it through, everyone is just trying to get pages of script down and that's all. There's little opportunity for thinking or concentrating on where the focus should be, or what the emotional payoff is.

It's just 'get it late, get it done' and so a moment that could be sad and poignant and bring a tear to our eye... doesn't quite pay off. It's okay, but that's all.

At the end of the day, Aaron's journey in Lazarus From the Mists is okay, but it's not the greatest rendition of this kind of story.

In contrast, the cavemen story is actually kind of fun. It's sillier and goofier. It's effective the first moments when they're just flitting around in the shadows. But once we actually see them it almost becomes a cartoon.

The sleeper story is absolutely sincere, almost too sincere. But with the cavemen, you have tons of extras, running around in fake wigs and beards, wearing the shredded remains of bright coloured uniforms, doing their Planet of the Apes shtick, rushing a makeshift battering ram, going 'what is this thing you call 'sky'?' It's almost like a variety show comedy sketch. But there's a lunatic energy there that's missing in the Sleeper storyline.

Starlost is typically visually bland, it's all softly lit, no harsh shadows, no starkness. It's often lit as if for a talk show or a soap opera and the colour scheme tends to be equally soft. We can understand the reasoning behind that aesthetic. The Ark is a designed space, and it's designed for living in or working in. So the aesthetic sensibility is going to be that of a hotel or an office space, not a haunted house, spooky forest, or factory. The whole structure of the Ark is supposed to be built as one piece, so an underlying uniformity of look and design makes sense.

But, for once, for the caveman scenes, the look is distinctive, the shots are underlit, full of shadows and debris. It's genuinely creepy and menacing. And most damningly, it's a sign of what they could have done with the show, if only they'd tried a little harder, pushed the envelope a little further. Or had the extra time and money, to be a little more ambitious.

But then, as I've said, it shifts into a cartoon, and the tone changes.

Oddly the caveman storyline leads to the best moment. The head caveman, some guy who wears a red construction hard hat as his crown, comes on scene. He's played by Doug McGrath, who starred in Going Down the Road. He's not biggest of the cavemen, and he's not the toughest, but he's clearly the politician of the bunch, the smartest and the most devious. He wears his thoughts clearly on his sleeve, his mental process is nakedly transparent. He's genuinely fun to watch as he interrogates Garth, shoots down challengers to his authority and schemes his way along the story.

He gets captured and accidentally shot by a crossbow, and his terror and helplessness when he's in Garth and Devon's hands is vividly shown without a line of dialogue simply through' just expression and body language.

There's something interesting in that scene. McGrath's caveman is fighting Garth and Devon, but the minute he's shot by the crossbow, everything changes. Garth, Devon and Rachel, shift smoothly from fighting to first aid, they lay him down, Garth holds his head tenderly, they reassure him and administer medical attention.

It's not the sort of scene we see in American television. When the villain gets shot, the hero either looks for the next adversary or challenger to deal with, more concerned with friend or foe. Or they rest and recover from their ordeal. We don't see this automatic empathy and ministration.

Again, this may be another aspect of Canadian sensibility expressing itself. Perhaps so subtly that no one really noticed it when they were making the episode.

Faced with an overwhelming implacable nature, a landscape that can't really be conquered, Canadians huddle together beneath it. All alone together, the only way to survive is to help each other, when someone needs it. We aren't conquerors fighting over possession, but survivors holding each other up. If someone's injured, doesn't matter whether they're a friend or enemy or stranger, you try to help. Just a thought.

Overall, the cavemen story starts out scary and becomes clownish, but somehow manages to acquire genuine heart. Its cliché, but I'm sentimental.

Later, as McGrath's character leads his people into a promised land, and plucks an apple sharing bites of it, it's a genuine affecting scene despite its corniness

Bottom line? It's decent. Not a bad story, or pair of stories, and it shows promise. The ability to use lighting, production design, and characters in interesting ways offers a lot of potential that sadly, wasn't explored much in subsequent episodes.

Creatives

Leo Orenstein, was a Montreal born writer, producer director, whose career in Canadian film and television stretched from 1954 to 1976. This was the first of two directing efforts for Starlost, his other episode being The Pisces.

For Douglas Hall, the first billed scriptwriter, I have almost nothing. In addition to Lazarus in the Mist, he's also likely credited as Doug Hall for Farthing's Comet. His works on Starlost are his sole credits under either name, and that name is sufficiently generic that further online searches were futile.

Don Wallace, the second credited scriptwriter was a Canadian whose earliest work was an industrial film for the National Film Board in 1944. His real background was as a soap opera man, for which he is credited with 1760 episodes as a writer, 1223 episodes as a director and 1336-episodes as a producer, across six different shows. Although I've speculated as to the possible influence of soap operas on the production, this is about the only crossover for a soap opera writer. This was Wallace's only writing credit for Starlost.

Credit where credit is due, this is one of the titles mentioned by Harlan Ellison as a story in development before he quit. The extent of Ellison's contribution is unclear.

Backstory and Continuity

I have no idea what a Radiation Virus is but it seemed to be going around. A virus is a lump of protein configured to infiltrate and take over our cells. Radiation is just a packet of energy. It's one of those terms that drove people like Ben Bova and Harlan Ellison crazy.

Of course nowadays we live in a world where space ships go 'whoosh' and lasers go 'pew!' So don't sweat it.

We do wonder if Doctor Aaron couldn't have just found them a more useful person to wake up, although in practical terms, anyone they wake up from an emergency medical cryogenic sleep was going to be in bad shape. Still, from a common sense point of view, it might have been worthwhile to hang around the cryogenics a bit longer.

There is a possibly grim denouement here. The 'cavemen' have been living in the tunnels, and presumably making use of the food delivery system there. Devon leads them to an empty garden/retirement habitat filled with light and fruit trees, and then seals them in. Is it large enough to sustain them, will they be able to feed themselves the way they did in the tunnels? Or has he inadvertently doomed them to starve to death when the fruit trees are finally picked bare.

Creators and Cast

Directed by Leo Orenstein

Written by Douglas Hall and Don Wallace
&&&
Devon: Keir Dullea
Rachel: Gay Rowan
Garth: Robin Ward
Sphere Projection: William Osler
Dr. Gerald Aaron: Frank Converse
Jane Aaron: Vivian Reid
The Sergeant: Doug McGrath
1st Tube Dweller: Clive Endersby
2nd Tube Dweller: Alan Bleviss
&&&
Original Airdate: September 29, 1973

THE GODDESS CALABRA – EPISODE THREE

Our heroes blunder into Omicron, a dome populated only by men.

There's one word that sums up The Goddess Calabra, and that's 'queer.' Welcome to the Pleasure Dome. Any doubt about that is dismissed early on when John Colicos, titled 'the Governor,' reclines on his throne and is entertained by a group of dancing men. Yep, this is gay all right. It is unapologetically ahead of its time.

The Starlost trio stumble into Omicron, their first dome since Cypress Corners, and are taken prisoner. They've found a dome occupied solely by men. With nothing else to do, the Omicron men have created a martial culture of warriors and machismo. Basically, it's an entire society based on going *"Hoo-Ah!"* to each other. Talk about culture shock.

At first, they're taken for mutants, but then Rachel is mistaken for the Goddess Calabra, which is good for her and her companions. Complications arise when the Governor, decides there's nothing else to do but marry her and imprison the others. And that starts the plot ticking away...

The threadbare production values that characterizes The Starlost work in its favour for once. The barren and antiseptic sets, devoid of lushness or clutter, all hard angles and utilitarian squares and rectangles is a left brain aesthetic taken to extreme. It's a male environment, through and through, blank and impersonal, a kind of amped up Spartan aesthetic.

Even the opening shot, featuring a superimposition of a tiny trio on a massive cyclopean landscape of cones and boxes, like some child's playground works effectively and convincingly for a change. We're given a sense of the kind of utterly impersonal, cyclopean architecture symptomatic of the Third Reich, but carried a step further as monuments are streamlined into primal Euclidean geometric forms.

In fact, the only exception to this sterile masculine aesthetic at work, is in the statue of the Goddess Calabra, which, although featureless, is rounded, full of the curves and details which have fallen away from man's world.

But as effective as the visual imagery is, this episode, like so many others of the Starlost belongs to its guest stars, John Colicos and Barry Morse. Both of these were very accomplished performers, and perhaps to take advantage of that, or perhaps the director simply took a little more time and care, much of the interplay with Morse and Colicos involves a lot of close ups.

John Colicos, as the Governor, comes across as a decadent Roman emperor, lounging around on his couch, being entertained by his dancing boys. But where a more clichéd script would portray Colicos as soft and decadent, inbred and effeminate, that's not the case at all.

Instead, he's the best his society can offer. Past his prime, but still tough as nails, fierce enough and strong enough and smart enough to hold his own against all comers, winner of twenty challenges, even as he feels the shadows lengthen around him.

Unlike other series adversaries, Smith of Manchester or Roloff of the Implant People, who are unapologetic villains, Colicos character isn't truly villainous. He's simply a man dealing with his lot in life. He's not even stupid, rather he's quite smart and insightful about both himself and his society. That contrasts with Smith, who is terrifyingly narrow-minded, or Roloff who revels in cynicism.

Colicos' Governor is even likeable in a way, as in when he points out his 'mother' - a gestation machine - with something like pride, or the bitter humour that's always lurking under the surface.

He wants to marry Rachel, but his real goal is to preserve his life and rule. He's getting older and he knows he's going to die in trial by combat sooner or later, that's how leadership works around here. And as he ages, it looks like it's coming closer and closer. But her presence gives him an opportunity to escape that fate. If he marries a goddess, he becomes divine himself and gets a free ticket out of inevitable death by combat.

Colicos never once descends to the level of cliché, but animates his Governor with life, energy and humanity. Say what you want about Colicos, he's trundled his way through more than his share of crap one-note performances, but he was also an actor who could share a movie screen with Jessica Lange and Jack Nicholson in The Postman Always Rings Twice and more than hold his own. Here, in this role, he's definitely on top of his game.

"John Calicos," Gay Rowan said in an interview with Bruce Calllow, *"was very professional and actually quite shy. But he was fun to work with. John Calicos was one of Canada's foremost Shakespearean actors and he took his scenes very seriously! Great fun to work with him."*

Robin Ward has a more vivid memory, *"There was an acclaimed Canadian actor John Colicos who played a Roman emperor type. He chewed up the scenery in true Caligula fashion and when he bellowed that he would "Crush his enemies!" while simultaneously crushing a bunch of grapes he was holding, I almost lost it."*

That's vivid and you'd expect it of a Shakespearean stage actor, a striking if slightly ridiculous image.

Colicos himself has his own story, related to Phillips and Garcia. *"There was a scene where Keir and I had a sword fight. We didn't have any stunt doubles. We thought we could handle it ourselves. Keir got a little carried away and he bonked me on the head and knocked me unconscious. You could hear the bonk echoing throughout the studio! I was rushed off to the hospital and there wasn't any permanent damage. The next day I went to work, and Keir was most apologetic. That shot was left in the final cut."*

Knocked unconscious? Did that actually happen? It seems a bit much.

"I think something happened. I don't know that he was unconscious. I think Keir might have knocked him down or something. I wasn't there, we weren't all on sets at the same time," Rowan commented.

The lack of stunt doubles or stunt coordinators, and the breakneck pace that saw even 'Ed Wood' style mistakes just ignored and going in anyway, suggest that even if Colicos exaggerated, some version of the incident occurred.

Watching the fight scene, there are a couple of blows, one taken by Dullea and one by Colicos that look a little real. And particularly, when Colicos is struck the shot cuts too quickly.

Anyway, while Colicos is trying to seduce Rachel; her friends Garth and Devon decide to escape. This brings them straight to the priesthood, the softer side of this warrior society. It seems in this dome, men are either warriors or priests, and there is an ongoing but subtle conflict between the two factions.

So, at this point, the leader of the priests, Shaliff, played by Barry Morse, gets involved. Shaliff as the priest is also sharp, although hidebound in a pointless religion, he's not a stupid man.

"I don't think Gods would need to escape by tying and gagging government house guards," Morse's character remarks.

Once again, he too avoids a cliché role. Rather than being either an underling or a simple adversary to the Governor, and rather than being a cynic, Shaliff's faith is genuine, and his relationship with Colicos' Governor is complicated and bittersweet, hinting at the long history between them.

"You gave me power, I even had power to stand up to you. And now, with a few simple words, you take it all away," Shaliff tells the Governor, and you can feel the tenderness between them.

There's an odd power to these words, a kind of remonstration that has more weight than a bitter tirade. There's pain and love mixed up in it, and it aches with the old wounds and thoughtfulness of a long married couple.

Morse himself was an accomplished actor. He played Lieutenant Gerard, a 'Javert' role, the ruthless policeman pursuing Richard Kimball in the Fugitive. Although he's got a huge list of credits, he's probably best known to the Sci-Fi community for his role on Space 1999, a Gerry Anderson live action production.

Robin ward remembers, *"The grotesque and monstrous characters in the show often seemed to be a licence to over act which many guest stars did with great relish, to the great amusement of we three regulars. Barry Morse did not however and gave a dignified and subtle performance as if he was playing Willy Loman."*

Some parts of the episode are almost tragic. The scenes with the monks spending their lives trying to find metaphor and symbolism in technical manuals is both funny and painful. The priests have wasted their lives in a futile and misguided study. At best, they might get some good poetry out of it all.

But then again, consider Colicos faction, the warriors. Warriors to what purpose? There are no mutants, no invaders, and no enemy within or without. They're warriors without a war, with nothing to do but fight and enslave each other in an orgy of pointless ritual.

It's no wonder that Colicos' Governor seems bored stiff when we first see him. He's an intelligent man coming to grips with the pointlessness of his own existence, of his own society. The fact that he's given the priesthood and the head priest some authority, as Barry Morse's Shaliff points out, suggests that he's well aware of the limitations and the futility of his world.

Rachel appeals to him, not just as a means of survival, but as an escape from boredom and ennui, which is why he bothers to talk to her at all, or why in the end, Shaliff, Rachel and Devon can reach him. He's already realized his society is a dead end, even if he's resolute about staying on top of it.

Speaking of Rachel, Gay Rowan has one of her best roles in the series, smoothly playing off Colicos, Morse and Dullea. Her character flirts coolly with Garth and Devon. She casually banters with the Governor but doesn't give an inch, pumping him for information, refusing to be cowed and even shaking him out of some of his preconceptions. She's fearless: At one point she tells him, *"Everything about you offends me."*

Things unwind in pretty standard fashion. Devon starts an uprising to rescue Rachel, he eventually has to fight the Governor and then beats him in the death match.

They win their way to the Ark's schematics and discovery they are hopelessly out of their depth. They're just bumpkins from Cypress Corners, like the priests, they have no idea how to read schematics or technical manuals. Nevertheless, they manage to work out that maybe there's a back-up Bridge that they can find.

Then they leave, but not before Colicos' Governor comes to them to say he's re-thinking this whole macho warrior society. Honestly, we see the same story beats in a Star Trek episode.

But what makes this story interesting is the nuance and thoughtfulness applied to the characters and their world.

As noted, it's a very queer episode. Star Trek would have stayed miles from that. By definition, if it's a dome composed entirely of men, all the relationships are between men. That said, it's handled with sensitivity and intelligence. It's outrageous yes, just the concept is outrageous. Colicos and Morse are both too talented as actors not to appreciate and sharpen the camp or gay subtext, but they never go overboard or make their characters clichés. It's amazing that this could be made in the 1970s.

The episode was based on a story by Ursula K. Le Guin, and it shows. It's hard to imagine that a male writer, or a non-sf writer could have handled a story like this with the intelligence and sensitivity she brings to it. Le Guin was part of Ellison's dream team of bringing real science fiction writers to the Starlost to write scripts. In hindsight, it seems a particularly daft vision. The requirements and skills for television writing as opposed to short story or novel writing are quite different. Except for the odd crossover artist, like Ellison himself, there wasn't a lot of overlap.

There are of course the creaky bits, plastic helmets and bits of silliness, awful fight choreography. The performances are more theatrical than natural, but it works. In the end, it's a compelling episode, driven by Colicos and Morse, their bittersweet relationship, and their poignant existences in a society which restricts and smothers both of them.

Creatives

Ursula K. Le Guin needs no introduction, one of the leading speculative fiction writers of her era, she produced a number of classic works, Earthsea, the Lathe of Heaven, and the Left Hand of Darkness among many others.

Harvey Hart, who had also directed Voyage of Discovery, was a Toronto born director and producer. He seems to have been well liked, and noted as having a warm relationships with his actors.

Martin Lager, 37 years old at the time, was a Canadian writer and producer working almost exclusively in Canada. He would write four of Starlost's episodes, putting him behind only Norman Klenman himself. Lager's episodes are The Goddess Calabra, the Astro-Medics, The Implant People and the deplorable Space Precinct. The Goddess Calabra is far and away his best work on the show, although based on Ursula K. Le Guin's story. In Astro-Medic he shares credit with Paul Schneider and in Implant People he shares credit with another American writer, John Meredyth Lucas. Space Precinct is his only genuinely solo work. Although a Canadian writer, I don't think that there's much in his episodes that's strongly reflective of Canadian culture or sensibilities. With the exception of Calabra, the scripts he's associated with feel mainly pedestrian.

John Colicos, featuring in Star Trek and Battlestar Galactica, and a character actor with a long history in Hollywood, was actually born Canadian. In fact, outside of Hollywood, he had a reputation as one of Canada's finest Shakespearean actors. I assume that despite his expatriate status, he ticked a box for Canadian content. From his point of view, I suspect that he'd been in so many productions, that his work on Starlost was just another Tuesday.

Similarly, his co-star, Barry Morse was once asked about his role on the Starlost, and replied that after appearing in 3000 productions, he simply didn't remember anything – just another role.

Continuity and Backstory

This episode reinforces the notion that most of the domes are on their own. Cypress Corners is not the only dome which seems to have largely forgotten about the rest of the Ark.

We get a glimpse at the level of technology that must have been around. There are no women in this dome, for all intents and purposes, there may never have been women in this dome. Men only are being reproduced by technology. Where did this come from? You would need an established infrastructure to turn out a steady population of new babies. Are all the domes birthing people mechanically, with Cypress Corners being an exception? Did this dome start out as men only, perhaps an established culture or subculture from the era of the Ark's construction?

Or was it established as some sort of social experiment? We see active social meddling in Only Man is Vile. The Beehive features ongoing biological research. Perhaps it was a thing. The Ark was venturing into deep space with no possible back up, so maybe there were ongoing research programs of all sorts, hoping to find solutions to the challenges of everything from an endless voyage to alien worlds or even extraterrestrial civilizations.

Beyond this, there's bits of continuity. In the previous episode, the trio had escaped danger, and Garth called them to go home. This episode, following on the heels, Garth complains that they should have listened to him when he told them they should go home.

The idea of the back-up Bridge is from Ben Bova's section of the series bible, inspired by American design of naval warships, which always have a secondary Bridge in case the main Bridge is destroyed in combat.

Creators and Cast

Directed by Harvey Hart
Story by Ursula K. Le Guin
Written by Martin Lager
&&&
Devon: Keir Dullea
Rachel: Gay Rowan
Garth: Robin Ward
Sphere Projection: William Osler
The Governor: John Colicos
Shaliff: Barry Morse
Priest: Dominic Hogan
Captain of the Guards: Michael Kirby
1st Soldier: Peter Langley
2nd Soldier: Ardon Bess
Deputy: George Narkowych

&&&
Original Airdate: October 6, 1973

THE PISCES – EPISODE FOUR

The Pisces Scoutship returns to the Ark after being lost for ten years, but on the Ark four hundred years have passed.

The Pisces, the Ark's scout-ship, sent out to chart potential new worlds, returns. But without their realizing it, due to time dilation from flying close to the speed of light, although the crew have experienced only ten years, four hundred and nine years have passed on board the Ark. Bummer.

As if that isn't enough, the long spell at super-luminal speeds means that the Pisces crew has been afflicted with 'space senility,' and they'll die soon, unless they go back to their ship and light speed.

Yes, literally a couple of episodes after Lazarus in the Mists, it's another 'The Sleeper Awakens' episode, right down to the old crew members, having shown up out of the past, now having to return to where they came from to save their lives. This time it's a variation on the Flying Dutchman.

This episode is characterized by fairly static direction. After some impressive opening shots of vast empty corridors bringing home the immensity and desolation of the Ark, we switch over to Devon, Garth and Rachel sleeping in their makeshift quarters. Devon wakes up, has a snack. And then an alarm rings. It's hardly opening with a bang.

They rush to a viewport, there's another remarkably static shot of the three of them staring out into space, all lined up like a kindergarten class picture. That sort of composition, the three of them lined up shows up a lot, both in this episode and others.

After that dismal beginning, the episode improves, lightened and brightened considerably by Lloyd Bochner's no nonsense Colonel

Garoway. In fact, so commanding is the force of his personality that he actually gets Garth to start unloading the ship. That's kind of a thing with Garth, he just seems to instinctively do what he's told, providing that the person giving the orders is sufficiently authoritative. He does the exact same thing later in Circuits of Death.

Devon and his friends try and tell them of the disaster. Garoway just doesn't get it. This is a running thing, he is simply in complete denial. He refuses to believe he's been gone for four hundred years. He refuses to believe that his family is dead. That his home has been abandoned so long no one even remembers. It's weird, he'll be faced with it, have his nose rubbed in it, but an instant later, he's back to denial. Even when he acknowledges it intellectually, you can see that he's not accepting it emotionally.

His first response is to go out for a scouting mission in the Pisces to survey the Ark, and he invites Devon and friends to come with them and see the Ark from the outside.

Cue the long long scenes of the Ark, shots of Garth, Devon and Rachel looking at the Ark, shots of their faces superimposed on the Ark. The whole thing is clearly trying for one of those *"Ooh Ahh"* sense of wonder moments.

Does it work?

You have to remember when this was made, the space age wasn't even fifteen years old. Sputnik, the first satellite, was only 1957, sixteen years before. The first men in space from both the USSR and the US were only 1961, twelve years earlier. The American two man Gemini program was 1965, eight years previous. The first three man rocket and first moon landing, the American Apollo program was 1969, four years before and lasted until 1972, the year before Starlost. The first space station, 1971, was the Russian Salyut, two years before. Throughout this period, unmanned probes like Mariner and Voyager were being sent all over the solar system, bringing back startling images of Mars, Jupiter, Saturn and their satellites. Meanwhile Canada, Europe, China and Japan were all putting their own satellites in orbit. This was happening right in front of us, the future literally unfolding before our eyes as a documentary.

While all this was going on, Hollywood was making its own pseudo-realistic space exploration movies, starting with Destination Moon in 1950. This would peak in 1968, with Stanley Kubrick's 2001: A Space Odyssey, depicting a technological near-future with all these slow tracking shots, loving visual explorations of technology and space, filled with documentary realism, portraying space stations, moon bases and a mission into the far reaches.

This was 'sense of wonder' stuff, with the wonders happening right in front of us, with the images and imagery of television and movies being extensions of what was actually happening. Breathtaking miracles of technotopia leaped from headlines and were rendered in movie theatres.

Douglas Trumbull would extend that 2001 aesthetic in his own film, Silent Running. And further into the designs for the Ark prop. It was a kind of techno-porn back then, these long, loving shots of spaceships. This trend would continue right onto the ponderous Star Trek: The Motion Picture.

Star Wars washed it all away in favour of Whiz Bang, but even there, that loving, lingering techno-porn sensibility was still evident in Lucas' opening tracking shot of the surfaces of two immense spaceships chasing each other.

In a sense, this is the 2001: A Space Odyssey moment - just being in space and flying around the Ark, seeing its immensity, the achievement it represented. It was very much a part of its age. It was about sense of wonder. This was the big money shot.

And you know what? It worked. Ten year old me, watching it, would have just been riveted. It was of the age when the average television audience would have just found it awe inspiring.

This is the thing with Starlost, or with any production like this. It's very much a product of its time, and indeed, of its place. The sort of things that blew people away then, the issues that animated people, even the references as we'll see in Circuit of Death, these things are lost to us and we look at it with a different sensibility.

This is a more jaded age, used to seeing more impressive special effects. Still, the detailing of the Ark, the slow tracking shots, are impressive.

But while they are touring, problems arise. To our trio's horror, the Pisces crew fall asleep right in the middle of piloting. The scout ship is drifting away from the Ark.

Oh no, crisis! There have been a couple of wobbly moments with Garoway and Janice, but this is the first clear sign of the senility that will infect each of them to varying degrees, and establish the imminent danger that propels the episode. Cue the dramatic music and commercial break.

What's happened is that the Pisces departed four hundred and nine years before on a scouting mission, and they were apparently hit by the same disaster that struck the Ark. They lost contact, and in trying to find the Ark, travelled up to sub-liminal speeds, somewhere between 90% and 99.9% of the speed of light. Because of time dilation, they only experienced ten years' time in all those centuries.

The problem is that when humans travel at these relativistic speeds, it affects their neural pathways. They acquire 'space senility,' an irreversible, fatal decay. The only escape is to return to relativistic velocities.

There's some genuine heart here. I've complained about the rather restrained emotion of Doctor Aaron's farewell to his wife in Lazarus from the Mists. They do it a little better here. But just a little.

The episode has the ideas all right. A lost crew returning to find everyone they ever knew dead and gone. The horror of their premature space senility, the fact that their minds are literally disintegrating before each other's eyes. There's some real emotional potential here.

The guest cast go through the motions effectively and hit all the right marks. But having said that, there's often a failure to follow through to deeper levels that may have made this episode a classic.

Never once does Garoway get the chance to express horror at his condition. We see him suffering spells of space senility, but we never ever go deeper. What does it feel like to know you've had a spell, and that you may have another one? What's it feel like to know your mind is going to rot? That it's unstoppable? The problem is that Garoway only has the one note, he never gives up and never wavers. He's relentlessly cheerful and businesslike. There's no moment when he really seems to grasp his condition, or comes to grips with it. It's always stiff upper lip with him.

In fact, this makes Garoway seem insufferably stupid. It's as if he's incapable of comprehending his environment. The Ark is deserted, he blithely ignores every sign. Persuaded to tour the damage, he refuses to accept it happened centuries ago. Even when he tours the ruins of his quarters, when he has it rubbed in his face, he just doesn't stop. That obstinacy may be more subtle symptom of his 'space senility' but it becomes almost annoying. Wake up, man!

Teale says *"Colonel Garoway is as shattered as we are."*

But he never ever gives a sign of it. Instead of a man bearing up under strain, he seems oblivious to it. I suppose that's one way of coping. But it makes him seem oblivious rather than sympathetic.

On the other hand, Teale and Janice are allowed to freak out. Of the two, Teale comes off best. She's least affected, but also the most open. Her character actually gets lines, delivering a lot of the exposition and explanation underpinning the story, but also acting decisively, arguing with Garoway, and pulling a stun-gun on Devon.

But they don't appear to suffer the same level of disease. At best, their symptoms seem to be panic, which isn't necessarily proof of the condition.

Instead, it's Garoway who experiences the worst of the sickness, and Teale and Janice who react to it. This produces a distancing effect on both sides. The audience doesn't truly become involved, or perhaps, not as involved as they could be.

Eventually, Janice and Teale, get tired of Garoway's denial and mutiny in a lunatic plan to abandon the Ark and fly back to Earth. Devon struggles with them causing Pisces to flounder. Cue scenes of everyone swinging wildly back and forth, pretending that the floors are tilting.

In the end, the Pisces crew realize they have no choice but to go back into space and cruise at relativistic velocities. They'll be the Flying

Dutchmen, forever doomed to travel at the edge of the speed of light, barely aging as centuries pass outside, never able to slow down, no home to go to.

It's poignant. It's tragic. There's something mythic there. And they, the creative team in front of and behind the camera, don't really do as much with it as they could have.

It's not necessarily badly handled in the way it's dealt with. But it never does reach the heights it could. Whether this is the fault of the writers, the script, the actors or the direction isn't clear. But stop a moment and think what a writer like Harlan Ellison could have done with it.

It could have been brilliant, it sits as merely ordinary. Not awful by any means, but simply ordinary. It's not a bad episode, and played the way it is, it could have made a slightly better than average episode of Lost in Space or a slightly sub-par episode of Star Trek.

Creatives

This episode was written by Norman Klenman, who we've discussed. This is one of four official credits.

Leo Orenstein, was a Montreal born writer, producer director, whose career in Canadian film and television stretched from 1954 to 1976. This was his second directing effort for Starlost, his other episode being Lazarus in the Mists.

Lloyd Bochner, who played Captain Garoway, was a Toronto-born actor whose work encompassed many mediums. Starting out in radio as an announcer, he began appearing on screen in 1946 and by 2002, had amassed a staggering 219 film and television credits. Like many other actors of his era, he moved to the United States early on to pursue his career. His work was primarily television and he was in pretty much everything, a notable credit was voice over work in the Batman animated series. Working and living mainly in the U.S., his role in Starlost probably related somewhat to his Canadian citizenship.

Carole Lazare, playing Teale, an unusually substantial role, was a Canadian actress active in the 1970s and 1980s, appearing in film and television, usually small roles, ranging from high end productions like

Cronenberg's 'The Fly' to B-Movies such as Ed Hunt's 'The Brain.' She wrote for an erotic television series, Bliss, and became an entrepreneur and consultant.

Diana Barrington was an English actress whose career ran from 1959 to 2002, who worked extensively in Canada.

Backstory and Continuity

The Pisces launched on its current mission on January 1, 2381. Its mission was to search for planets suitable for colonization. In order to do this effectively, it would have to be travelling much faster than the Ark, likely very close to the speed of light, 99% or better. When the disaster hit, the Ark went off course, and the Pisces spent ten years in relativistic time trying to locate them. That translated into a voyage of four hundred and nine years Ark time.

The Ark itself is travelling more slowly. Ben Bova's portion of the Starlost bible says that the Ark is moving at about thirty per cent of light speed. Otherwise, the Pisces could never have caught up with it.

Thirty per cent of light speed after a century or so would put the Ark about thirty to thirty-five light years out from Earth. The fact that the Ark was sending a ship out to scout for habitable worlds suggests that they believed that they were sufficiently far from Earth that they were relatively safe from the 'disaster of galactic proportions' at that distance. It seems they may have been wrong.

It's implied in the series, but not outright stated, that whatever disaster hit the Ark was the same one that afflicted the Pisces and killed half of the six person crew. If true, this must have been an incredibly wide spanning disaster, since the Pisces was well distant from the Ark. We might be looking at the shockwave front of a Supernova perhaps.

Ellison in his bible, drops a few hints that the cataclysm that hit the Earth, the fate of previous interstellar expeditions and the disaster that hit the Ark are all connected, and would be revealed in the final episode, but he never gets there. All we get are hints and some muttering about a giant black hole.

The fate of the Earth might still be in question. When Teale mutinies, she wants to take the Pisces all the way back to Earth. Ultimately, after dropping off the protagonists, that's the destination they settle on, hoping to find survivors. This may be delusional and her own version of space senility. But presumably she had some idea of the expected magnitude of the disaster and felt that there was a reasonable chance of survivors.

If the disaster that hit the Ark sufficiently widespread to cripple the Pisces, it could be that it was the same phenomenon that hit the earth decades earlier. Ellison's bible doesn't connect the two events, but within the series there are possible hints.

Assuming that the source of the threat was known, and the Ark was moving directly away from it, and assuming the threat was moving at or near the speed of light, the Ark would have been thirty light years out from Earth at the time of the disaster. Which would place Earth's catastrophe around 2351.

There's an interesting throwaway line when Colonel Garoway refers to something called the 'Dome Wars. 'Don't treat me like an old veteran of the Dome Wars, I can walk.'

This implies two things: 1) The Dome Wars had taken place in Garoway's lifetime or immediately prior. 2) That they had taken place so long ago that the veterans were retired and becoming extremely frail. Given that the reference was one of contempt, its unlikely many veterans were still active in the command structure. The Captain's age is given as forty-four years. Based on this, we'd hazard a guess that the Dome Wars occurred thirty to fifty years before Pisces left.

Given that the plural is used, it's likely the Dome Wars were likely not a single conflict, but more likely a series of conflicts and may have taken place over a period of several years.

It's possible that the Dome Wars resulted in some or perhaps all of the domes being locked down. Both Goddess Calabra and Mr. Smith of Manchester feature militaristic societies that might be products of these wars. Certainly Manchester is intent on resuming the Dome Wars, if it ever breaks out.

We have to wonder about Space Senility, as silly as that name is. Apparently, on this show, travel at relativistic velocities, over ninety per cent of the speed of light or closer, does some peculiar things to the human neural system, which can manifest, as narcolepsy, mania, obsessive behaviour, hyper-emotionalism, compulsivity and cognitive deterioration.

The crew of the Pisces have a bad case of it with Garoway being the worst. But having watched the rest of the series, I find myself starting to wonder. As the series progresses going to be meeting mad scientists and other people who exhibit deranged behaviour. The Ark is travelling at thirty per cent of light speed. Perhaps much milder form of Space Senility, or Relativity Senescence are occasionally cropping up throughout the Ark? It might explain a lot.

Sadly, chances are zero that Klenman or anyone else involved with the show had this or anything like this in mind, it was just that they needed to tell stories, and so they had to come up with demented and grotesque characters. But they did put it out there, and it does explain a lot.

Finally, a bit of internal continuity. As Garoway falls ill, Teale refers to the medical center, and Rachel tells her that they've been there and it's empty. This is a direct reference to Lazarus in the Mist.

Creators and Cast

Directed by Leo Orenstein
Written by Norman Klenman
&&&
Devon: Keir Dullea
Rachel: Gay Rowan
Garth: Robin Ward
Sphere Projector: William Osler
Colonel M. P. Garoway: Lloyd Bochner
Captain Janice: Carnes Diana Barrington
Navigator Teale: Carole Lazare
Old Man: Ted Beatie
Old Woman: Lillian Graham
&&&
Original Airdate: October 13, 1973

CHILDREN OF METHUSELAH – EPISODE FIVE

Our heroes discover a group of immortal children who believe that they are piloting the Ark

This is actually quite an interesting episode. Devon and his posse think they've discovered the back-up Bridge, only to find it occupied by creepy immortal children with psychic powers who believe that they're the real Bridge crew running the ship and that Devon and Garth are dangerous lunatics with an insane story.

It works, with heavy shades of John Wyndham's Midwich Cuckoos (made into a film as Village of the Damned). Creepy children are a bit of a minor staple in science fiction and horror. We have very definite ideas of what children are and how they should behave, and when they don't, it's deeply disturbing. There's a bit of that in Lord of the Flies. You also find that disturbing quality in the twins, in The Shining. It's a variation of the Uncanny Valley effect, a juxtaposition of something that seems normal, but isn't.

It's this cognitive dissonance, this sense of 'unearthly children' that really makes the episode and gives it its drawing power, all the while sneaking some fairly subtle ideas in under the radar.

In this case, we find that the children are actually over five hundred years old. They literally precede the launching of the Ark and their faded memories stretch all the way back to old Earth. Their aging process has been stopped so they'll never grow up (at least not until they're given an injection to jumpstart their maturation process).

Instead, they've been part of an experiment or project to train a Bridge crew, and they've been running the simulations so long and so perfectly in their hermetically sealed environment, that they've forgotten they were a lab experiment, if they ever knew it. After five hundred years, they believe that they're the real Bridge crew and that they're really piloting the Ark.

Because they're cut off, and they've been fed nothing but simulations, they don't realize that the Ark's been disabled by a disaster, that it's been drifting off course for centuries, and that it's about to plunge into a sun. And they don't believe a word of it, because it contradicts everything they know.

Even worse, five hundred years of monotony, of running repetitive simulations over and over, have worn down their identities. I don't know what five hundred years of rote repetition would do to a person, but it's probably not healthy.

They've become almost robotic. They believe that what they're doing is real, that they bear the weight of safely piloting the Ark and looking after three million lives, and so they've been forced into adult responsibilities.

The children are creepy because they don't act like children, they act like small adults; sober, attentive, professional and impersonal. The Captain plays like James T. Kirk, calm, collected and in command. The others carry on efficiently, there's no sense of play-acting their roles – they really are Captain and Bridge officers doing their job. At least, when they're on mission.

Off mission they don't speak, they stare. They've lost the ability to live outside their professional roles. They wear and identify themselves by numbers not names. They don't play games. Essentially, they've been robbed of their childhood, or had it eroded away.

So obviously, when Devon and friends show up, they're not welcome. They're seen as insane trespassers, and put on trial. The children being professionals attempt to check Devon's story, but they can't verify it because they're in their simulation. But even the existence of the adults is so disturbing that the Captain eventually decides to put them to death, Garth and Devon at least.

Rachel gets a dispensation and will be made a ward – there's a role reversal there, the mother figure becomes a ward of the children. Under Rachel's guidance, the children begin to recover their identities and even learn to play again, something the Captain finds deeply disturbing and unwelcome, because it's chaos and a break from the routine.

Ultimately, things are exposed when they're caught up in another simulated Bridge emergency and Devon deliberately screws things up by pressing a button. The kids are going 'Damn you, you've doomed us all!' But at the end of the countdown, it just goes 'Simulation failed, try again.'

That's when we realize how they became trapped – they were doing their simulations so perfectly, they never got an error message, they never made a mistake, and so they never got called out on it.

In the end, Devon and company move on, the kids remain behind. Through Rachel, they're now playing, their humanity is restored, and they're taking on names instead of numbers.

But the Captain, the leader, is left alone, staring off into space. I would imagine it's pretty traumatic to discover that the life you've lived for five hundred years, the weight that you thought you carried, was all a lie. I'd expect, after playtime, there's going to be some deep existential crises all around. There is just enough note of disquiet at the end.

Overall, it's a very watchable episode. Early in the season, there's enough budget that they've got decent production values in terms of sets and props built. I did catch a Spirograph design (that was a seventies children's toy which involved drawing geometric circles and arcs) (We were so easily amused in the seventies) though.

And the cast is large – counting both extras and speaking parts, there were at least seventeen kids of various sizes and ages. I'm quite impressed by that – children are notoriously difficult to wrangle, but they all manage to hit that creepy uncanny valley child/adult/robot vibe. The kids with speaking parts acquit themselves well.

"The kids were really fun," Gay Rowan remembers. *"I had quite a maternal instinct. So it was a lot of fun for me to do the mothering role. The Director was*

very patient with the kids and he worked hard on getting good performances out of them."

That sea of bodies is its own sort of production value, in some later episodes, there are only two guest actors and no extras, giving the episode a threadbare feel.

For once, Gay Rowan as Rachel, gets a decent role, interacting with the children and becoming something of a mother figure, not entirely metaphorical, she brings them through their emotional rebirths.

This is cliché of course but actually a positive thing, at least her character got something meaningful to do. Here she's a mother figure. In the preceding Goddess Calabra, she's the object of desire, which gives her a platform to build a performance. Basically, mother and sex object. Beyond that?

In many of the later episodes, Rowan didn't actually get much of a role. In part, that was the limitation of the character – Rachel is a pseudo-Amish woman from Cypress Corners with all the baggage that comes that. It's established in the first episode that she's brave and passionate, and willing to violate norms and rebel against convention.

In Pisces, there's a moment where talking to Janice and Teale, she feels frustration and loss at how much opportunity was denied to her growing up in Cypress Corners. In The Alien Oro, when speaking with Idona, she expresses a similar frustration with the opportunities that have been denied to her, a resentment of the restrictions and inherent sexism of Cypress Corners.

But often not much was done with her character. The reality is that often the scripts didn't really have much of a role for her, apart from standing around. She was the love interest, and in a potential love triangle, but that didn't pass muster with chaste Canadian standards.

"I think they were trying to create a romance between myself and Robin's character. I don't think that the romance took off the way they expected between myself and Keir's character. It was supposed to be myself and Devon. That didn't take off the way that they wanted it to. That was my sense," Gay Rowan recalls, suggesting perhaps it was a lack of sexual or romantic chemistry between herself and Dullea.

A lot of the problem came down to the stumbling sexism of the seventies. Feminism was becoming a thing, but no one knew what to do with it. There were no almost women involved in the creative side of Starlost, the producers, directors and writers literally all men. The only exceptions were writers Helen French and Marion Waldman, each co-credited on single episodes, and Ursula K. Le Guin, who was not directly involved, but a story contributor – someone else turned her story into a script. Outside of that, only casting and wardrobe, traditionally female occupations, were held by women.

"We all had Director's chairs, and someone wrote on mine "Hello my name is Rachel." It was a joke, because that was my line, in every episode - "Hello, my name is Rachel, what's yours." Rowan remembers.

"I got into an argument with one of the White Shoe Boys about my role, and he said 'What are you, a Woman's libber?' I said I guess I am!' We would try to change lines. I wanted to change lines all the time, that's when I got labeled a woman's libber. We would try our best to change things, we weren't always successful. I think they knew that the underutilized me. Definitely," Rowan said.

Underneath the surface, there are interesting ideas floating around. Children being forced into adult roles, and losing themselves. The crushing weight of routine and immortality. That notion that we only truly discover when making mistakes, or that perfection is a dead end.

It's a quietly thoughtful episode with a compelling premise, a potent central idea, and for once, it offers all the characters a useful role.

Creatives

Joseph L. Scanlon is credited with directing six episodes, starting with Children of Methuselah. The remainder are Mr. Smith of Manchester, the Alien Oro, the Implant People and Space Precinct, as well as an uncredited directing role on Gallery of Fear. Gay Rowan recalled him as her favourite director, *"I remember Joe Scanlon. I think Joe Scanlon took his job a little more seriously than a lot of the Directors did. He got into his work, and it showed in the way that he worked with us."*

Jonah Royston, forty-three years old in 1973, is actually the pseudonym of John C.W. Saxton, also known as John Saxton, a

Canadian writer and producer. His eclectic output included the Littlest Hobo, a children's series about a crime solving german shepherd, and Ilsa-She Wolf of the SS, starring Diane Thorne and shot on the sets of Hogan's Heroes, as well as low budget horror movies like Class of 1984 and Happy Birthday to Me, and a documentary/concert film about a Canadian country singer named Stomping Tom Connor. He seems to have bounced around in his career between Canada and the US, and between B-movies and eclectic projects. This is one of his two script credits for Starlost, and he has a separate credit for original story on this one.

George Ghent is also credited with the Starlost episode Gallery of Fear. He is fairly obscure. The Starlost episodes are his only writings credit on the IMDB. He has two dozen acting credits, almost all British, and is recorded in the UK comedies database. It may be that he was born in Canada and immigrated to England. But really, he's a blank spot on the map. An English actor with no known screenplay history.

This is the third episode whose title was expressly mentioned by Harlan Ellison as expressing a 'mythology' motif, making it one of the scripts he commissioned and worked on, although the nature and degree of his contribution is unclear. Ellison indicated he had selected six stories, but only mentioned only three. It's not clear whether the other three ever made it into production.

Backstory and Continuity

In the original Starlost Promo, Magicam is used to a man making his way through a gigantic child's fantasy landscape of toys, including a cymbal clapping monkey. This may have inspired a passage from Harlan Ellison's bible where he lists story ideas.

"In another dome they might find children who had been made immortal, frozen at the age of their adolescence, the remnants of a crèche, forced by survival to build a children's fantasy world."

In turn, this idea, may have inspired the immortal Children of Methuselah, although the child's fantasy landscape, and the Lord of the Flies motif was abandoned, in favour of them becoming miniature adults and the back-up Bridge crew.

The 'back-up Bridge' of course, is directly referenced from the Goddess Calabra, which is a concept that can be traced back to Ben Bova's contribution to the bible.

In this episode, one of the children reveals that her parents were left behind on Earth when the Ark launched, which means that she and her peers are at least five hundred years old, forever children trapped in ageless child bodies. Apparently, old Earth before the launching of the Ark appears to have worked out immortality, or at least prolonged life extension.

On the other hand, the children's tutors on the Ark eventually died of old age, the suggestion is that effective immortality only seems to be an option before you're grown up. But the Admiral offers to share the injection with Rachel, if she's compliant, which implies that this kind of molecular freezing/life extension is at least somewhat viable, at least for some adults.

That raises interesting questions for the population of the Ark. There's a presumption that most of the people on the Ark are living normal lifespans, otherwise it would be a lot harder for the isolated cultures to forget the nature of the world they live in. But there may be a few people here and there who were given or obtained extended lifespans. The characters of Doctor Asgard and Tabor, and Doctor Farthing and McBride, may be hard to rationalize without advanced life spans.

In terms of Devon's quest, this is a major advance. He's now found a group of people trained to actually pilot the Ark, all he has to do is find the genuine back up Bridge. One wonders though, why none of the Ark-wide organizations have thought to access these kids. Did they know about them? Or was this another secret sociological project, like Only Man is Vile.

Looking at Garth, although he's nominally a blacksmith at Cypress Corners, he's more than just some guy that pounds iron lumps with a hammer. Through the episode, he displays knowledge of electricity and wiring and is able to subvert security systems. I'm assuming that although Cypress Corners was rustic and traditional, the role of blacksmith also involved some higher technical training to maintain and repair the local systems. This isn't the only time Garth shows impressive technical ability.

This also raises the interesting notion that while Devon needed a key to get out, Garth had the technical skills to walk out the door and discover the Ark any time he ever wanted to. He just never felt the need.

Creators and Cast

Directed by Joseph L. Scanlon
Story by Jonah Royston (John C.W. Saxton)
Written by George Ghent and Jonah Royston (John C.W. Saxton)
&&&
Devon: Keir Dullea
Rachel: Gay Rowan
Garth: Robin Ward
Sphere Projector: William Osler
Captain/#1: David Tyrell
#2: Michael Tough
#4 (Jacob): Scott Fisher
#5 (Sarah): Susan Stacy
#6: Ricky O'Neill
#7: (David): Mark Lynas
#10 (Elizabeth): Gina Dick
&&&
Original Airdate: October 20, 1973

ONLY MAN IS VILE - EPISODE SIX

Our heroes fall into a strange dome of dysfunctional people, while shadowy forces watch.

Shimon Wincelberg, the scriptwriter, had written episodes for Star Trek, Lost in Space, Logan's Run, Planet of the Apes, Wild Wild West, The Immortal. Those are pretty solid genre credits. If you look him up on the IMDB, he has literally dozens upon dozens of credits in television, and a long history with stage plays.

So you would think he would have known what he was doing.

Because this is peculiar.

This feels like somebody's experimental, Avant Garde stage play put on in a converted garage and advertised by leaflets taped to lamp posts in a trendy district. It's got that odd feeling. Very stylized, very mannered. The characters aren't even really characters. They're 'archetypes.' Every line drips with 'importance.' It's all so 'meaningful' and 'art house.'

It also feels weirdly brief, like this is a thirty minute script, but it's been stretched out to full running time with a lot of pregnant pauses.

Not what you would expect from a guy who wrote everything from Mannix to Trapper John M.D.

We kind of wonder if it was even a Starlost script. As opposed to some art-house thing he did for a lark and pulled out of the closet when the program was accepting submissions. Or perhaps it was a rejected or abandoned Twilight Zone, or Outer Limits or Star Trek script that he just kept dusting off and submitting until someone finally bought it.

So what's the story? Devon and friends visit the 'Dome of Dysfunctional Asshats' also called 'New Eden.' Check that, 'New Eden' the heavy-handed symbolism starts early and doesn't let up.

It's a dome where everyone is riven by factions, no one trusts or likes each other, and everyone is terrified of the 'outsiders' - indestructible monsters who want to take their stuff, not that anyone has anything worth taking.

Devon and friends show up to an apparently empty community. Everyone has vanished. Food is left on dinner tables. Clearly, people have been living here, literally up to moments ago. But there's no sign of anyone anywhere, except for one terrified girl.

It seems that everyone freaked out and has been hiding in the basement, terrified of indestructible invaders. But we don't find that out for a while.

It all goes badly. Frankly, Devon and his pals should have just taken the hint, turned around and walked away. But then there'd be no story.

Anyway, it turns out that this supremely dysfunctional society is the product of two 'godlike scientists', from something called the Institute of Re-Education who sit in a cramped little room and watch proceedings.

Actually just one: Doctor Asgard, who believes that humans are just selfish shits and actively manipulates situations in order to screw with people's lives. His name, of course, is Asgard because that's the Norse home of the Gods. It's just a bit of meaningless pretentiousness. Asgard pontificates that he's doing it for the greater, good creating an improved, tougher, more aggressive race of humans who will be able to tame the new worlds that they settle on.

But the people he's produced are frightened, cowardly, bitter and selfish. They're backstabbers rather than world tamers, and they're clearly unable to maintain the society they've got even under the optimum conditions of the dome.

This doesn't bother Doctor Asgard, who continuously pontificates on human flaws and seems bent on bringing out the worst in the interlopers. It's pretty clear that Asgard doesn't really care about the official purposes of his experiment, he's just the sort of person who likes pulling the wings off of flies. This whole social experiment is simply petty sadism.

Which makes you wonder how long it's been going on? And how did Asgard get the authority to turn people's lives into a living hell?

But no worries, because the script doesn't even bother to think about questions like that, because this is 'Art' and the characters are 'Archetypes' in an abstract situation with no actual history - it's all supposed to just be there.

His companion, Doctor Tabor, is the good scientist. More heavy handed symbolics. Tabor is the name of a dome shaped mountain in Israel. Domes you see? It's also the site of a battle between Israelites and Canaanites, so you got your good vs evil. And it's the site of the transfiguration of Jesus. So... domes, good guys, holiness, got it going.

But it's not clear how 'good' Tabor is. She doesn't actually do anything, she simply hangs out with Asgard, as they watch the proceedings. She argues with Asgard that people are better than he thinks. And that's it. That's her whole shtick.

But when Asgard manipulates the situation, she does nothing. She doesn't even challenge his right to do so. She takes no actual action at any point, and fails to intervene in the proceedings in any way.

If we accept the premise of the episode, she's stood by observing and doing nothing while Asgard has turned the dome into a dysfunctional nightmare. Instead, she just has passive aggressive satisfaction when Asgard is eventually foiled and so she can tell him he's been proven wrong in his theories. Although Tabor's supposed to be the voice of 'good,' she's effectively irrelevant. Yeah, thanks for nothing, bitch.

Tabor's real purpose is simply to be there to give the antagonist someone to talk to. She's a sidekick, and a passive one at that. Unfortunately, we see this a lot in Starlost, McBride in Farthing's Comet is very much the same character, passively allowing another mad scientist to pilot the Ark into a comet.

The show, on the whole, had weak roles for women, something Gay Rowan herself has pointed out. Tabor, however, represents the nadir. Of course, this was 1973, but we haven't progressed as much as we might hope.

This is actually some sort of pseudo-biblical morality play. God and the Devil have gotten into an argument over whether humans are innately good or bad, and God has given the Devil carte blanche to prove his case. So God sits by while the Devil imposes all tribulations on the selected victim. We've seen this kind of story before.

To be fair to Wincelberg, he was Jewish, and his faith was a genuine part of his life and thinking, so it's not surprising to find him reaching for these themes in his writing.

But frankly, it doesn't speak well of a God who permits a supernatural sadist to randomly torture people. And it's not exactly edifying to see it play out here. Tabor in this story is far from the role of God or even 'good.' She gives no evidence of any kind of power. She's just the 'weak tea' voice of goodness, utterly useless, except to give Asgard someone to talk to. She has no impact on the story or plot whatsoever. Take her out, you'd never notice.

The two Doctors are omniscient observers, not actually interacting with anyone, or taking any actual action. They spend most of their time sitting down and just making snarky comments at each other.

Seriously, this is low impact acting, in only one shot does Asgard even bother to stand up. The rest of the time, he's seated at a table in front of a stationary camera. Occasionally he dramatically pushes a button.

Actually, you could take both Tabor and Asgard out, and it wouldn't change anything. All they're doing is fatuous commentary and moralising, which has been done to death. Neither of them actually take any direct action.

Our protagonists never actually meets or even communicates with Asgard or Tabor. Through the whole episode, including the end, they remain oblivious to them.

Edit them out completely, and you still have the same story of Devon and friends finding that the inhabitants of New Eden have made their own lives into dysfunctional hells, having fallen for the designated serpent in the garden. Of course then you've cut out ten minutes of what is already a thin, thin script.

There's also a girl that Doctor Asgard sends to sew dissension and depression among the protagonists. Her name is Lethe after the Greek mythological river of forgetfulness, and a tributary of the Styx, because, pretentiousness!

We think she's a robot though, or possibly a grad student, same thing really. She's exactly that colourless. In the pseudo-biblical narrative of the story, she's the official 'Serpent in the Garden' whose job is to bring out the character's darker sides and drive them apart. And yes, at one point Asgard actually calls his agent a 'serpent,' because, you know, pretentiousness.

She does this by getting alone with each of them, giving them a gun, and going *"Your friends really don't like you."*

Again symbolism – she does her shtick on Rachel when Rachel is caring for her and being a nurse, so Nurture. She hits on Devon when he's trying to activate a dead sphere projector, because, Seeker. She approaches Garth when he's standing among trees, because... Down to Earth? More ham-handed symbolism.

It genuinely is that lame. The actress approaches her role with the earnestness and the utterly wooden declamation of a junior high school morality production.

I'm surprised that at some point she doesn't say *"Have some drugs, kids! Drugs are cool!"*

Although, now that we think about it, she does get Garth drunk, so maybe they hit that cliché after all. Turns out, Garth is a mean drunk by the way.

But it's okay, she's not a character, there is no person there. There's no need for her to be persuasive, or seductive, or to express any emotion, or for her dialogue to be lively or convincing. She's an 'Archetype' dammit, in a 'Role,' dammit, doing 'Important Art,' dammit.

Devon goes off and gets himself captured, leading to a tedious conversation with the Eden people which goes like this:

Eden: You are our enemy. Our enemy is indestructible, and they want to destroy us.

Devon: I don't want to destroy you. I'm bleeding, therefore I'm not indestructible, so I'm obviously not your enemy.

Eden: Aha! Our enemy can bleed!

It goes around like this over and over. The repetition is painful and stilted. Slow learners.

Rachel isn't fooled by the serpent/robot/grad student. But Garth gets all depressed and just wants to lie down, until Rachel comes around and kicks him when its time to rescue Devon.

At first, he's under Lethe's spell, you can tell because all of a sudden his acting is as wooden as hers, and he's going 'Devon is my enemy. But later, he catches Lethe talking to a wall about an 'experiment' and figures out that he's been had.

He returns to save Devon, and because this is a heavy-handed pretentious script, he does it by cutting himself to show he can bleed and is mortal, and then melts the Edenites stony crazy hearts by offering to sacrifice himself in place of Devon.

Then there's a lecture about something - humanity maybe, or friendship, or just not being dicks. Our heroes leave.

New Eden is still a dysfunctional nightmare. Tabor has the last laugh while Asgard grumbles, but nothing in their relationship changes. End of story.

Honestly, this feels generic. There isn't anything here that you couldn't imagine as a Star Trek script, or a Lost in Space script or an Outer Limits or Twilight Zone script. Or more accurately, a rejected sci-fi script. This feels like somebody made a quick buck, dusting off an old file.

If there is any actual subtext to be found, it's that the people of the New Eden are ultimately a mirror reflection of the people of the Ark that Devon is trying to save. Everyone is isolated, they are, on the micro and macro levels, selfish, self-absorbed and indifferent to the larger world around them, unable to grasp the need to rise above their own concerns, to embrace the larger community.

Perhaps this may have been the reason that the Canadian producers bought it. Who knows? One can imagine the producer and the script editor sitting around going *"Hey, this script is like a microcosm of the larger situation with the Ark, let's go with it."*

Which in turn might resemble a microcosm on the often toxic regionalism and angry division in Canadian society. The 1970s were a cranky era when Albertans were outraged by French writing on the back of corn flakes boxes, and Quebecers were bluntly asking why they were even in the same country with the rest of us.

It feels farfetched. But who knows? The only support for that notion is that through the series, there's a consistent Canadian bias, so there may have been some degree of conscious or unconscious selection.

But there could be any number of other more prosaic reasons for this story. Maybe they were just awed by Shimon Wincelberg's credentials. Or maybe Norman Klenman owed him a favour. Or maybe they were short of scripts, and this was what was available. Maybe they just liked it for whatever reason. There's no way to know.

Wincelberg did travel to Canada to adapt the script, and he seems to have enjoyed his visit. So perhaps we're just being harsh.

But the Canadian/Ark metaphor is thin, if it's there at all. The Ark faces actual destruction, its dysfunction is the product of accident and isolation, not some meddling jerk.

For the people of New Eden, their danger is largely imaginary, and their dysfunction is the work of a malicious, god-like scientist meddling in their lives.

Still, there may be some degree of significance to be had, some contribution to the idea or subtext of Devon's quest for community, or to rebuild a shattered community.

Regardless, this one is pretty tough going, unless you like shallow, pretentious and wooden.

Creatives

The Director, Ed Richardson was Associate Producer or Producer for all sixteen episodes of Starlost, and likely one of the creative forces for the actual production. He likely had an outsize influence on the shaping of the show. He went on to produce or executive produce a half dozen Canadian television series, including the Littlest Hobo, the Lost Satellite and Cold Front. This was the first of four episodes that he would direct, the others being Gallery of Fear, Farthing's Comet and an uncredited directing role on Mr. Smith of Manchester.

Writer Shimon Wincelberg, was born in 1924 in Germany, he became an American in the 1930s when he and his family fled Nazi Germany. He served in US Army Intelligence during WWII. Starting in 1953, he began selling short stories, and branched out into books and scripts for stage, film and television. His genre work was substantial, but literally, he wrote everything. Wincelberg actually travelled to Toronto to work with the production, and had a pleasant experience.

Backstory and Continuity

You kind of have to wonder just how messed up the Ark is, that a character like Doctor Asgard would be allowed to carry out his demented social experiment. It begs all sorts of questions. How long has this been going on? Or allowed to be going on? Is Asgard immortal or somehow long lived, like the Children of Methuselah? How did he get his authority?

A peculiar observation about Doctors Asgard and Tabor, they didn't know that the Ark is in danger of plunging into a sun. Asgard flatly doesn't believe it. But as we'll see, other advanced societies on the Ark, as in the Astro-Medics or Farthing's Comet, are well aware of it. So Asgard and the Institute for Re-Education seem to be disconnected for whatever passes for mainstream Ark society these days.

There might actually be some justification for elaborate social research projects. All the eggs were being loaded into one basket and sent off into deep space. The domes, large as they were, were finite, which seems to have led to the Dome Wars within a century of departure. The conditions of the Ark and its situation were unique and unprecedented, and eventually they'd come to completely alien worlds.

Maybe the builders of the Ark decided it would be useful to set aside self-contained modules for social experiments – hence the Institute for Re-Education. But if so, they blew it, letting a sadist like Asgard run things. Still, this leaves the possibility that some of the groups encountered, the back-up crew in Children of Methuselah, or the all-male society of Omicron may have been experiments.

Or maybe the Ark just has a problem with mad scientists? Further on in the series, we meet Doctor Farthing, who also has an ineffective sidekick, and who manages to endanger everyone by steering the Ark into the path of a comet because... Science! And there's also Doctor Sakharov who gets frustrated and tries to blow the entire Ark up in Circuit of Death.

Thinking out loud, we discovered that in Pisces, there's a thing called 'space senility.' If you travel to close to the speed of the light, it can induce an Alzheimer's-like condition. The Ark is moving at 30% of light speed, presumably to avoid the syndrome. But maybe a very mild form of it is striking individuals all over the Ark.

Creators and Cast

Directed by Ed Richardson
Written by Shimon Wincelberg
&&&
Cast
Devon: Keir Dullea
Rachel: Gay Rowan
Garth: Robin Ward
Sphere Projector: William Osler
Dr. Asgard: Simon Oakland
Dr. Diana Tabor: Irena Mayeska
Lethe: Trudy Young
Village Elder: Tim Whelan
Village Man: John Bethune
&&&
Original Airdate: October 27, 1973

CIRCUIT OF DEATH EPISODE SEVEN

A renegade scientist triggers the Ark's self-destruct, to stop it, Devon and Garth must miniaturize.

I will confess: I was all set to despise this episode. The plotline is that Devon and Garth get miniaturized to go inside a computer.

Can't you just feel the stupid rolling off the very idea?

Miniaturizing people is one of those hoary 1950s B-movie clichés. You have your Fantastic Voyage, where a miniaturized crew takes a submarine around someone's blood vessels. There is also the Incredible Shrinking man, Attack of the Puppet People, Irwin Allen's Land of the Giants and many similar productions.

In the 80s there was a new wave of these movies – Honey I Shrunk the Kids, the Incredible Shrinking Woman. Always played for laughs.

It's always struck me as one of the most insultingly stupid tropes. It just makes no sense at all. But it's appealing because it does make good visuals as cast members wrestle their way through sets of oversized props. But it's a gimmick, its nothing but a gimmick.

So, imagine my surprise when I actually found it engaging, and the miniaturization wasn't absolutely stupid! The rationale doesn't actually make a sense, but its engaging bafflegab.

All right, let's get to the story: There's this guy, he's middle aged, black, focussed and confident. He absolutely knows what he's doing and why he is doing it.

He and his daughter show up on Bridge, and they get to work. His name is Doctor Sakharov Richards, played by Percy Rodrigues, and his daughter is Valerie Richards, played by Nerene Virgin.

Oddly, the name Sakharov only appears in script, and in places like IMDB credits, or VHS box information. I don't believe it's spoken aloud. Throughout the episode the character is called Richards. The Sphere Projector gives the name as I.A. Richards.

Sakharov, by the way, was the name of a famous Soviet (Russian) dissident from around this era. Dr. Andrei Sakharov was a nuclear physicist who became a peace advocate and human rights activist.

Starting around 1972, the Soviet government began to persecute him for his activism. Sakharov had been a dedicated communist, but between his activism and the resulting persecution, he became bitter and disillusioned, eventually coming to describe the Soviet Union as a cancer on humanity. Repression escalated, and he ended up as a political prisoner in the 70s and 80s.

Since this was the middle of the Cold War, Sakharov's dissidence, his advocacy, and his repression made him famous in the West. He became an international celebrity, was nominated for the Nobel Peace Prize in 1973, and won it in 1974. Sakharov Richards, as we'll see, is a deliberate nod to the Russian Sakharov.

Getting back to the episode, Richards doesn't explain what he's doing initially, he just sets about it, very purposefully. This, by the way, is the fourth episode that makes use of the Bridge set, they were getting their monies worth.

We find out gradually that he's planning to blow up the Ark, and escape with his daughter in the Ark's 'black box' module, which is designed to seek out and land on the nearest planet with all the Ark's records.

As far as he's concerned, the Ark is doomed, the domes are deteriorating, the systems are degrading and there's no saving it. So he's just doing people a favour by putting them out of their misery while he gets the hell out of dodge. He's practically a humanitarian by his lights.

It's insane. But the thing is, he does this with such reasonable conviction and certainty that for a second, you almost go along with it. He never rants or raves, he's always controlled, rational and competent, which makes it insidiously compelling. You're going 'Oh yeah, that makes sense...Wait! What?'

Devon and friends show up in response to an alarm he sets off. In this episode, they are out of their Cypress Corners duds and wearing silver jumpsuits. No explanation is given for the wardrobe change. These are the Ark's space suits, they're also worn in The Alien Oro, Farthing's Comet and Space Precinct.

Richards is not thrown by their appearance at all. To his credit, he's always icily calm and rational, even if his goal is demented. He gives them a story, and then enlists them, putting them to work loading up the escape pod. He's so confident and commanding, that they actually do what they're told.

Luckily, Devon notices that something isn't right - why load food on an unmanned probe? Unfazed, Richards invites our heroes out to discuss the matter and then locks them out of the Bridge.

Unfortunately, it all goes wrong. The escape pod gets jammed. Sakharov and his daughter are stuck on the Ark with the rest of us. At that point, he's got to cancel the self-destruct. But the circuits are fried. It has to be repaired before they all die. Richards will need to repair it, but he can't do it alone.

By the way, I just want to say, it's pretty flawed design when you have to trigger the self-destruct in order to be able to launch an escape pod. Even if it's the black box pod. Is it really that hard to imagine circumstances where you might want to use an escape pod, or launch a black box, without destroying the Ark?

At this point, another character, Cort, played by Calvin Butler shows up to arrest Sakharov. Nobody cares since the Ark is on a self-destruct count-down, and he doesn't actually offer anything to the plot. He's actually just there to show a little bit of Sakharov's background – the Doctor is not in good with the powers that be. Cort is also the love interest for Sakharov's daughter, but nothing is done with that either.

Nerene Virgin, playing Sakharov's daughter, is another of the female sidekicks that the show tended towards. In this case, she's almost unnecessary as a character. Since our protagonists encounter Sakharov almost immediately, she doesn't get much to do. On the other hand the existence of the character helps to define and soften Sakharov. Still, Ms Virgin is not well served. But then again, neither is Butler and his character.

But through this, and through various other means including conversations, references, and exposition from the sphere projector, we get a detailed background on Sakharov. Like the real life Sakharov, this Sakharov was a progressive, a human rights activist and populist. He led the Citizens party in his dome. Unfortunately, after the rival Control Party won election, they ended democracy and imposed a totalitarian state, imprisoning thinkers and scientists. With scientists and technicians in jail the environment of the dome began deteriorating, but the Control party was more interested in politics and power. Sakharov was the last dissident, when we met him he was on the run and fleeing arrest, all hope and faith gone.

The trajectories and fates of the real and fictional Sakharov's track each other, loosely. Both are dissidents and idealists crushed by totalitarianism. Both end up disillusioned.

There may also be an American race relations subtext, Sakharov Richards is a civil rights advocate who loses faith in a broken, repressive system and wants to burn it down, perhaps a reflection on some level of the Malcolm X frustrations and disillusionment with the civil rights movement and the reactionary persecution it faced.

Which brings us to the Sakharov we see at the start of the episode. Underneath that cold-blooded approach is a broken man, an idealist who has lost faith in humanity. He believes the Ark is doomed, if it doesn't hit the star, its systems will fail. Kinder to blow it up. This seems like a rather genocidal over-reaction, but it is a fascinating character study.

Back to the story: The self-destruct is counting down, to stop it they'll have to go inside the computer. We're about to get into the miniaturization. It turns out it's not that bad.

Rather than physically miniaturizing Devon and Sakharov, they're essentially placed into light comas, and their minds are projected into tiny telekinetic avatar-constructs that can wander around inside the computer. Yes, it's stupid. But it's not intolerably stupid.

It works dramatically. The inside of the computer is represented as polka dot land. A series of white boxes and levels filled with dots, salted here and there with what are supposed to be computer chips, transistors and diodes. It's a rather abstract representation of what an electronic micro-circuit would look like in the early 70s. It's also a dangerous environment because if you step wrong, you can make a connection between two live elements and get electrocuted.

So... none of those idiotic gigantic prop versions of tiny household objects, which is kind of a relief. Instead you have this weirdly interesting production design, like something out of an Austin Powers movie. It doesn't, in any way, look realistic, but it looks fake in a good way.

Sakharov treats Devon as little better than a half-trained dog. He's got a point. Rodrigues is very good at giving a sense his character is blindingly intelligent.

But then Sakharov nearly electrocutes himself, which is kind of embarrassing, particularly when he does it in front of Devon. Garth joins the miniature crew to help, and together he and Devon rescue Sakharov. It seems that in order to interrupt the self-destruct circuit, he'll have to sacrifice himself.

In the end, Sakharov sends Devon and Garth away. It's an important point, and maybe a redemptive one. At the start of the episode he was willing to destroy the entire Ark. He just didn't care. And at least initially, he simply didn't care about Devon and Garth, or anyone else. He has to save the Ark, at the cost of his own life, that's the only way to save his daughter. But in ensuring the survival of Devon and Garth he has redeemed himself, rediscovered his faith in humanity, and recovered some of his ideals.

Frankly, it's a much better episode than I was expecting. The correspondence between the real and fictional Sakharov is deliberate, and the story explores the progressive idealism, persecution and disillusionment of Richards in an interesting way.

The fictional Sakharov, is a fascinating character. Despite his attempt at cold blooded mass murder, you respect the man for his intelligence, clinical drive and his genuine conviction.

It would be easy to play him as a villain or a madman, but he's never anything but coolly analytical. His backstory is revealed gradually and effectively, and it adds nuance to the character with each step. Even as he's dying, he sticks to his conviction that the Ark is doomed, but he's willing to die for the chance that he can be proven wrong.

Setting aside the miniaturization nonsense, this episode marks a critical thematic shift for the Starlost. The episodes up to now have been basically standard Sci-Fi tropes, the sleeper wakes, the Flying Dutchman, unnatural children, etc. We still have that here with the miniaturization gimmick.

But suddenly, there's a hard shift to politics and political and social issues. The episode dwells on Sakharov's life and experiences, the sustainability of the Ark, the challenge of totalitarianism. There's almost a hesitation in bringing it up, hence the wrapping of the episode in a Sci-Fi cloak of miniaturization.

But still, there's a palpable shift from generic Sci-Fi to something more political and issues based, through Manchester, the Implant People, the Oro Episodes, and even the Gallery of Fear.

Bottom line? The show managed to take an idiotic Sci-Fi gimmick and render it in an unusual and visually interesting way, and used it as a driver for an effective drama.

Creatives

The Starlost was the first Directing credit for Peter Leven, although he had a handful of second unit or assistant directing credits going back to 1965. His career as a Director ran from 1973 to 2010, including eighty-one credits, all either television series or television movies, mainly based in California.

For writers we have the ubiquitous Norman Klenman, covered extensively elsewhere.

Percy Rodrigues, who plays Sakharov Richards, was actually a Montreal born African-Canadian actor. Distinguishing himself on the Canadian stage, offers of film and television roles drew him to the United States in the 1960s, where he accumulated over a hundred acting or voice credits. Among his notable genre credits, he did voice work for Michael Jackson's Captain Eo and the animated Heavy Metal movie, he also appeared in Star Trek, Planet of the Apes and Mission Impossible. As was common for the time, he was a political activist involved in the civil rights movement.

Nerene Virgin was a Canadian actress from Burlington, Ontario, whose film and television career ran from 1971 through 2000. She passed away in 2024.

Backstory and Continuity

So... the only way to launch this black-box escape pod is to activate the self-destruct for the entire Ark? Wow. Talk about bad design! It's one thing if an external force destroys the Ark, sure launch away. But self-destruct? Why would anyone build a self-destruct for the entire Ark anyway? Why would that even be necessary? How would that be a good idea?

But Sakharov's plan begs the question: Where were they going? Sakharov is going to blow up the Ark? So then what? Starve to death in the escape pod? Was there a destination? It's never mentioned, never discussed and never resolved. Of course, in other episodes, we find that the Ark is passing near two human civilizations, Exar and the Federation. Does Sakharov know about either of these? Is he trying for one of them? And if he knows, then how widespread is this knowledge on the Ark?

Sakharov is convinced the Ark is doomed because his own dome is failing, and he asserts that failure and deterioration is widespread. Actually, we've seen or heard of several domes that appear to be in deep trouble – Manchester is verging on ecological catastrophe, the dome of the implant people appears to be in decline, the Egrek dome mentioned in Oro suffers from toxic contamination, our protagonists frequently encounter areas of broken structure, failing mechanisms or people reverted to savagery.

Is the deterioration of the domes related to the disaster? Possible. At the very least, four hundred years without active maintenance is doing it no favours. On the other hand the Ark is well over five hundred years old, it may well be nearing the end of its physical life-span. It may not have actually been intended to last this long.

A small continuity nod. When Richards and his daughter visit the Bridge, they observe that someone's been here before. It's been cleaned up and the bodies are gone.

That's a reference to the Pisces episode, where we saw the Pisces crew visit the Bridge with our heroes. They had dinner there and we saw Garoway try to fix some of the circuitry and giving up. Clearly, as part of the failed effort to restore the Bridge, and before their dinner/party they did clean up. It makes sense, who wants to eat with corpses laying around?

Creators and Cast

Directed by Peter Leven
Written by Norman Klenman
&&&
Devon: Keir Dullea
Rachel: Gay Rowan
Garth: Robin Ward
Sphere Projection: William Osler
Sakharov Richards: Percy Rodrigues
Valerie Richards: Nerene Virgin
Security Officer Cort: Calvin Butler
&&&
Original Airdate: November 10, 1973

GALLERY OF FEAR – EPISODE EIGHT

Driven into a mysterious Art Gallery, our heroes encounter an unnatural foe.

As Devon, Rachel and Garth are walking through the Ark's vast empty corridors, a strange dusty wind kicks up. Not something you would expect on a spaceship, and probably not a good sign. The spooky wind grows in intensity, until Devon and his friends are literally hanging on for dear life, and are forced to seek shelter in a vast ... art gallery?

As Devon and his friends wander the bright, clear gallery, they discover that the artwork is alive, or at least psychically responsive, it changes and interacts with their thoughts and aesthetic. It's an interesting idea in and of itself.

The curator, Daphne, appears out of nowhere to guide them through the gallery and offer refreshments. They're given rooms. They change into Ark uniforms. They are treated to a high class dinner party.

It gets strange. Rachel's mother appears to her. Garth's father shows up to argue with Garth and Devon. Both of these characters are played by their actors, Jim Barron and Aileen Seaton respectively, from the pilot episode Journey of Discovery

Garth and Rachel act weird as if under hypnotic spells. There are trippy psychedelic light effects. Devon eventually realizes that it's all illusions and head games.

The name Magnus keeps coming up. Devon goes to the Computer terminal to ask about Magnus, but it flatly refuses to tell him anything.

Gradually he learns that everything that's happening is the work of a rogue AI named Magnus, which has been trapped in the Gallery and wants someone to let it out.

Okay, so what we have here is the stereotypical 'Aliens screw with people's minds' shtick. This goes all the way back to Journey to the Seventh Planet, or Star Trek's pilot episode, The Cage. And probably more than a few episodes of Outer Limits, Twilight Zone and so forth, all the way back to the pulp magazines of the 1930s. It's one of those classic concepts.

But that really sells it short, there are some interesting things going on here.

For instance, this reads as an ultramodern ghost story. There are a lot of ghost story elements, the creepy wind, the mysterious room, the apparitions. It eschews the creaky old haunted house and dark corners for a brightly lit landscape.

Some of it, particularly the dinner scene, feels like direct allusions to 2001: A Space Odyssey, a reference to the final phase, where the unseen aliens have Dullea's astronaut, and there are these surreal scenes of living his life and having dinner before mutating into the star child.

The another allusion to 2001 is the way Devon's destruction of the AI Magnus, parallel's Dullea's 2001 character's destruction of the AI Hal, even to the point of pulling out the circuit plates. In both, we see the death of the AI: Hal's childish sing song, and Magnus' vanishing face.

Typically, with a lot of these 'aliens screw with people's minds' stories, it usually wraps up when people figure out 'hey these aliens are screwing with our minds!' At which point, the mask comes off, and you move directly to the final throw down.

Here it's a little more complicated, the narrative unspools slowly. We hear about Magnus a lot before we find out what he is - an AI powerful enough to manufacture psychic re-creations of people, including the curator, Garth's Father, Rachel's mother, the deceased Admiral of the Ark. Within the gallery, Magnus can create literally anything. We only slowly grasp Magnus' abilities.

As we figure out what Magnus is and what he can do, we learn his intentions. He wants out of his cage. He's the genii in the bottle that needs someone else to set him free.

The rest of the episode becomes a battle of wills between a desperate Magnus, trying every tactic from threats to blandishments to bribes to get Devon to free him, and an increasingly stubborn Devon.

I don't know that I'm entirely satisfied. The script calls for all sorts of creepy things, as with the whole ghost story, weird shtick. This is attributed to Magnus playing head games, but it feels a little gratuitous. It's just an AI that wants to be free, is all that dancing around necessary? It strikes me that Magnus pulls stuff that just doesn't advance its agenda.

In the end, Devon stops just short of releasing the rogue AI, and instead opts to destroy him. Devon's argument is that there's no way to control an intelligence smarter than humans are, Magnus' freedom means Magnus' rule.

There are a few things that I find interesting, and a bit unusual.

One is that there's actually a debate among the trio. Rachel challenges the morality of destroying Magnus. Garth wonders if perhaps it can be bargained with.

Star Trek never debated that. Crazed AI? Captain Kirk just snuffed it and went on his way. That's kind of the American way. There's no quarter given with crazed robots or computers. If anything, it actually seems easier - they're not technically alive, so way easier to kill.

Except here, there's a discussion? Is it right? Doesn't Magnus have a right to exist? It's interesting, and it's kind of Canadian, we're a lot less certain in our morality, more ambiguous and reflective.

In terms of a sentient's right to exist, this is probably a stretch, but in the United States Rowe v Wade had just come down from the Supreme Court in 1973. Canada did not legalize abortion until 1988 after a long controversy. Abortion remained a hot discussion topic.

It whether to destroy Magnus or simply leave it trapped is a live issue in the episode, and there isn't a pat conclusion. The morality of destroying Magnus is openly challenged.

There's a freeze frame and some effects, which suggests that it was added in post-production at the last minute. A ringing voice addresses Devon and announces that they are the community of artificial intelligences of the Ark, and that they've seen what he's done, and basically denounce him as a murderer.

Well, that's a definite lack of validation. No one ever did that to Jim Kirk. The clear implication is that Devon has made the morally wrong decision, that he is a murderer.

And it's true - he didn't have to. He could have walked away, or tried to escape. Magnus would have been left trapped, but 'alive.' The episode is refusing an easy moral resolution, I like that.

The other interesting subtext comes from looking at the series as a whole. Magnus offers the salvation of the Ark, and it's at least a credible offer. It is the most powerful AI on the Ark, and it has access to the personal life information of the occupants.

Freed, Magnus might be able to pull it off. But it also offers the genuine risk of enslavement. That's the choice that Devon faces - survival and enslavement, or taking chances with his own destiny even if it risks destruction. That's the choice he makes when he decides to destroy Magnus.

That's also the same choice he faces in Return of Oro. It's the crux of the conflict between Oro representing survival and enslavement, and Devon, advocating freedom and risk, which culminates in an actual debate.

Now maybe this is just the comfortable cliché for the standard hero. But it does seem to suggest a thematic consistency for both the hero, and the overall philosophy of the show, and perhaps foreshadows the debate in Return of Oro.

It's also interesting that the debate in the Return of Oro is ultimately judged by the Ark's coalition of Artificial intelligences. The same group that called Devon out in this episode.

So, although this episode isn't referenced in Return of Oro, there's an arguable case that the Gallery of Fear is a thematic and practical forerunner for that later episode.

Creatives

Both Ed Richardson, the series producer, and Joseph L. Scanlon are credited with directing this episode. Ed Richardson appears to be the listed Director on the titles, and worked on four episodes. Scanlon, who directed five other episodes, is recognized in IMDB as a Director, but is not officially credited on screen.

George Ghent appears to have been a British actor. This episode and Children of Methuselah are his only recorded film or television script credits.

Alf or Alfred Harris, is a remarkable footnote. Thirty-eight years old at the time of Starlost, he was yet another Canadian writer, who went to California seeking fame and fortune. His career, stretching from 1953 to 1980 included Mission Impossible, Wild Wild West, Bionic Woman and Jason of Star Command. His first credit on IMDB, however was 51 episodes of a Canadian Broadcasting Corporation show – Space Command, a Canadian science fiction television series, from 13 March 1953 till 29 May 1954, starring James Doohan, later Scotty of Star Trek, and with William Shatner and Barry Morse, in a guest roles. Space Command seems to have been a Canadian entry in a flurry of space opera television serials from the early fifties including Rocky Jones Space Ranger, Space Patrol and Tom Corbett Space Cadet, Buck Rogers and Flash Gordon. This was the Canadian Broadcasting Corporation's first dramatic series. Very little hard information exists, some sources suggest that Alf Harris was the creator, the actual number of episodes is uncertain and may be as few as fifty-one, documentation is scant, the original records are gone, and only a single episode, available on YouTube, remains.

Backstory and Continuity

There's a trace of Harlan Ellison's bible here. In his story ideas, he posits strange living crystals, altered by centuries and radiation. They evolve into psychoactive, dream crystals that bring a person's thoughts to life, confronting the heroes with their own actualized fears. This is reminiscent of the psychically reactive artwork in Magnus' 'gallery' and some of Magnus' head games.

Brave New Ark – Magnus is able to manifest holographs or projections of Garth's father and Rachel's mother. Which poses the question of how does it know these things? Neither explanation is a particularly happy one. Either Magnus is a telepathic AI able to dig into their minds, which is actually proven...

Or the surveillance systems of the Ark are recording practically everyone everywhere including Cypress Corners. In which case, Magnus, although confined, is able to access that information, at least some of the time. Magnus does say that it has been accessing information for centuries as it's been evolving and improving itself.

The notion of an Ark-wide surveillance comes back up again in Space Precinct. The implications of such surveillance are disturbing. Particularly since the Ark is allegedly going into a sun and no one is doing anything about it.

Does this mean that our protagonists' efforts are basically futile, all the work and danger they encounter trying to figure things out and work towards saving the Ark, it's actually all known and accessible? That someone(s) are watching them like rats in a maze? If so, why isn't anyone saving the Ark? Or at least help and tell them where to go? Give them a map? An instruction manual?

Or there's a worse possibility that maybe the danger and the quest are not entirely real, and as in Only Man is Vile, Devon and his friends are being manipulated and are the subjects of a sociological experiment? Or perhaps they're being tested for worthiness?

The bleakest possibility is that the Ark is genuinely and irretrievably doomed and beyond saving, Devon's quest is futile, and it's all just the band playing on, going through the motions before the end.

There are no answers, it's just a rabbit hole.

If Magnus is able to access Ark-wide information, what exactly are the terms of its confinement? It just seems forbidden from controlling, manipulating or perhaps even communicating outside its gallery.

The fact that Magnus went rogue so soon after the launch of the Ark, together with the Dome Wars, implies that the launch was premature.

There were clearly a lot of things not fully tested or planned out. This may speak to the desperation to escape.

Finally, as pointed out, Magnus is not alone, rather, there seems to be a confederation of Artificial Intelligences on the ship, although they seldom manifest. They'll show up again, to throw their support behind an Admiral, in Return of Oro.

This confederation seems to include the Sphere Projector. In this episode it shows surprising volition, openly arguing with and eventually mocking Magnus. This implies that there may be an active intelligence there, which puts a slightly different perspective on its initial conversation in the pilot, Voyage of Discovery. It seemed very concerned then about the Ark's impending destruction.

Which I suppose leads to another rabbit hole. Perhaps the Ark really is in danger, but the Artificial Intelligences are prohibited by their programming from interfering directly, and the other shipboard societies are conditioned against taking control under any circumstance.

One day, an Artificial Intelligence finds an unconditioned human from Cypress Corners wandering around outside his habitat and decides that he and his friends would be a perfect tool to get around their programming limiters and save all their asses.

In which case, the whole series amounts to the AI struggling to subtly manipulate and guide Devon and his friends around the Ark carefully training and positioning him so that he can eventually save them all.

I guarantee you, no one connected with the show when they were making it, put this much thought into it. When you're running ahead of the tidal wave, you're just running, and that's all. But they did do a series of stories featuring sneaky manipulative AI. So maybe some of this was going on, on some subconscious level?

Creators and Cast

Directed by Ed Richardson and Joseph L. Scanlon
Written by George Ghent and Alf Harris
&&&

Devon: Keir Dullea
Rachel: Gay Rowan
Garth: Robin Ward
Sphere Projector: William Osler
Magnus: Allen Stewart Coates
Daphne: Angel Tompkins
Admiral Austin: William Clune
Monster Devon: Danny Hodgkins
&&&
Original Airdate: November 17, 1973

MR. SMITH OF MANCHESTER – EPISODE NINE

Our heroes find their way into a sealed dome and encounter a threat to the entire Ark...

I will confess that in the opening moments of this episode I laughed out loud. The guards' uniforms with their tight jackets and high cut collars reminded me of nothing so much as a posse of Elvis impersonators.

Given the tenor of the episode, I can't say that this was entirely accidental. Mr. Smith himself, when he makes an appearance looks like nothing more than a paunchy middle aged Mr. Spock gone to seed.

Then I stopped laughing.

Mr. Smith of Manchester is a searing and terrifying meditation on the corruption of power, and the inevitable logic of such corruption.

The story: Our protagonists wind up in a high technology, industrial biosphere called Manchester. They're arrested as spies by armed Elvis Impersonators, and taken to meet the dome's ruler, Mr. Smith, and his assistant, Trent. Smith is played by Ed Ames, best known as cowboy actor, so this is an unusual role for him.

Smith believes that they are spies, tortures them, but eventually turns around and decides to be friendly. Whoever Devon and his friends are, they're from outside the dome and Smith desperately wants out.

Trent attempts to warn them, but is taken away by police. Devon confronts Smith about her arrest and discovers that Trent had drawn up plans to conquer the Ark. But Devon and the others become suspicious of Smith himself as they discover that Manchester is stockpiling weapons.

Garth and Rachel find their way to the outer city, and we are shown the polluted, devastated sections of Manchester. They encounter desperate people in rags, sick and dying children and a corpse collector calling out 'bring out your dead.'

They're told that Trent has been released, but she's been released to the Outer City, a polluted ghetto, where she's been left to die.

Smith isn't really bothered by this misery. He's proud of Manchester's achievements in setting production records. For Smith everything needs to be bigger, bolder better. Manchester is all about industrial production at any costs. The decay, degradation and pollution is a small price to pay for that industrial production. Manchester needs weapons to defend itself from the enemy outside the dome that they haven't seen in five hundred years. And defense won't be enough, Manchester needs to conquer.

Devon and his friends, after a confrontation with Smith, finally escape the dome, leaving Smith and his plans of invasion trapped for the time being.

As with many episodes of the Starlost, the main cast is underplayed. Devon proceeds to unravel the riddle of Manchester, bouncing from Smith to Trent, from Inner City to Outer, but Rachel and Garth have almost nothing to do. This episode, like many others, belongs to its guest stars, particularly Smith, but also Trent and a couple of others.

Trent is clearly the smarter of the two. Although Trent starts as another female sidekick, the character fleshes out and becomes integral to the story. She's the brains behind Smith and they play it that way. It's Trent who first accepts that Devon's story is true. It's Trent who grasps the consequences of that truth: That the Ark is in danger. Something that Smith never does.

It's an interesting testament to Smith's paranoia and single mindedness that learning of the Ark's imminent destruction doesn't alter his agenda in the slightest, where for Trent, it changes everything.

It's Trent and not Smith who's drawn up the plans for the conquest of the Ark. And it's Trent who in the end outmaneuvers Smith to allow Devon, Rachel and Garth to escape. It's Trent who stands up, falls from grace, and in the end shows conviction.

Another significant role is that of the nurse, whose role, more than anything else demonstrates and exposes this society's paranoia. She's terrified of Smith, and terrified that he's watching her. And in fact, he is.

There's also the babe factor. Mr. Smith's assistant actually has remarkable sex appeal. Not much of a role, overall, but definitely sex appeal. She's not really in the episode for anything but window dressing, at one point Smith actually calls her a 'dumb bunny.' But it fits Smith's shallow character: Of course his assistant would be young and sexy. It's an interesting juxtaposition to Trent, and encapsulates Smith's sexism perfectly.

That's quite striking for this series, because there isn't a lot of sex appeal or sexual chemistry floating around. Generally, the Starlost was almost entirely sex free. Once in a while, a character might look longingly at another character, but that was about it.

The occasional romantic subplot, as in The Alien Oro or Pisces was so chaste as to be almost neuter, one got the feeling that after a year or so, people might have gotten up to holding hands. So, in this context, to have a character like Smith's assistant stroll through was quite unusual.

There are some striking moments to the episode. There is a remarkable scene where Devon is in the warehouse, shouting into the empty building for Smith to come out that makes him look stupid and paranoid.

Until the scene shifts, and we discover that not only is Smith there, but he'd brought an entire army with him! The sheer shock and overkill of Smith's hidden army is one of the most startling scenes in the entire series.

Another powerful scene is where Rachel, in the Outer City, meets a mother with a child. They sit there, quietly and without fanfare, as Rachel realizes that the baby is dying, and that it is such a common tragedy that there are no tears left for it.

My ex-wife watched this show as a child, and this particular scene haunted her for years. In her memory, they show a clearly dead baby, a corpse, adding horror to the heartbreak. She was surprised, watching it decades later, to find the scene different than she remembered. But it's a testament to the emotional power of the scene that it made such a profound impression. Despite the fact it wasn't exactly as she remembered, the emotion of the scene is genuine and raw, and it's that rawness that shaped her memory.

Even the sets and miniatures come in for praise here, although, as always in Starlost, they're betrayed by their budget. Nevertheless, the grimy, smoky hell of the Outer City is powerful, with its dying babies and corpse collector.

The miniature model of Manchester is, as with the Implant People, pretty tosh. The model makers could have done well to have learned a few things about detailing or forced perspective, or scale of any sort. The miniatures of Gerry Anderson's puppet series make them look sick.

But for all of that, the image of Manchester as a series of factories constantly belching smoke, and the use of that image throughout the episode and as a final scene is quite powerful. The continuous smoke of the factories actually give it a sense of movement and life It's one of those moments when we accept the unreality while accepting the message behind that prop.

This is also one of the episodes where they make an attempt to give a visually expansive scope, particularly the scenes of the weapons warehouse and outer city. The production also moves through a series of sets, giving an expansive feel to Manchester as more than just some generic rooms.

The star of the episode, of course, is Ed Ames as Mr. Smith, the ruler of Manchester. His character's name is clearly an allusion to Mr. Smith Goes to Washington, a Jimmy Stewart movie about American idealism. In contrast, Ames' Mr. Smith is Nixonian, the dark face of the American dream, the worst aspects of the American character, an American nightmare.

Smith is nothing less than a dictator, a monster, who rules his dome with an iron grip and who has or is destroying literally everything around him. Smith is mad, or he represents madness. A manager, he drives his people to exceed all production goals. But to produce what? And for whom? And at what cost? None of these matters concern

Smith. His dome is choking to death on its own pollution, but his solution is simply to build an inner city and to drive production ever forward. He schemes for the conquest of the Ark.

Smith is consumed by paranoia. He trusts no one and nothing. Everyone is lying to him. Everything must be watched. He listens to Devon's story under hypnotic torture, a device he's believed infallible, and when it fails to accord with his paranoia, he simply concludes they've beaten the machine. He condemns Trent because in his eyes, disagreement is tantamount to betrayal. His paranoia is infectious. As with Roloff in The Implant People, everyone in Manchester fears that they're being watched and spied upon.

Smith never backs down. He lies knowingly and sincerely, caught in one lie, he simply moves on to the next lie with equal sincerity. He demands absolute loyalty, but has absolutely none himself. He is utterly protean, saying or doing whatever serves him at the moment.

Unlike Roloff in The Implant People, he never drops the mask, never stops playing a role. Even at the end, looking down at the dying Trent, a woman he has condemned to death he plays the part of a wounded parent. It's all about him, it's always all about him. And the people he murders, well they forced him to do it. Smith does terrible things, which are always justified, and he's never responsible.

He's not that bright, as we've said. Trent is clearly smarter. She's the one that drafts up the plans. But this is meaningless to Smith. He either never understands, or he simply doesn't care. He's entirely self-absorbed in his ruthlessness. Contradictory evidence doesn't make him think. He simply bulldozes his way through.

There is something chilling about Smith and his continuing insistence on playing his part to the hilt. Whereas Roloff in the end is happy to play the villain, Smith will accept no other role but as the hero of his story. His lies and betrayals are necessary, even justified. He admits to sending his own parents to the outer city to die, an action he found regrettable but necessary. He killed his own parents, but he sees himself as the victim of that action.

His lies are so earnest, and so adamant, that one wonders if he even somehow believes them himself on some level. He's so sincere that you almost find yourself believing. The horrible thing about Smith is that deep down, he may believe that he's doing the right thing at every step of the way, no matter how awful it is. It may not be a role, but some kind of political schizophrenia or a pointless ruthlessness.

He is an Orwellian monster, able to sincerely and with great conviction, hold contradictory principles within himself, to lie truthfully, to betray with integrity, and to create a society embodying those Orwellian principles where misery equals success, suffering means plenty, where everyone is watched and no one is beyond suspicion, but somehow everyone is free.

Yet, as frightening as Smith is, I suspect that he and his contradictions have more resemblance to modern dictators and even modern politicians than Roloff does. In Smith we see the echoes of the bland hypocrisy of a Reagan or Trump, sincerely contradicting themselves without a care, or of the defensive brutality of a Hussein or a Milosevic, destroying their companions at whim. If Roloff is Nixon, then Smith is Reagan or Bush, or especially Trump.

The subtext of Manchester, is of course, pollution. Manchester is a British city which in the 19th century was ground zero for the Industrial revolution, known for industry, poverty and squalor and pollution. It's also the place where Karl Marx and Frederick Engels met, and the subject of Engels railing about 'The Conditions of the English Working Class.' So the name is not chosen randomly, there was a lot of political and social freight.

Pollution and unconstrained industrialism is another Canadian issue of the era of the show, although it was hardly restricted to Canada. However, Canadians, because of their unique position had special concerns. We were a comparatively underpopulated nation with large reserves of wilderness, and perhaps a more socially cautious and leftist people. Despite vast size, the places occupied were fragile and small, pollution was far more devastating.

More than that though, we were the neighbor to a heavily industrialized state, and thus, became concerned about pollution spilling over the border in such forms as acid rain or contamination of fish or wildlife. Cross-border pollution was a major issue for Canadians, while that particular issue simply didn't exist in America. This is actually alluded to in the episode when Trent warns them of the danger of Manchester's pollution contaminating the rest of the Ark.

The episode highlights the logic or illogic of runaway industrialization. To Devon the situation seems irrational, even insane, but clearly to those trapped within it, Manchester's economy is inevitable and inescapable and more than anything else, it's good. It's growth at all costs, even if the price is destruction.

Smith is honest in his pride over his people's great achievements, the construction of the inner city, the record-breaking production levels. But his logic is merely the logic of our own western culture, with its commitment to continuing endless growth, to development at whatever the cost and to bypassing the consequences of such a course, at least for a few people.

In short, like the best science fiction, Manchester is a distorted but all too accurate reflection of our own society and the shortcomings and illogic that we've trapped ourselves in.

The episode has the courage to avoid easy solutions. In another series, people might have realized their errors, overthrown or reformed Smith, and joined hand in hand to rehabilitate their biosphere.

Here the conclusion is bleaker, Devon, Rachel and Garth escape. But Smith is left in charge, and the logic of Manchester's society is unassailed. Perhaps it is even reinforced, because now for the first time, Smith knows that there are enemies and opportunities out there.

Our heroes are left glumly realizing that sooner or later, they'll have to do something, without knowing what, or one day, Smith will be out there.

The final shot, of course, is of Manchester's mills and factories ceaselessly churning away and endlessly spewing their poisonous by-products. A visual hint that Manchester's pollution is ready to invade the Ark as well.

Again, this ambiguous resolution is distinctly Canadian, Margaret Atwood in her book Survival, examining Canadian literature says that Canadians don't win, we survive. The world is too big and implacable to truly conquer, so we endure and survive.

Mr. Smith of Manchester is not nearly as ambitious as the Implant People in the sheer variety and scope of its ideas. Manchester has fewer targets, but it hits them more profoundly and with greater force. It may be one of the best episodes the Starlost produced.

Creatives

Joseph L. Scanlon was an American director brought in to direct. He is credited, officially or unofficially with at least five episodes, including this one.

Norman Klenman, co-writer of the episodes, was also the Story Consultant for the series, officially credited with four episodes, and unofficially credited with as many as four more.

Arthur Heinemann, scriptwriter, and also separately credited for the story, was born in Mexico in 1910, but is best known as a prolific American scriptwriter, mainly for television. His major genre credit is for three episodes of Star Trek. This was his only credit on Starlost.

Backstory and Continuity

There's an interesting and indirect callback to Pisces here. There's a direct reference to the Dome Wars in dialogue. We discover that Manchester has been locked away from the rest of the Ark for five hundred years. It's not a stretch to see the militarized, aggressive warmongering society of Mr. Smith as a key player in the Dome Wars.

It's interesting to observe that Smith didn't even know about the Disaster that hit the Ark four hundred years ago. It looks like Manchester completely missed that. Also due to long isolation, they were unaware the Ark is heading into a sun until Devon told them.

Creators & Cast

Directed by Joseph L. Scanlon
Written by Arthur Heinemann and Norman Klenman
From a story by Arthur Heineman
&&&
Devon: Keir Dullea
Rachel: Gay Rowan
Garth: Robin Ward

Sphere Projector: William Osler
President Mr. Smith: Ed Ames
Trent: Pat Galloway
Smith's Secretary: Pattie Elsasser
Old Nurse: Doris Petrie
City Man (Bring Out Your Dead): Les Rubie
&&&
Original Airdate: November 24, 1973

THE ALIEN ORO – EPISODE TEN

Our heroes confront an alien who is cannibalizing the Ark to fix his own ship.

Planet Exar sends scout ship 531 to check out the Ark, detected on long range micro-sensors. Something goes wrong, and the scout crashes into the Ark. About a year later, Devon and friends are travelling through the modules, and they come to a section open to vacuum.

Luckily, they manage to access space suits with the guidance of the sphere projector's voice, allowing them to pass through the damaged section. It's actually an imposing image, the three suited characters marching across the desolate wreckage with the great gaping tear in the hull open to space above them.

Crossing through to the other side, they encounter Idona of the Egrek dome, and her companion Oro.

Oro, they learn is an alien from Exar, played by Star Trek's own Mister Chekhov, Walter Koenig.

Koenig was a close friend of Harlan Ellison, so it's tempting to wonder if that connection was how he ended up on the show. It's possible that he was cast or committed early on, through Ellison, before his departure. But as nearly as we can tell, Koenig became involved, and the Oro scripts written, long after Ellison had burned his bridges and walked off.

It's possible though. When Ellison dictated his original twelve minute audio treatment he expressly had Walter Koenig in mind for the part of Devon. When Dullea was cast, Ellison was quite upset. Later, when writing the bible and creating the character of Garth, Ellison again had Koenig in mind. It's likely that the Canadian producers and/or Koenig were aware of this history. There may have been some baggage.

Actually, we suspect Koenig's participation might have resulted in a little friction with his friend Ellison, but we're not aware of either ever mentioning it.

It must have been a little weird, knowing that you are guest starring on a show where the main lead and second lead parts were originally written expressly for you. Or working on a show where your close friend was so burned that he immolated the place. I imagine there may have been some odd things going on in the back of Koenig's mind.

Robin Ward commented, *"Walter Koenig who was a regular on the very successful Star Trek series, seemed to think our show was slightly beneath him. He appeared as Starlost was staggering towards the end and the cast and crew were exhausted and demoralized."*

Apart from the Ellison connection, which might have helped or hurt, Koenig's almost certainly cast as Oro because of his Star Trek history. Trek had become the definitive Sci-Fi series, so there's likely a deliberate attempt by the producers to trade on that. Given the Canadian content requirements, I'm surprised they didn't bring in William Shatner or James Doohan.

Koenig's Oro was the only major character they brought back to the show, returning in The Return of Oro. It's possible the two episodes were shot back to back, although this seems doubtful, given the frantic pace and the need to get episodes in the can. Regardless, they were certainly produced within weeks of each other.

Anyway, since his crash Oro has been looting or dismantling sections of the Ark to fix his ship. This disturbs Devon, leading to this exchange:

"Do you mean to tell me that you've been tearing pieces out of the Ark?" Devon demands.

"It's raw material, good for nothing else," Oro replies.

Devon wants Oro to help to fix the Ark. Unfortunately, they're closing in on Oro's launch window, and Oro needs to leave to have any chance of making it home. He has no time to help.

To be frank, he just doesn't care. He doesn't care about the Ark, or its people. Oro is near emotionless. He regards it all as a lost cause, and he's simply indifferent. As he says, for him its raw material, and nothing else. He just wants to leave and take Idona with him.

Idona is another of these female sidekick roles, but with a little more meat, since she's got a fatal disease and a romantic subplot. Or perhaps the romantic angle is the main plot.

Garth gets a crush on Idona, mainly because he's lonely. Idona reciprocates because he's the first man she's seen, apart from the scrawny Oro. He shows off his blacksmith skills, which include alien spaceship repair. She's quite a chilly person but she warms up to him. They end up together, making small talk and working on Oro's ship together, which includes blacksmithing with an open flame, and using an actual arc welder. The relationship grows to the point where they're touching each other, although they never get to an actual kiss.

This romantic subplot was a recurring thing with Garth, by the way. Unlike Jim Kirk, Keir Dullea's Devon wasn't a single man available for romance, he was with Rachel, even if it was an asexual pairing. So that left Robin Ward's Garth to play a romantic lead, such as it was.

The Starlost was pretty chaste, so mostly it translated to longing looks and vaguely emotional monologues. This episode invests far more in the romantic subplot than most. They actually take time to develop it through several scenes.

Unfortunately, she's with Oro and planning on going back with him to his world. This sets up a love triangle between Idona, Oro and Garth. She decides she wants to stay with Garth.

There's a further complication to the triangle, if Idona remains on the Ark, she'll die. Egrek's dome is contaminated, males can barely survive to eighteen, so women rule. But that means they have to have a lot of kids, and Idona can't bear children. She left Egrek but can't survive long outside her biosphere, because her body is adapted to the contamination. She was dying, until she met Oro, and she has to go with him to survive. It's a bit of a soap opera situation.

Oro gets a message from home telling him to leave soon. This escalates a chilling low key confrontation between Devon and Oro, as

Oro keeps dismantling the Ark. Devon walks off with a key component, but eventually gives it back. Oro repents slightly offering to help before he leaves. It's a tentative careful reconciliation at best.

Idona collapses. Garth puts her on Oro's ship, and she and Oro fly off. That's about it. It's very soap opera, with its doomed romance, love triangle and mutual self-sacrifice.

I've suggested elsewhere that a lot of the Starlost's writing and acting was probably influenced by theatrical tradition.

American television developed in Hollywood and its writing and acting evolved out of thirty or forty years of movies. It's not mysterious, that's what was around. If you were hiring actors, they were going to be movie actors, who acted a certain way. Your lighting people, your directors, they'd all learned their trade on movies. So when they needed to work on television, they just did things the way they'd learned.

In other places, such as England or Canada, what you principally drew on was theatre people - your actors were stage actors, the directors were stage directors. People used what they knew. You can see that with the Starlost, there's a certain 'stage oriented' style to a lot of the production that's reminiscent of British television.

But another influence in Starlost was almost certainly soap operas of the 1960s and 1970s, a half hour or hour broadcast daily. That's a pretty breakneck pace for everyone involved. So you often had fairly basic acting. You also had fairly rote series of camera set ups and moves - alternating close ups, two shots where people had conversations while both of them faced the camera, seldom more complicated shots as characters moved around each other. You had a lot of dialogue, because dialogue was just easier to shoot than action. It's not terrible by any means, but it often had to be fast, simple and cheap, simply because of the constant demand of production.

Ambition was a luxury on the soaps, it was about getting the scene done and going on to the next one. So you weren't doing wild cinematic camera angles or scenes framed or edited like in the movies, or dramatic fight scenes, there just wasn't the money or time. In Canada in 1973, if you were looking for people who knew how to light a set, and shoot characters for a video screen, direct actors or edit a sequence together, you were going to be drawing your technical people from daily talk shows and soap operas, and that's the kind of experience and style they would be bringing to it.

You see this influence in a lot of the Starlost's cinematography, in terms of where they put the camera and the kinds of shots and scenes they edit together. It's not necessarily a terrible thing, and some of it is quite effective. You can also see it in the relatively slower pace of the episodes, and in the dialogue driven stories.

The thing is, that this was pretty acceptable, even normal, for a lot of the television of the 60s and 70s, even in America. Over the decades, as technical skill and investment has ramped up, and soaps have faded somewhat, we're less tolerant of this slower, more formal pace.

Setting aside the Idona/Garth romance, it is the Devon/Oro storyline, and particularly Oro himself that interests.

This episode was shot close to, possibly concurrently with Return of Oro. Although the writers and directors for the two episodes were different, there's an underlying thematic continuity between the two episodes, most likely driven by the script editor, Norman Klenman, and the producers, William Davison and Ed Richardson.

Oro's name is Spanish for gold, and not coincidentally, he wears a metallic gold uniform. It's also a pretty obvious tag to the direction of his character. He represents greed and selfishness, the allure of gold. Oro's lack of emotion, is perhaps, simply the selfishness of not caring about anyone or anything else.

He's from the planet Exar, which we see in space as a reddish Mars-like body, surrounded by six moons. This gets rendered variously as Ixar, or Xar, but it's most probably Exar.... as in X.R. Which is a few letters off from U.S. This is probably not a coincidence. Rather, Oro and Exar represents America, and his interactions with Devon and the Ark are really about uneasiness with Canadian-American relations.

The core of the episode's conflict is that Oro is literally dismantling the Ark for his own needs. To him, the Ark is just raw material, resources. Devon, in two separate scenes is outraged.

'We live here,' he says, 'we may need that!'

They see the Ark in radically different ways, and Oro's casual looting horrifies Devon.

There's more to it. Oro simply doesn't care. He's not interested. He doesn't hate the people of the Ark. He's cold, but he's polite, he's even relatively friendly. But it doesn't matter. To him it's impersonal, it's all just business.

On the other hand, Oro's important to Devon. He represents the potential to save the Ark. Devon needs Oro, his knowledge, his skill, his technology. So there's an uneasy tension with Devon, forced to rely upon and to try and build bridges with a man whose views and values, whose priorities, are so alien to his own.

There's the Canadian/American relationship in a nutshell. Canadians think a lot about America. Americans don't think about Canada at all. They're vaguely aware of it, and they have nothing against Canada or Canadians. It's just not on the radar, even when they're up here visiting. Despite a century of amity, the American attitude is largely indifference and dealings come down to 'nothing personal, it's all just business.'

It goes a little bit deeper: The early 1970s were the high water mark for Canadian Economic Nationalism. In the postwar era, into the 1950s and 1960s, Canada had industrialised. Part of that was increasing economic engagement with the United States.

There was a lot of foreign investment from the U.S. into Canada, American companies purchased or built plants and factories in Canada, they bought land, they bought mines and minerals, they bought resources. The Canadian economy was starting to look like an economy of branch plants. Our raw materials, and our money headed south. We were becoming second class citizens in our own country, our economy owned by and run from south of the border, for the benefit of foreigners.

This crossed over with the emerging environmental movement. Pollution from American-owned factories crossed over the border and poisoned our air and waters. American owned companies extracted our minerals, they cut down our forests, took up our green spaces. There were objections to Americans buying up our land.

To the U.S. we were raw materials. Our country was raw materials. For Canadians, it was, 'Hey wait a second, we're living here!'

There was a real concern that our forests would be clear cut away and shipped south so American timber barons could make a few bucks. And then what? There was a fear that our nation would simply be looted and despoiled by big American conglomerates, leaving nothing but pollution and garbage.

For all its immensity and implacability, Canadians had an oddly delicate view of nature, that it was fragile. Or maybe the fragility was the part of nature we depended upon. Nature in Canada is vast and unyielding, but we live on narrow margins.

So while the soap opera plot of the doomed romance tends to take up a lot of space, the interplay between Devon and Oro feels much more intense. Koenig plays his Oro with studied indifference, a man for whom the Ark is resources. Devon is impressed, hopeful, distressed and at times almost violently angry.

Devon, expresses deep shock and horror when he finds out that Oro's been dismantling the Ark, he's genuinely outraged and angry. It doesn't feel like soap opera in those moments, it feels real. That might be Dullea's acting.

But I also think that it was tapping into issues that people were talking about, that were being discussed intensely in Canada, particularly in the city where the show was made, and among the social classes, and even the specific people who were working on the show.

To an American audience, it probably went right past them. It simply wasn't a discussion they were having. At most, they would have seen it as a parable about environmentalism. Fair enough. Some, in the post-Vietnam era might have had the awareness to suspect that maybe someone was talking about them.

But for Canadian audiences, this probably resonated strongly. These themes and ideas in The Alien Oro cut very close to the Canadian debates of the era, and they return, expanded and developed to take center stage in The Return of Oro. That feels very deliberate.

Creatives

Joseph Scanlon, born in New Jersey, relocated to California and between 1965 and 1952 worked on 58 television series. The Starlost came early in his career, and he ended up directing five, possibly six episodes, over a third of the series. Other genre credits included Land of the Lost, Star Trek: The Next Generation, Quantum Leap, War of the Worlds, and the rebooted Outer Limits.

Marian Waldman was a Toronto born actress and screenwriter. Starting as a chorus girl she became an active stage actress and playwright. Mainly involved with the theatre she also accumulated a small handful of film and television credits in Canada. Among these was a CTV syndicated program, Police Surgeon, where she co-wrote four episodes with Mort Forer. Along with Helen French, a co-writer for the Implant People, and Ursula K. Le Guin, story contributor for the Goddess Calabra, these were the only women with creative impact on stories behind the camera.

Mort Forer, the other credited writer, was a Canadian screenwriter active with a handful of credits between 1973 and 1981. The Starlost was his first credit, his last an episode of the Littlest Hobo, about a travelling german shepherd who solved crimes (don't laugh, I grew up on it) in 1981. I don't know much more about him.

Walter Koenig needs no introduction, but we'll do it anyway. Koenig is best known for his work as Chekov on Star Trek. His friendship with Harlan Ellison dates from that time. He also featured as Bester, on J.M. Straczynski's Babylon Five.

Alexandra Bastedo, a multi-lingual polymath, was arguably more famous at the time than Koenig, having recently starred in the 1968-1969 Sci-Fi/espionage series The Champions as well as the espionage series, Codename, in 1970. She appeared in movies such as Casino Royale and Blood Spattered Bride. Bastedo was born in England, with a Canadian father and an ancestry that included indigenous, French, German, Spanish, Italian, Dutch and Scottish elements. She lived in Canada for a time. In addition to acting, she wrote several books, mainly about animals, and was active in animal welfare.

Backstory and Continuity

Garth's blacksmith skills are truly impressive if he can use them to rebuild and repair an alien spaceship. This may not be as ridiculous as it seems. Garth is from Cypress Corners, which is a pseudo-Amish dome, but the Elders use computers and talk genetics, without wholly understanding it. It's possible that Garth's blacksmith training may have involved a lot more sophisticated technical skill than simply hammering pieces of iron. His job in Cypress Corners may well have involved sophisticated maintenance and repair work covered over with pseudo-Amish brainwashing and narrow mindedness.

It's rather interesting though, that the Ark's components can be readily adapted to Oro's ship. That suggests perhaps a common technological origin?

We don't learn much about Oro and Exar, beyond the fact that Oro is something of a jerk. Exar is estimated to be less than half a parsec (roughly a light year to a light year and a half maybe) away.

Exar's technological capacity is unclear. On the one hand, they don't have the resources to send more than a single one man scout, and no ability to send a rescue. On the other hand, a light year or so is a long way. Does Exar have faster than light travel? If so, why a single scout? Overall, FTL doesn't seem to exist in this universe, and Oro's concern over a launch window suggests his ship is sub-liminal. Perhaps extended solitary voyages of a year or more explains his personality.

To be completely fair to the production, they did go to the trouble of building Oro's spaceship as a full sized prop/set piece that Gay Rowan is able to walk completely around, and even walk inside of on camera. It is a rather ugly looking, silly kind of thing, a crude idea of a flying saucer, with lots of tail fins and bubbles all around. They also built a two-foot long miniature model for space shots as Oro arrives and departs, used in both episodes. On the other hand, when Oro is shown in his ship pushing buttons too aggressively, the viewing window wobbles.

In this episode, the Sphere Projector isn't visible, but its voice is heard. Actually, through the course of the series, several different computer voices are heard, suggesting distinct Artificial Intelligences. What's notable about the Projector voice in this episode is that it tells Devon to shut up. When Devon yells, the Projector voice informs him that it will not respond unless he modulates his voice.

There may be a continuity issue. In Circuit of Death, episode seven, we see the trio walking along in their silver space suits. But it's only in the tenth episode, that we see them acquiring and putting on the suits, suggesting that perhaps the episodes were out of order, and that Oro should have come first, and been followed immediately by Circuit of Death.

Oddly, IMDB and other sources list the airdate for this episode out of order, November 3, 1973, immediately prior to Circuit of Death, November 10, 1973, while still listing this as the tenth episode in series. Very peculiar.

Another, less embarrassing continuity issue – at the start of the episode, Exar announces that they've only recently detected the Ark on long range scanners. But later on, Oro notes that the disaster that struck the Ark was observed and recorded.

My interpretation is that it's either sloppy writing, or that the disaster that hit the Ark was cosmic in nature, widespread enough that it hit Oro's world as well. In other words, something like a supernova wave front, travelling at light speed or close to it.

Creators and Cast

Directed by Joseph L. Scanlon
Written by Marion Waldman and Matt Forer
&&&
Devon: Keir Dullea
Rachel: Gay Rowan
Garth: Robin Ward
Sphere Projector: William Osler
Oro of Exar: Walter Koenig
Idona of Egrek: Alexandra Bastedo
&&&
Original Airdate: November 3, 1973

THE ASTRO-MEDICS – EPISODE ELEVEN

When Devon is injured, the Astro-Medics come to the rescue. Also... aliens.

I am rather more fond of the Astro-Medics than I really ought to be. There's something old fashioned and retro to the episode, even for the era it was made in.

There are two main stories here: The first: Devon is injured and near death. Garth and Rachel manage to summon the Astro-Medics, a kind of Ark-based space ambulance, providing us with a life and death medical drama. Medical dramas, Dr. Kildare, Doctor Marcus Welby, General Hospital, etc., were quite popular in this era. So once again, the Starlost is scooping off the surface and adapting the popular culture of the time.

The second story and the big Sci-Fi idea here is that there's an alien spaceship passing near the Ark calling out for assistance. Their crew is sick and dying from some kind of unknown medical crisis and they desperately need help. Luckily, the Astro-Medics are on the job.

The alien contact story is a gentle echo of the Campbell era of Science Fiction when the stories were all about experts or engineers encountering a science-ish problem and figuring out how to solve it.

Don't knock it. Such stories may have been simplistic with wafer thin characters, but there's an innocent appeal to them.

Someone once said that the golden age of science fiction is twelve. There's some truth to that.

When you're young, problem solving, the skill of how to solve problems, and the faith that you can figure things out, is a really important thing. A literature which is fundamentally about problem solving is a damned good thing. A literature that teaches you that problems can be solved, that difficulties can be assessed rationally, approached through open minded learning, that intelligence and perseverance can lead to a solution. Yeah, that's a good thing for young people.

The Astro-Medics take up the cause trying to reach and help the aliens, who call themselves Rillians, while also trying to learn the details of their problem and figure out how to save them. At first it seems impossible, how do you even begin to diagnose, much less cure an alien disease?

The Rillians relate their symptoms, questions are asked, inquiries go down apparent blind alleys but even that is useful information. The Doctors keep asking questions, accumulating information which doesn't seem to help or make any sense, until finally, there is a Eureka moment that pulls it all together.

Mystery solved! The Doctors eventually figure out that the aliens are cold blooded reptilians, similar to lizards on Earth. Temperatures on their planet are so stable they have no experience with the overheating on their ship. The solution is to just bring the temperature down.

Yes, this is a spoiler, but it's been fifty years, so get over it. The aliens manage to be sympathetic, and the struggle to find a solution to their plight with its careful accumulation of puzzling data and 'eureka' moment works well.

It's a tease, we barely see the aliens. They don't appear on the Ark at all. Rather, they're on their ship communicating remotely. Visually the alien is shown as series of indistinct blurred images, slowly improving with each appearance. Maybe this is poor reception given distance, or perhaps a slow process of two incompatible radio/television systems slowly coming into synch. Eventually in the final scenes we get a good look the alien himself - which turns out to be a sort of flat human/reptilian face with rough gray scales and a peculiar Beatles era wig. It's not a bad make up for the minute we see it, or for the available budget and resources, or for that matter, for the era. The payoff builds slowly but works. As always with Starlost, it's a 'no-budget' bit of cleverness, and there's something old fashioned to the presentation.

Throughout, we hear them as a slow sibilant voice without apparent emotion, but relatively benign - they're desperate and in distress, but at the same time they're warning the Ark it's heading towards a sun and to change course.

A note on the alien ship, which is also part of the slow reveal - it actually looks like an orbital satellite. Canada was the third country in the world to launch a satellite - Anik, basically a big bronze colored drum with a radio dish on one end.

Through the sixties and early seventies, Canada, China, Japan and Europe would join the space race with more artificial satellites. There were a variety of looks and designs up in orbit. Drums, antenna, projections and solar panels sticking out like wings were common features. We can't match the alien ship to any particular satellite, but its configuration would be immediately recognizable and authentic as just another orbital satellite. It's another sign of how Starlost tended to draw strongly on contemporary space age aesthetics, both in fiction and real life.

The shots of the Astro-Medic and the Alien Ship, are 'Space Age' fan service, drawing on contemporary 'space age' aesthetics and tropes, very much along the lines of similar fan-service in the Pisces or Farthing's Comet.

Oddly, the Astro-Medic shuttle in comparison looks like plasticine model, bright red, with Lego studs. It's comparable to the Pisces and fits in with the overall aesthetic of the Ark exterior and interiors. Actually we've read that it's just the Pisces model repainted red, which seems likely. It lacks the visual authenticity of the alien ship.

The Sci-Fi medical mystery, however, can't sustain the whole episode, so we have a series of human stories revolving around the A plot. A lot of human stories, actually. In addition to the main trio we have seven principle speaking roles, and a soap opera's worth of sub-plots.

The episode manages to handle this by backgrounding the main cast much of the time. Keir Dullea, the star of the series barely has a few lines right at the end, he spends most of the episode lying unconscious on a medical gurney.

I can't imagine William Shatner or most stars being willing to be relegated to background characters in their own series. Was this a source of resentment or conflict for Dullea? From what I understand, he considered himself an 'actor' rather than a star, and more a team player?

In long running series like early Doctor Who, or soap operas, where shooting is continuous through the year, sometimes the actors would need a rest or vacation. So in the script, they'd get bopped on the head, or thrown in a dungeon, and their character would be written out, or written down to a few minimal appearances, while they rested up.

It might be the case here. Dullea might have had a cold, or wanted a break, and it could have been as simple as that. This is an episode where literally all of the protagonist roles seem interchangeable, it could have been Garth or Rachel lying unconscious, for instance with the others interchangeably dealing with guilt and anger.

Or the script may have simply called for Dullea to lie down for a while, and as a dedicated actor he just gave it his all. You never know.

The main subplot focuses on the guest stars, the physician's triangle. Doctor Christopher Trask is the young Doctor, smart, skilled, overly ambitious, callous and a colossal jerk. His father, Doctor Martin Trask, is the old wise physician who cares about patients but has lost faith in himself. Doctor Jean Pelletier is the heart, trying to bridge these characters.

Young Trask wants to abandon Devon to die, so he can work on the 'sexy' alien problem, which ultimately defeats him. Old Trask believes Devon, and every patient is worth fighting for, but no longer has the confidence or skills to save them. Rounding out the trio is Pelletier, who works to reconcile them. It's only when the young and old Doctors are reconciled work together on both missions that things work out. In the end young Trask learns humanity, old Trask regains his confidence, and everyone realizes they're better together.

Doctor Pelletier also works with Garth, helping him confront his guilt over almost getting Devon killed. Garth actually has a role in this episode. It's his error that almost gets Devon killed. Subsequently, he gets to talk about his feelings. Ultimately, Garth has a critical moment where he sabotages the shuttle's mission, by pressing a button.

Rachel, on the other hand, is mostly under-used. But this is a consistent thing. She doesn't really have anything to do but stand around and wring her hands. She does get to express anger at Garth for getting them in this mess.

The final subplot revolves around the Astro-Medic flight crew. Their job is to fly the Doctors around and it's a mission they clearly believe in. They need to fly out to the alien ship, but in doing so, it increasingly looks like a one way trip, and in the end, they face dying in space. Oddly, there's an intriguing quiet stoicism there, they believe in their mission to help people, even aliens, and if it costs them their lives, so be it.

If this feels like Soap Opera fodder, it is, and it's handled that way. It's very much soap opera direction, with similar camera set ups, both stationary and moving.

It's all very carefully managed and restrained. There's no fight scene, no romantic clinch. By the action standards of Star Trek or a lot of contemporary American television, this was visually quite tame. When Garth derails the Astro-medic's launch, the ship doesn't shake violently and the actors don't toss themselves back and forth. It's actually quite low key in a weird Canadian way. In American version, there'd be a confrontation, a struggle over the button, maybe a threat, a speech or two, and the ship would roar and rock about. There might even be sparks or a small explosion.

Instead, he just pushes a button. That's it: Button. Pushed. It's similar to the low key way Devon simply pushes a button in Methuselah's children. It's an oddly Canadian lack of flair.

The most aggressive thing we have is Garth's threat - *"Tell everyone to stay where they are, or I'll press every button on this console!"*

The actual drama is conceptual: The crew inexorably calculate that rescuing the aliens will cost them their lives, but never really doubt that saving others' lives is worth it. Devon will die without help but the Doctor is unwilling. There's the crisis of the young Doctor being unable to figure out the riddle of the aliens and rediscovering respect for his father and others and commitment to patients. There's the old Doctor rediscovering his value. There's Garth's guilt over his screw up, and Rachel's anger.

All of it is played with restraint. Maybe too much restraint? But that itself may be typically Canadian. Do we really need histrionics? Or perhaps the decision was to make the drama low key, so as not to overpower the puzzle of the Aliens and their problem.

Overall, it's a modest episode, which manages to introduce and solve a reasonably engaging Sci-Fi medical mystery, and buttress that with a scattering of human interest subplots.

Unlike the Oro episodes, I'm not sure how to gauge the 'Canada culture' significance. The rather chaste relationships and lack of violence or action may speak to tamer, more conservative Canadian sensibilities.

Or perhaps it showcased the limitations of shooting in Canada. But honestly, this isn't really a 'Can-Con' episode, not in the way that the Return of Oro is.

Mainly this is a competent old school Sci-Fi story, crossed with the contemporary medical dramas of the era.

Creatives

Behind the scenes, the Director was George McGowan, born in Paris, Ontario, Canada. He was educated in Toronto, started out working in Theater, and got in with the Canadian Broadcasting Corporation. He built a respectable career as a working journeyman director moving back and forth between Canada and Hollywood, the IMDB records a stunning seventy-eight directing credits between 1960 and 1990, most of it television or B-movies. His genre credits include the Invaders, the eco-horror Frogs, Seeing Things and the Star Wars-inspired Shape of Things to Come. For Starlost, he also directed the regrettable Beehive.

Paul Schneider, one of the credited writers, was a New Jersey boy who moved to California. The IMDB lists forty-one writing credits, all of them for television. Notably, however, his credits include a couple of episodes of Star Trek, an episode of the animated Star Trek series, two episodes of Buck Rogers and three episodes of the Six Million Dollar Man. Interestingly, he'd also written several medical shows, including eleven episodes of Marcus Welby, two episodes of Doctor Kildare and an episode of Ben Carson. This suggests that he was likely the one to pitch a Sci-Fi medical drama.

Martin Lager, the other credited writer, was entirely a home town boy. From 1965 on, he was writer for a series of short films with the NFB, with some independent local film and television productions. Pretty much all of his work has been in local Canadian productions. Lager had writer or co-writer credits on four of the Starlost episodes.

Stephen Young, who plays the young Doctor Trask was a popular Canadian character actor and leading man of the era. Bud Knapp, playing the older Trask; Meg Hogarth playing Pelletier; and Michael Zenon playing the alien were all local Canadian actors.

Backstory and Continuity

We learn that the Astro-Medics consist of five medical shuttle modules - basically flying ambulances that 'orbit the ark' and apparently are based out of the Medical dome. There used to be more, but when the disaster hit many of them were destroyed.

The Astro-Medic crew know all about the disaster that struck the Ark, though they never bother to explain to Devon and friends exactly what happened. They also know about the Bridge being destroyed and the Ark on a collision course with a star, but have fatalistically decided that they can't do anything about it, so why bother. What the hell is wrong with these people?

The same thing shows up again in Space Precinct at the end of the series, where we are shown another Ark-spanning service organization, this one law enforcement, with remarkable abilities and information, which also doesn't seem to be motivated to avoid disaster. There may be a comment here about the tunnel vision of bureaucracy, but gee whiz!

There's a slight feeling of missed opportunity. The end of the episode has the crew of the Astro-Medics getting the call and going onto their next mission, coincidentally carrying our protagonists along. This is a fairly typical television series ending for the time. But these medical modules presumably have complete information about the status of the Ark, its domes and command modules, and appear to be able to travel and communicate through the Ark and most of its different biospheres.

Surely, even if they're completely fatalistic, they could give Devon and friends a leg up in their quest. Again, it's one of those things that don't seem to hold up, or at least begs the question.

Finally, the Ark seems to have drifted into a crowded area of space. The previous episode featured another alien, Oro, and revealed the Ark was passing close to Exar. Now we have another alien ship passing through the same neighborhood? And at the end of the series we encounter a third civilization, the Federation. What are the odds? Or is there some connection?

Creators and Cast

Directed by Georg McGowan
Written by Paul Schneider and Martin Lager
&&&
Devon: Keir Dullea
Rachel: Gay Rowan
Garth: Robin Ward
Sphere Projector: William Osler
Dr. Christopher Trask: Stephen Young
Dr. Martin Trask: Budd Knapp
Dr. Jean Pelletier: Meg Hogarth
Astro-Medic Captain: Bill Kemp
Alien Ship Commander: Michael Zenon
Astros-Medic Astrogator: David Mann
&&&
December 1, 1973

THE IMPLANT PEOPLE – EPISODE TWELVE

A Dome where a villain has used cybernetic implants to become a tyrant.

The idea of sticking a chip into people's heads is pretty old as far as science fiction goes. While it's a staple of Cyberpunk it probably goes back at least to the sixties. The possibilities of direct machine-human interface, the potential to control machines with mind, to overcome physical and mental disabilities, the ability to download information directly, that's all some heady stuff (no pun intended).

Of course, Sci-Fi also offers a cautionary tale – if you can download information directly into people, if you can chip them, then you can also control them. This is the crisis that our heroes encounter – one where a well-meaning effort to help humanity by implanting chips has led to the precipice of a totalitarian dystopia.

In this case the Implant is supposed to enhance brain function and cognitive ability, but Roloff has used it as a personal torture device to trigger excruciating pain. Roloff uses this as a means to slowly subvert the state, isolating the Queen, undermining and by-passing the elected Council, and ultimately imposing an outright dictatorship.

In many ways, the Implant People plays like a paler version of Mr. Smith of Manchester. The central villains in each, Roloff and Smith, are tyrants, ruling their communities through a combination of coercion and social paranoia and presenting themselves to Devon and the others as benign leaders. But beyond that, they take off in different directions. It's interesting to juxtapose tem for contrasts.

This episode, like so many others belongs to the guest cast. In particular, Donnelly Rhodes as the villainous Roloff owns the show. Rhodes is a veteran Canadian character actor who's appeared in everything from Disney to the X-Files. He was particularly well known for his roles in Danger Bay and in the spoof Soap.

Here, he plays the secret, de facto ruler of the dome, who has usurped power by controlling access to the Queen, Serena, played by Pat Collins. As her aide or spokesman, he has effectively gained control of the military and scientific establishments, using them to further consolidate his position.

The appearance of Devon, Rachel and Garth, and their unprecedented access to the Queen in which they threaten to speak the truth galvanizes Roloff to consolidate his power.

First he lies to Devon and his friends to get them on his side. But of course, that won't last, so he dissolves the Council, ostensibly on the orders of Serena. Then he rushes back to Serena, announcing that the Council has dissolved itself as a prelude to a coup. With Serena in hiding and the visitors sidelined for the 'crisis' he moves to neutralize them by rushing them all to get implants to put them under his control.

Devon and Garth get suspicious, so Roloff knocks out Devon and has him implanted anyway, while Garth, with the help of Jardy, escapes to the resistance.

Even when his plot is foiled, and Devon and Garth join the resistance, he's undeterred, in short order scheming to blow up the resistance and eliminate Serena. It is immense fun to watch him scheme and plot away, always a jump ahead of everyone else.

Donnelly plays him for all he's worth. As an aide to Serena he's deferential and supportive; speaking initially to Devon he's the voice of reason; and with the council he's a sadistic bully. When he triggers an implant to inflict excruciating pain, there's a cut to him grinning with pleasure. Exposed by Devon he's sly and mocking. Unlike Smith of Manchester who never ever drops the mask, and who is perhaps unaware he's even wearing a mask, Roloff knows he's a villain, and he enjoys it thoroughly.

In Roloff's world everyone is blind, they're hypocrites or cowards, ineffectual and impotent, wrapped up in their illusions and sentimental morality. He can barely restrain his contempt.

Roloff believes he sees clearly, he's unleavened by sentiment or morality, he sees himself as a superior man and glories in it. At one point, when Devon asks him why he's done his deeds, he simply says with a mixture of sarcasm and honesty *"It's because I'm evil and corrupt."*

Interestingly, Robin Ward commented, *"The grotesque and monstrous characters in the show often seemed to be a licence to over act which many indulged."*

That certainly describes Rhodes performance to a T. Oddly, Starlost didn't have that many 'grotesque and monstrous characters.' Rhode's Roloff, Ed Ames' Smith and Simon Oakland's Asgard are all that really come to mind.

Most of the guest star characters on Starlost were often sympathetic, even tragic – doomed characters like Dr. Aaron on Lazarus from the Mist, Colonel Garoway and his crew in Pisces. Koenig's Oro was less a villain than simply a man going about his business, indifferent to others. Sakharov Francis is a broken man. Farthing is clueless. The characters of Children of Methuselah and the Goddess Calabra were people trapped in their respective worlds.

Starlost seems to have consistently tried to avoid villains and 'good versus evil' plots, Roloff here and Smith in Manchester are the most vivid exceptions.

Devon is also a lot crankier this time out. At the opening, he snaps at Garth when Garth complains in the tunnel. Oddly, Devon is taken in by Roloff's lies, in part because Roloff holds out the prospect of helping the Ark. Garth is the suspicious one this time. Devon becomes increasingly hostile to Roloff and when Roloff is finally honest, he literally loses his temper.

In previous episodes, Devon's tended to focus on his mission and merely wanted to leave whatever dead-end dome he's stumbled into. But as the series has progressed, his character has become increasingly frustrated, stubborn and suspicious. Here, he actually goes after Roloff, joining and leading the rebellion. In the scene where he fights a guard, he really does look like he's punching the guy out. Devon has always been driven, but here, his performance takes on a harsher edge, as if continuing frustration is making him harder and bitterer.

This actually represents a shift for Devon, or perhaps highlights the evolution in the character. In Manchester, he simply wanted to get the hell out and get away from Smith. Here for the first time he's committed to revolution, to changing the state of affairs, rather than just searching and moving on. He's very intent on getting rid of Roloff.

Through the series, we may be able to discern elements of a character arc. As Devon progresses on his mission to save the Ark, he becomes steadily angrier and more driven, more alienated from his friends right up to 'Return of Oro.'

Garth has more of a role in this episode than usual. Too often, he's relegated to standing around like a lunk, but here, he actually gets some opportunities to do things. When the episode opens, Garth is chewing out Devon. He's clearly tired of the whole quest, exhausted and irritated about being dragged all over the Ark on Devon's pointless mission.

Compare this antagonistic Garth to that of other episodes like the Pisces or Circuit of Death where he just seems to meekly obey anyone who appears to be in authority. Again, there's signs of a personal evolution, culminating in Garth's abandonment of Devon and Rachel in Space Precinct (an otherwise bereft episode).

The animosity and frustration growing in this episode, with both Garth and Devon, seems to lead directly to the next episode the Return of Oro, which develops the emotional splits we see between both men.

In any event, this is a fairly prominent episode for Garth. For once, he's the one making things happen. He's the one going down the rabbit holes, discovering the biosphere, facing off with Roloff, developing a real bond with Jardy, the mute boy played by Jeff Turner. His actions set the stage up for Devon, but he's still a key figure in driving the episode forward.

The episode borrows from Alice in Wonderland, the opening scenes have Garth pursuing a thieving street urchin through claustrophobic tunnels, a rabbit hole, into a large, brightly lit laboratory whose green clad inhabitants react to him in nonsensical ways, alternately paranoid, pleading, threatening and boasting. As Alice would say: Curiouser and curiouser.

Later, Jardy, the urchin, again leads Garth away from Roloff's schemes, from that same room and into yet another warren of claustrophobic tunnels where he meets the resistance movement. They fill him in so he can come popping back up to rescue Devon from Roloff.

Of course, Jardy isn't quite the white rabbit. His inspirations seem to be some combination of Peter Pan and Oliver Twist. He's clearly a lost boy, outside of society but with pretty much a free run of everything, living by his wits, more brave and competent than the adults and repeatedly saving the day and moving the story along. In look and action, he strikes me as a sort of transitional character between Peter Pan and the later Feral Child of the Road Warrior movie.

The episode is much more kinetic than other episodes, with people running or rushing about. The chase through the warrens is quite well done, there are sudden attacks, and dramatic shifts of direction throughout, often echoed by changes of scene or sets which give the episode real pace and gloss over its shortcomings.

There are definitely shortcomings, as with Mr. Smith of Manchester, the episode is hampered by the 1970s TV convention of the omniscient observer. We know who the good guys and bad guys are because we watch them being virtuous and villainous. Smith's and then Roloff's attempts to lure our heroes into their traps are obvious to us, but not to Devon, Garth and Rachel.

This sort of storytelling works because the audience identifies strongly with the protagonists so that we have a real investment in their lives and conduct. Thus we react to danger that they are not yet aware of. It was a staple of storytelling for many action and mystery series through this period.

For me, it is a lot more interesting when our viewpoints are confined to the protagonist. It would be more satisfying if we were allowed to honestly wonder 'Is Smith/Roloff really the bad guy?'

A big difference between this episode and Manchester is clearly budget. By the time we get to the Implant People, money must have been tight indeed. The generic sets this time out are particularly generic and quite sparse as if the set dressers or designers have run out of money or imagination.

The Queen's chambers appear to be furnished in nothing more esoteric than 1970s office furniture, complete with plastic tropical plants.

Even the tabletop model is tosh, although the golden tower rising high above gray fortress walls that separate it from the rest of the biosphere is suitably symbolic. It works as a metaphorical landscape, if not a literal one.

Although the poverty and misery of the people are mentioned several times, the budget does not extend, as it did with Manchester, to showing us any of it. At best, we see a single ragamuffin and some darkly lit dingy corridors where the conspirators plot. The costumes don't look as if a lot of time and money was spent on them and even the extras appear particularly muted. This tends to blunt the effectiveness of the episode. It's hard to animate that sense of outrage if there's no real portrait of misery.

Another weakness is the child actor who plays Jardy. This is a shame, since much of the episode depends on him. It's hard to tell whether Jardy's performer is a good actor or not, since he has no lines. At some points, as when he puffs out his chest to simulate Roloff, he comes across quite well.

But there are too many points where the camera focuses in on him for a reaction shot, and for all the expressiveness he shows, they may as well be shooting a potted fern. I have a sneaking suspicion that the decision to make him a mute was because he wasn't able to handle lines, even though it's a major plot point.

But having said that, the real problem is the writing around the boy. Particularly embarrassing are two scenes:

The first is underground with the resistance where Devon sends the Jardy out with a long elaborate messages for Garth and Rachel. The kid can't speak. How does Devon think the child is going to be able to transmit all that information? Devon doesn't even write it down?

The second is where essentially Garth is questioning Jardy and it comes across a lot like 'What is it Jardy? Has Lassie fallen down a well?' Again feels like Jardy is somehow transmitting an impossible amount of communication.

Later, Jardy shows up at Roloff's quarters. Obligingly, the villain reveals his master plan for no good reason. He even shows the boy the detonator he'll use to blow up the resistance, and then conveniently forgets about it, allowing the child to steal it. Roloff then compounds this stupidity by allowing Jardy to run around free while the other hostages are safely incarcerated.

This is typical of the whole episode: Early on, when our heroes are being arrested by Roloff's guards, Jardy simply runs up, steals Garth's crossbow from one of the Guards and runs away, apparently without anyone noticing.

In short, other people are written to behave like idiots around Jardy. This extends even to his grandfather, who's apparently worked for years on scientific devices to help Jardy, but apparently couldn't be bothered to feed him or give him a bath.

Perhaps the biggest shortcoming is the resolution. Roloff is defeated because he trips and falls. Hardly the most dramatically satisfying conclusion. In the end, Roloff is undone because he has two left feet? That's equivalent to Darth Vader dying of a heart attack on the Death Star.

It's shocking in its apparent incompetence, it's as if the episode was drawing to a close and they just had to pull a rabbit out of a hat. It may happen in real life, but its bad storytelling because the incident, the fall, has no relationship to any of the prior events contributing to the plot. It's dropped in out of left field, a bush league 'Deus ex Machina.'

One can imagine the conversation on set....

Director: "Okay, he's got hostages, they can't get in, he's got his security guards.... Darn, he's going to win."

Donnelly: "I know, I'll just fall down and they'll get the drop on me."

Director: "Great...roll!"

I'm tempted to attribute this to bad writing, and certainly, it is lazy writing.

But there may be a bit more to it than meets the eye. Perhaps it was meant to work on a metaphoric rather than literal level. Consider this: Roloff's power came from Serena's blindness, from her unwillingness to see what was happening around her. As Roloff delights in telling her, she ignored reality and chose to live in a little fantasy world of meaningless gestures, and so has lost everything. Roloff, in contrast, prizes his ability to see clearly.

But literally, the same thing happens to Roloff, throughout the whole third act, he remains absolutely confident that he's in control and he's on top of things. But most definitely, he is not. His plot to blow up the resistance is forgotten, they run wild through the complex, searching for him, his guards nowhere to be found. The situation proceeds to escalate, but he seems indifferent, even dismissive, confident that he'll come out on top. In the end, he's just as blind to reality as Serena was.

He's like Hitler in the last days of the war issuing orders to non-existent divisions. By the time he trips and falls, Roloff has lost. His physical fall is just the punctuation of his fall from power, it's the sudden stop at the end.

The episode functions well on metaphoric levels. Impotence, or disability seems to be a running theme of the episode. The Council doesn't function they haven't passed legislation in years and provide nothing more than a scapegoat, the scientists are crippled, even Garth loses his ability, the hostages are paralyzed. The leader of the resistance batters ineffectually at a door. In fact, every character seems to face some form of disability that prevents them from taking action.

The only effective character (in the sense of one who actually accomplishes things, not in the sense of credibility or persuasiveness) is the only truly disabled one, the mute boy, Jardy, which must surely be a deliberate irony. In fact, Jardy is loaded with so much metaphorical freight that the poor boy seems almost doubled over under the weight. Consider that the whole implant fiasco comes about because of Bateman's attempts to 'help' Jardy.

Good intentions pave the road to hell? Useful technology has unintended consequences? Consider that Jardy isn't implanted and functions quite well, unhindered by his apparent disability. In short, he's not disabled, he's just suffering from the preconceptions of people who see him as handicapped. How utterly politically correct, it brings a brave little tear to my eye.

Just take a look at Devon's 'coming of age' to and about Jardy. Recall Serena's 'that dirty starving little boy, is that what all my people are like?' in which Jardy gets to sub for the unseen oppressed masses. And while we're at it, let's not forget the Peter Pan and Alice in Wonderland influences.

The episode is freighted with obvious messages. Roloff says nakedly that poverty is a means of control, that a population busy with subsistence has no time to protest. Elsewhere, the notion of a society corrupted and ruled by lies is explored.

There's a message tyranny will come to pass if people stand and do nothing. That freedom is something that must be fought for and defended or it will be chipped away. The genuine threat to freedom is gradual surrender and erosion by the well-meaning, which allows brutes into power. As opposed to open direct threats.

Both Roloff and the Implants themselves also stand in for metaphoric concerns. Dealing with Roloff, its interesting how he usurps power. He's essentially a bureaucrat. Unelected, representative of nobody, he takes power not through elections or conquest, but through administration and isolation.

From the 50s through the 70s, many people felt that Canada was really ruled by a class of senior bureaucrats, an old boy's network, nicknamed Mandarins.

These Mandarins superseded elected officials and even cabinet ministers, reporting directly to the Prime Minister, forming and directing policy regardless of the wishes and directions of the elected government. In modern American terms: The deep state.

The power of the Mandarins was something that became painfully apparent during the Diefenbaker years, as the Prime Minister fought with his own staff. And again in the Pearson years, when the elected officials seemed to have no real direction of their own, but were led by bureaucrats.

There's a possibly apocryphal story of a bureaucrat deciding the Prime Minister Diefenbaker, the highest official in the country, didn't have the security clearance to look at some papers, and simply took them off his desk, literally in front of him.

In Canada, the traditional Mandarins were eventually brought to an end in the 1970s, as the next Prime Minister, Pierre Elliot Trudeau undertook a number of initiatives to break up the existing map of power and to make government more inclusive and open to Canada's differing ethnic and regional groups.

Based perhaps on his observations of the Mandarins, Canadian-born economist John Kenneth Galbraith went on to speculate that bureaucracies would come to rule the world, that business administrators would supplant Boards of Directors as the real shapers of the corporations' actions and activities. The old business models, Galbraith trumpeted, were obsolete. The future belonged to managers or bureaucrats. Although Galbraith never had the nerve to take his ideas to their logical conclusions there was, especially in Canadian society, an unease that we had lost touch with democracy.

Again, this thread was probably not unique to Canada. Consider the British comedies, Yes Minister, and Yes Prime Minister. I'm sure that people everywhere in any advanced state have railed against the bureaucrats, and it undoubtedly forms a staple of the loonier American right wing ideology. Nevertheless, the particular fractious circumstances of Canadian history and politics undoubtedly meant that the issue had a special significance for us. The idea that bureaucrats had somehow become de facto rulers resonated strongly with a Canadian population which felt disenfranchised and unrepresented by elected officials. Although that's faded, it still feeds some sense of regional grievance in parts of Canada.

Of course, the matter can be viewed another way. Roloff is clearly not of the patrician classes. Rather, he has rough features, a five o clock shadow, a blunt means of speaking and factory worker's sideburns. He has none of the refinements or features of good breeding associated with the elite. If Serena looks the part of a queen, Roloff looks the part of a bricklayer.

Even his name sounds suspiciously foreign, probably Russian, with its hints of communism. With typical Canadian schizophrenia, Roloff also represents the upper classes fear of the working classes. Roloff embodies the terror of the ruling elite at having their powers and privileges usurped.

In short, to different groups, Roloff represents on the one hand, the tyranny of the entrenched bureaucracy, and on the other hand, the usurpation of the masses. In short, a typical Canadian solution in having one character represent contradictory impulses, inviting the viewer to choose their flavour.

Of course, in the end, one has to wonder if sometimes, that cigar isn't simply a cigar? Are the literary or intellectual themes we see in the Implant People deliberate? Or is this post hoc rationalization? Did the writer really intend these things, or are we just reading into it.

My own judgement is that it's really there. Simply put, much of this is not subtle stuff, but is applied with hammer blows. This is not reading into things, the script is dropping anvils on us. Roloff's victory speech to Serena isn't much more than the writer calling a halt to the plot and lecturing us directly.

There's painfully deliberate symbolism in the way the Council leader makes a speech and then breaks Roloff's wand, the symbol of his rule, across his knee.

All too often, the messages are couched in fairly blunt terms, and the subtexts feel conscious and deliberate. The whole episode has the feel of a young, inexperienced writer who has studied too much Shakespeare in University and hasn't quite got it out of his system. It seems very clear that the writer didn't just want to tell an adventure story, but that he wanted to say *meaningful* things.

Overall, the Implant People is a fairly strong episode. Although constrained by numerous flaws, it has strong, if occasionally muddled, literary and intellectual subtexts. It is about things and it has things to say.

The intelligence which courses just beneath the surface, the array of social concerns and themes elevates this episode well above its mediocre production values and ham handed plot. It is literate science fiction with more in common with 1984 and Brave New World than with Buck Rogers.

Creatives

Director Joseph Scanlon was an American television director, who officially or unofficially, is credited with at least five episodes of Starlost.

The Episode credits Helen French and Martin Lager as writers. Helen French is obscure, she has only a handful of Internet Movie Database entries, from the mid-60s to the mid-70s. Her earliest work is for the CBC in 1964, and CTV in 1972, so we can assume she's a Canadian writer. She is one of the very few women with a creative credit on the show.

Martin Lager, on the other hand, was a Canadian writer credited with four episodes of Starlost. We suspect that Lager might have been a bit of a merkin, a Canadian name to put on a script, in order to satisfy those all-important Canadian content requirements. Of his four credits, only one of them is solo and that one is a bit dire.

The Internet movie database lists two additional uncredited writers. Alan Spraggett shows up. He is another Canadian artist with minimal credits, and we don't know much about him.

The second uncredited Scriptwriter John Meredyth Lucas was a prolific writer, producer and director for American television from 1950 to 1989. He was notably active with Star Trek. This was his only work for Starlost. He was, however, a prolific director and writer on another Canadian syndicated drama, Police Surgeon, a show that Helen French also wrote for, and that Marian Waldman and Mort Forer were connected to.

The presence of four writers, two of them uncredited, along with Norman Klenman as the story consultant, seems puzzling given the slender story and its gaps. Did this really take five people, even with all the symbolic and metaphorical baggage? It suggests a difficult story process. But whatever went on there is lost to time.

Backstory and Continuity

Once again, we see a dome in a state of rapid decay, with people impoverished and starving. As appalling as Roloff is, we should consider the possibility that Roloff is a symptom, not the cause of the dome's decay, or even worse, a by-stander and opportunist taking advantage of that decay.

On the other hand, there's a more optimistic suggestion – the reports of deterioration and poverty we see or hear in the Implant People, Manchester or Circuit of Death, all appear to be human induced, and may simply be bad management. The Ark has massive resources, but these resources are poorly administered or captured by incompetent or tyrannical governments.

On reflection the Ark, as a whole, may not be decaying. The decay of the dome in this episode is directly from misrule, as is the case with Sakharov's home in Circuit of Death.

Manchester for instance, is highly polluted but seems to have been stable for centuries. Egrek, the women's dome, which we hear of in The Alien Oro is contaminated, but this contamination also appears to have been stable for centuries, long enough for its inhabitants to adapt.

Perhaps the problem is not the Ark failing, but the people?

And this offers an opportunity for a counter-narrative or counter-interpretation. Perhaps the real problem is Queen Serena, an out of touch autocrat, content to let her bureaucrats do her dirty work.

Perhaps the dome and Serena's order is fundamentally broken and corrupt, and Roloff is just a usurper. In which case, the restoration of order under her rule won't actually change anything.

Creators and Cast

Directed by Joseph L. Scanlon
Written by Helen French and Martin Lager (credited) and Alan
Spraggett and John Meredyth Lucas (uncredited)
&&&
Devon: Keir Dullea
Rachel: Gay Rowan
Garth: Robin Ward
Sphere Projector: William Osler
Queen Serina: Pat Collins
Advisor Roloff: Donnelly Rhodes
Councillor Dumal: Dino Narizzano
Professor Brant: Leo Leyden
Jardy: Jeff Toner
&&&
Original Airdate: December 8, 1973

THE RETURN OF ORO – EPISODE THIRTEEN

The Alien Oro returns with a plan to save the Ark...for a price.

The return of Oro is probably the single best episode of the Starlost, and in many ways the most intriguing, both in terms of dramatic structure and in terms of its thematic elements.

Unlike many of the other episodes which tended to start slowly, this one opens with a bang, showing us an apparently insane man, Williams, trying to break through a door.

Most of the time an episode will begin with a relatively static shot of Devon, Garth and Rachel, so this is a real shift of emphasis. A much more explosive beginning than usual.

Devon appears, to confront Williams. Immediately the two of them get into a shouting match. Even as they rant at each other, Williams is struck down.

Although they were almost fighting, Devon calls in Garth and Rachel and they react to the crisis of an injured man. It's reminiscent of a similar incident in Lazarus in the Mist.

But, it turns out, he'll be all right. Meanwhile, Devon walks through a door that was barred to Williams, to meet the Vice Admiral of the Ark, Tau Zeta, a robot!

Okay, Tau Zeta is a crappy robot. There is an unverified story that Tau Zeta was actually a promotional prop or model made for a shampoo or detergent company that the production bought or borrowed. We don't know if that's true or not, but you can sort of see it.

"It probably was," Gay Rowan laughed when asked. *"The things they brought on set to work, all the sets made from Javex bottles, the things they used, we would laugh hysterically. There were things in that show you had to laugh, or you cried."*

Tau Zeta's has extremely limited mobility, and the shape and look does remind you of those plastic bottles for shampoos or dishwasher liquid. The 60s and 70s were awash in really crappy looking robots. But if that's the worst thing in the episode, we can live with it. And frankly, it's such a demented story, that I kind of wish it were true.

The robot is voiced by Pat Moffett in a casual conversational manner, without electronic modulation or any of William Osler's mannered twitchiness when he does his sphere projector.

Now, let's stop a moment here and note that we've just had three plot twists thrown at us one after the other in practically as many minutes. That's pretty intense, especially considering that a man accidentally injured playing with the ship was about half of the entire plot of the Astro-Medics.

Here's an interesting development: Tau Zeta knows who Devon is. She's looked forward to finally meeting him. They know who the madman, Williams, is. Apparently, they've been watching. In short, Tau Zeta seems to have fairly complete knowledge of people on the Ark.

This isn't the first time we've seen this. Magnus, the Artificial Intelligence in Gallery of Fear also seemed to be able to access information on the trio. This is a disturbing revelation, because it suggests that Devon and his companions have been more lab rats in a maze than genuine explorers. That alone is an intriguing enough premise that you could spend an hour exploring it, but this is an episode that consistently makes unexpected left turns.

No sooner does the cast realize they've been lab rats, than they're about to meet the Admiral of the Ark, the person Devon's been searching for the whole series. And it turns out that its Oro! Let's just throw a couple more twists in.

Oro is back! Or at least, he's on his way back to the Ark in his little scout ship. But it's a different Oro in manner than the one we've seen. This Oro is convivial and friendly, he greets Devon like an old friend.

It's a change that leaves Devon suspicious. His explorations of the Ark have left him bitter and cynical, the mantle of trying to save the world when nobody else seems to care, has weighed him down. He refuses to take Oro at face value.

But Oro presents himself as a saviour. He's returned to rescue the Ark, just as Devon had asked, and just as he'd promised. He proposes to bring the Ark into orbit around Exar and offers a new life on his world, and even shows them pictures of what looks remarkably like the Canadian wilderness.

It literally is straight out of a National Film Board nature documentary. Notably, the river and rapids footage is strongly reminiscent of the image of Yukon's Otter Falls, which was on the Canadian five dollar bill then in circulation. The producers are clearly tapping an iconic national image of unspoiled wilderness. Williams, Garth and Rachel are won over, and even Devon comes to doubt himself.

This episode is structured far more dramatically than many others in the series. For one thing, information is parceled out much more carefully.

And most of the time, the viewpoint is that of Devon himself. The omniscient observer perspective is restricted. We, the audience don't know, for instance, that Oro has lied to them about his plans, until Devon discovers it. In an episode like the Implant People or Manchester, we were shown Ames and Roloff lying and scheming. Here, quite often, we only know what Devon knows, though Oro's conduct is just as self-serving and sociopathic as either of those villains.

Interestingly, this limited point of view allows Devon to come across unsympathetically, and it adds depth to his moments of doubt. Oro plays the friendly gentleman offering rescue, and he presents his case and persuades Rachel and Garth.

In contrast, Devon seems stubborn, obstinate, even unreasonable, not just to his friends, but to the audience. Devon's abrasiveness here isn't limited to Oro. He clashes with Williams. Rachel accuses him of putting his own need to be a leader ahead of the good of the Ark. In short, he's a jerk.

When Devon refuses Oro's help, Oro says that it needs to be unanimous, and promises to go back to Exar. Devon's suspicion and hostility sabotages the cause he's fought for through thirteen episodes.

This makes for an interesting role reversal, where the official bad guy comes across like the good guy, and our hero seems like a villain. The Starlost had always done well by its villains, but here the reversal is almost complete.

So when Tau Zeta tells him that the scenes of Exar are fakes, it has a particular shock. Because, up to this point, Oro had been winning the audience and Devon losing it. In this moment, we're told that Oro really is the villain and that Devon is right.

It's reminiscent of that moment in Mr. Smith from Manchester, when Devon seems to be crazy and paranoid, shouting at an empty room, only for the audience to discover an instant later, that Smith is waiting on the other side with a hidden army.

The few times the observing eye moves from Devon, for example, when Oro convinces Garth and Rachel that Devon has to be stopped, tend to add to the drama rather than diffuse it. Devon is being set up and we can't know what will happen in the confrontation.

The whole episode plays out like a chess game between Devon and Oro, with each making moves and counter moves, escalating the tension to the point of murder. It's a contest between the two which eventually results in a literal contest.

The episode is also laced with a fascinating ambiguity. Is Oro really the bad guy? Of course he is, but with Ames and Roloff, we were shown clearly that they were, their rationalizations merely that, rationalization. Because of the restricted perspective, we aren't shown that about Oro.

Instead, his arguments and proposals are compelling. When he sells Exar's beauty to the trio, he's selling it to us the audience. When Devon confronts him that the images are Old Earth, Oro dismisses it arguing he didn't have images of Exar and these are similar, he still sounds reasonable.

Even when we discover what he's really up to he is still disturbingly polite and civilized. He doesn't exult in villainy like Roloff, or wallow in power like the Commander in The Goddess Calabra, or even betray the ingrained paranoia of Mr. Smith.

Rather, he's mild and reasonable, a sensible person doing his job without particular animosity. He doesn't attack Devon, quite the opposite, his policy is a series of attempts to enlist or neutralize him.

He attempts to sway Devon with images. When caught, he simply makes his case anyway. When that doesn't work, he distracts Devon and then tries to lock him away. When Devon escapes, he attempts to neutralize him through his friends. Ultimately, Devon won't back down, and it's only after running out of other options that Oro decides he's got no choice but to execute him. That's when the robot steps in, and Oro agrees to a debate.

Each action, though increasingly villainous, is reasonable on its surface. At first, he doesn't even seem bad at all, and even though we see he might be in a situation where he's compelled to do increasingly bad things. The whole point of the series is to save the Ark, and he's actually doing it.

Even exposed he still has a compelling logic on his side. He's offering the Ark a choice, destruction on their own terms or survival on his. As the computer admits, his arguments may be better.

In short, he's as much an opposing point of view as he is a bad guy. Certainly he's convincing and compelling enough that he makes Devon doubt himself, he nearly persuades the artificial intelligences, and pulls Garth and Rachel over to the side.

Devon's victory is a remarkably telling one. Framed as a debate over arguments, a battle of logic, Devon wins because of his values.

The debate, and the entire struggle, in the Return of Oro is quintessentially Canadian. If the series was a branch plant production imported from the US, by the time we get to this point, it's got the maple leaf stamped all over it.

What the Return of Oro is really about, is the decision as to whether to be a colony or not. To seek a measure of safety and security, and accept a guarantee of second class status and lifetime mediocrity, by accepting status as a satellite. Or trying to go your own way, trying to master your own destiny and risking destruction. It's about whether to survive as part of a larger body, if that means losing your identity.

You just don't see that in Star Trek. Superior beings or races were occasionally encountered in American science fiction, but they were always, in the end, defeated, overcome, sometimes revealed as lesser beings or exaggerations, or simply dealt with and then ignored. The possibility of inferior status was dealt with quickly with an automatic 'no.' American science fiction simply refused to deal with the whole notion.

This is probably because it's never been a serious issue for American or even British society. These societies have always confronted the world on their own terms, dominated or at the very least been equals in their own spheres. They've never really confronted the idea of marginal status or of being faced with an overwhelming adversary. The worst they've ever come up against was a stalemate.

The ideas and debate in Return of Oro is inescapably Canadian. It's framing a current ongoing Canadian debate from 1973, and even using the language and arguments of that debate.

If we see the whole story is a kind of metaphorical version of the Canadian national debate over our future, then maybe Williams appears in a different light. He's a throwaway character with very little to do with the story – but he's also a loud, obnoxious guy with an exaggerated sense of entitlement who demands access everywhere. An 'Ugly American'?

It's notable that Devon, who's normally fairly civil, reacts to him with anger shouting back. The ship's AI refuse him access. The message is that he's an interloper who doesn't belong, even Devon senses it.

If that's the case, then the metaphor is that Williams is the ugly, entitled American, barging in and Oro is the smoother version, come with cash and promises, with the two of them getting in each other's way.

The notion of the Return of Oro as a metaphor for a national debate certainly has nothing to do with Harlan Ellison, early on he'd divorced himself from the production. This stuff was coming from Norman

Klenman, Bill Davidson, Ed Richardson, and the other Canadians who were the brain trust for the series.

Return of Oro posed certain problems for the writers of the series. Where do you go from there?

The usual rule for television back in this day was to hit the reset button. Every episode had to return to the status quo, because everyone had to start off from the same place for the next episode. Nothing substantial or lasting could ever be allowed to happen.

Except that fundamentally, irrevocable things had just happened. Devon had made contact with, and gained the support of, the community of artificial intelligences that monitored and controlled many of the ships function. Oro had diverted, or was on the threshold of diverting, the ship from its doomed heading towards a star. At the very least, Oro had put all the pieces in place for a course change. Devon had become Admiral of the Ark, awarded gold security clearance.

Essentially, the problems were solved. The Ark wasn't going to fly into a sun. Devon now had access to the knowledge and resources to steer and fix the ark. He didn't need to search for an alternate Bridge any more, he could just ask the AIs for directions. All of Devon's motivations for the initial episodes, practically everything he was striving for, had been accomplished.

In a sense, this episode completes the quest. Harlan Ellison, in his bible, talked about the Starlost as a television novel. In that sense, he was far ahead of his time, anticipating Babylon 5, Breaking Bad, the Sopranos and LEXX.

But if the Starlost was equivalent to a television novel, that novel had been completed, or at least a major section of it had been concluded. The quest established at the beginning of the series had been fulfilled.

Maybe the Starlost really was a television novel after all. A small one, but a genuine novel across thirteen episodes. Maybe it was genuinely ahead of its time. Let's examine that a little bit.

This episode is not just a sequel to The Alien Oro but builds on and extends the ideas and concerns of that episode. It's also, loosely, a sequel to Gallery of Fear and the establishment of the community of artificial intelligences we see there, that community is back, through Tau Zeta, to judge once again. In fact, it's arguable that the AI have been active through Devon's first contacts with a sphere projector in Voyage of Discovery.

It's not only these three episodes that we can connect to each other. Voyage of Discovery connects directly to Lazarus in the Mist, with Doctor Aaron in Lazarus explaining to the trio what their discoveries in the previous episode mean.

From there, each episode, in some way advances their mission and their knowledge, whether it's encountering remnants of the Ark's infrastructure, or confronting increasingly toxic societies more and more aggressively. There may be stand-alone episodes, but there's actually something of a progression leading a hardening Devon.

The debates between utilitarianism and idealism are echoed repeatedly through Only Man is Vile, The Implant People and Circuit of Death and even Gallery of Fear. A lot of the show's episodes, when you come right down to it, amounts to a series of debates which ultimately culminate in the great debate to the death in this episode.

Again and again, Starlost wrestles with the idea of community, and people's place in it. It wrestles with the idea of limitations, of a finite and delicate world.

Perhaps it doesn't do so perfectly, and perhaps some of its ideas and notions are addressed erratically. Not everything necessarily fits into arcs and themes. But there is enough there, to be worth critical, even literary evaluation.

There are signs of a character arc for Devon and his companions. This episode sows be an escalation of the angrier snappish Devon, briefly fooled and now wary of promises, in the previous episode, Implant People. An aggressive Devon fighting with Garth and committed to overthrowing Roloff.

That earlier person in turn is an escalation from the Devon of Manchester, seeing through Smith and merely wanting to escape. It's subtle and uneven, but Devon seems to slowly be getting angrier and more frustrated as the episodes go on. Is this an actual character arc?

On episodic television, under the traumatic pace of production that the show demanded? Normally, I'd say no, everyone wants to hit the reset button, everyone is too busy getting pages of script in the can to think of character arcs. But there are some things to give pause.

For one thing, the show maintained a brutal production pace of nonstop eighteen hour days. Weeks of that on end would wear anyone down, and Keir Dullea, might actually have been increasingly exhausted and cranky. So there may be a character arc, reflecting the actor's personal arc.

Another possibility is that Dullea is a genuinely gifted actor, he's inhabiting the character eighteen hours a day, through dubious scripts which really throws the character in his head in sharper contrast, and he may well have deliberately or unconsciously been moving Devon through an arc, evolving his personality.

There's actually some support for that, Robin Ward felt that towards the end, Dullea was deliberately fashioning a more impatient, frustrated Devon.

"Keir inexplicably decided in one of the last episodes to give his character Devon a John Waynesque flavour which did not sit well with Mr. Koenig and they both had a slightly nasty argument on the set during which he accused Keir of being unprofessional," Robin Ward recalls.

The friction between Dullea and Koenig is interesting. As we've noted, Koenig had been a close friend of Ellison, and Ellison's choice for the roles of both Devon and then Garth. So there was definitely possible baggage. Robin Ward had the sense that Koenig found the role beneath him. The antagonism or rivalry onscreen between their characters may have had deeper roots.

Beyond Devon, less obviously, there are signs of growth or change with the other characters. Garth slowly becomes more assertive and self-possessed, still deferring, but ever more his own man.

In Pisces he starts out doing simply deferring to authority, any authority, but through Astro-Medics, Implant People and the Return of Oro, he's increasingly inclined to follow his conscience, even if it means challenging authority or friendship.

Rachel herself makes the effort to be more assertive, and we know that behind the scenes, Gay Rowan was pushing her character.

Finally, there's the overwhelming presence of Norman Klenman, a credited or uncredited writer for half the series, and story editor for the whole series. If Starlost had a multitude of writers from all over, that would be one thing. You wouldn't expect consistency, or homogeneity or any kind of continuity or arc. But Klenman was this presence through the show and inevitably had a huge influence on the narrative.

The thing with writers is that when they work with the same material, they tend to build continuity and progression into it. Even if they don't mean to, it happens almost unconsciously. Ideas and characters are recycled and re-examined in different ways. Tropes and themes recur in the work of everyone from Edgar Rice Burroughs to William Faulkner, H.P. Lovecraft to Steven King. This appearance of connectedness, of narrative progression, of something resembling a television novel may have just been an organic result of the heavy presence of a very few people, maybe just Klenman, or maybe Klenman, Richardson and Davidson. So it may come down to Klenman deliberately or inadvertently laying it in.

So for any number of reasons, conscious or unconscious, whether it's punchiness, or a consistent creative team, or simply being immersed in culture and reflecting the issues of the time, Starlost seems to evolve character and narrative arcs that build and culminate in the Return of Oro? For whatever reason, or combination of reasons, there is a whole that is greater than the sum of parts.

I find myself wondering if I'm just reading tea leaves, projecting pattern and form into something that was simply episodic television produced under breakneck circumstances. The reality is definitely that Klenman, Richardson and Davidson were all just scrambling desperately to get each episode done, and on to the next.

That's not really a basis for vision or planning. And honestly, the notion of a television novel was anathema to television at the time. The idea that you should be able to run episodes in any order, and that your audience should be able to start watching at any point.

Then again, I argue with confidence that individual episodes, particularly the Oro episodes, but also Manchester and others, directly wrestle with different themes and questions of Canadian identity, or reflect Canadian attitudes and experience. Honestly, I can't watch Return of Oro and not see the great Canadian debate about our own future.

I've argued that the show was simply picking these ideas from the environment, from discussions and media that everyone was having. It was literally the water that the fish was swimming in, so it's impossible to avoid.

But if we accept that the show and characters were animated by the larger national discussion that was going on throughout, is it really a stretch to say that a continuous national dialogue which animated individual stories could also animate the series as a whole, that it would drift to the architecture of some larger story?

Would the quest nature of Devon's mission not require some kind of commitment to progression, to resolution, however erratic and imperfect? Maybe it was just baked into the premise.

But when I look at Voyage of Discovery and the progression to Return of Oro, there seems to be a whole, a journey, which is more than the sum of its parts, more than random disconnected episodes.

But if we argue that the thirteen episodes constitute a novel, and the novel is completed, then... What now?

The Return of Oro was episode thirteen in a commissioned sixteen episode series. Was this a natural progression – do the main story, and leave a couple of episodes for wrap up? What about the eight episode option for a possible extended twenty-four episode total? Was the last third pivoting to a new direction?

Had they decided to wrap up the arc in the face of declining ratings and cancellations and impending cancellations by syndicated stations? No, that wasn't it. The series fate was still up in the air. The decision not to pick up the option for the next eight episodes wasn't made until the second last show.

Why have an apparent arc or conclusion at all in the thirteenth episode? This wasn't being done in America, and Klenman and other expatriate writers worked in the US, they knew how it was done and what was demanded.

But Richardson and Davidson weren't really connected to Hollywood and not wedded to its conventions. They might have seen things differently and been open to a coherent story. Or perhaps with less Hollywood experience they policed things less effectively and didn't prevent it. Or maybe it was inexperience, they hadn't quite learned to follow the Hollywood formula.

What was the thinking?

We don't really know.

This is literally a 'Death of the Author' situation, the key creative persons making decisions have all passed away and can't explain themselves.

We can only sift the actual episodes and recurring evidence of a 'novelistic' continuity, and try to parse it.

Harlan Ellison had come up with the television novel idea, but he never fleshed it out. He was long gone by this time. In the end, he was just spit balling a notion. Nevertheless, Williamson, Richardson and Klenman each clearly read that bible carefully. Williamson and Richardson needed to parse it for production decisions. Klenman was unimpressed, but still read it. Perhaps Ellison's idea about a television novel sank in and influenced the thinking and progression of the show. At the very least, it is there.

Ultimately, it's a matter of opinion. Perhaps one can read too much into it. It's easy to dismiss it as all just unconnected episodes and sloppy writing, amounting to nothing much.

Or maybe we're not punching at ghosts, and the shape of a novel is genuine and buried in the episodes. For what it's worth, we choose the latter. But assuming that Starlost was something of a television novel, that novel had reached a conclusion with Return of Oro.

So what next?

Where would they go next? Where could they? Would we see Devon, Rachel and Garth hitting the reset button? Would they blithely forget the episode and continue wandering randomly around, looking for answers they should already have in their pockets?

That's possible.

And perhaps the last three episodes read that way. It would really undermine the 'novel' concept.'

Equally possible, we may have seen a shift in the direction of the series, and a shift in Devon's mission, moving from exploration to reconstruction, from trying to find something to trying to build something.

Following The Return of Oro, the remaining three episodes show a tentatively different narrative direction. The political subtext that appears in the series starting with Circuit of Death seems to fade away. Starlost had featured a run of increasingly political episodes, increasingly open about being political, increasingly about issues. The final three episodes aren't really political at all. The subtext seems to vanish.

They're visibly cheaper, narratively and structurally weaker; clearly more generic.

Perhaps that goes without saying, the decision whether to pick up the option for the next eight was being delayed, money was running out. The costs of episodes that had gone over budget were now coming due with less money available for the final episodes. Everyone had been doing eighteen hour days for months on end and were exhausted and ragged.

After the climactic episode, the series visibly descends. Each of the subsequent episodes are weaker in every respect often with glaring problems.

Farthing's Comet and The Beehive show a different Devon and his friends. They're no longer wandering from dome to dome aimlessly. They are directed, focused, they are seeking out trouble and solving problems.

Farthing's Comet, actually has Devon making slight repairs on the Ark and altering its direction, at least out of the path of an immediate menace. Devon's spent the whole series looking for someone to steer the Ark, and now he's doing it. It's a monumental step, and actually remarked upon by Rachel in the episode, in terms of its significance to the narrative.

In the Beehive, Devon, Garth and Rachel show up at the beehives because they've been setting off alarms, and they're there to find out what the problem is. They're actually wearing Ark fleet uniforms, and they're acting like official investigators and trouble shooters. They literally assert authority. This speaks to a dramatically different role and mission.

Even Space Precinct, wretched as it is, sort of fits. Space Precinct is about Garth leaving Rachel and Devon behind to go home. But would he really do that, unless the danger was past? Unless their mission was complete, and he was just refusing to sign onto Devon's next protracted mission? Garth was always the most down to earth of the characters, he wouldn't leave them in the lurch, but he also wouldn't stay past the end of danger. Just a thought.

Creatives

This was Francis Chapman's sole directing credit for Starlost. Chapman forty-seven years old at the time, was born in Toronto and seems to have made his entire career in the arts working in Canadian film and television production.

In contrast, the Return of Oro is Alex C. James sole writing credit on IMDB. No other information on him.

Norman Klenman, on the other hand, seems to have been one of, if not the single, critical person, to the shaping of Starlost. He is the credited writer on the Pisces, Circuit of Death, Mr. Smith of Manchester, and uncredited writer for Voyage of Discover, Return of Oro and Farthing's Comet.

Backstory and Continuity

The main AI is Tau Zeta, Vice Admiral of the Ark, but it's clear that she cooperates with other intelligences to run the ship. The presence of a community of Artificial Intelligences on the ship dates back to

Gallery of Fear, and may be hinted at as early as the first episode, Voyage of Discovery.

It is established that although the Artificial Intelligences are in communication with each other and aware of the danger to the Ark, they seem unable to do anything about it directly. This implies that they have been actively limited in various ways, much as Magnus was involuntarily limited in Gallery of Fear.

Given the distances, it is likely that Oro never actually returned to Exar. It is, after all, estimated about a light year or more away, and this universe seems to lack FTL. Perhaps he only got far enough out to report and receive new mission orders which sent him back. This poses a larger question of what happened to Idona.

Random thought: Given Exar's proximity, is Exar's star the one the Ark is on course to collide with?

Oro's final fate suggests that there was some sentiment to bring Koenig back for a third or continuing appearances as a troublemaker if the series had continued. This was confirmed by the producers, Davidson and Richardson.

Williams's apparent insanity, as we've seen, is not unique and amounts to a further hints at the possibility of widespread cases of dementia from travelling at significant fractions of light speed.

Creators and Cast

Directed by Francis Chapman
Written by Norman Klenman and Alex C. James
&&&
Devon: Keir Dullea
Rachel: Gay Rowan
Garth: Robin Ward
Sphere Projection: William Osler
Oro of Exar: Walter Koenig
Tau Zeta (voice): Pat Moffatt
Tau Zeta (body): Phillip Stephens
Williams: Henry Beckman
Earthship Ark Computer: Jim Barron
&&&

Original Airdate: December 15, 1973

FARTHING'S COMET – EPISODE FOURTEEN

A Mad Astronomer diverts the Ark into the path of a comet... for science!

The Ark is under attack! The episode begins with genuine drama. The Ark is shaking, there are booming sounds of impact. Devon and his friends are cowering and running. But who is attacking? It's actually a fairly dramatic opening with genuine tension.

They're wrong, it's not an attack, but it's still a good hook. And in terms of the Starlost's subtle continuity, it's justified.

In the previous episode, our heroes had saved the Ark from being taken over by Oro of Exar. In the episode before that, they'd encountered the Rillian's ship passing near the Ark. Devon and his friends know that aliens are real, that they have already tried to take the Ark, and this might be the next move. It's reasonable for Devon and the audience to think its aliens.

The trio make their way to a Sphere Projector, and a fairly effective scene, where they manage to tease useful information that sends them to the Astronomy section looking for answers.

It turns out its not aliens after all. It's just Doctor Linus Farthing, chief astronomer and jovial mad scientist, recklessly putting the Ark in danger.

The name is obviously a reference to a Nobel Prize winning scientist, Doctor Linus Pauling, who was a chemist rather than an astronomer. Pauling is one of the few men to win two different Nobel prizes in two different fields – one in chemistry and the other for his work as a peace activist. Later on, Pauling's reputation declined as he became fixated on Vitamin C as literally the cure for everything including cancer. But in 1973 he wasn't the Mayor of Flakytown yet and was still famous and highly respected.

A Farthing is also an obsolete unit of English currency, typically a trivial amount, essentially equivalent to a nickel or a dime. So there may be a comment about triviality there.

But physically and in his bluff mannerisms, Doctor Farthing also resembles another famous chemist, Isaac Asimov, practically down to horn rimmed glasses and side burns, although Asimov's were much woollier.

The Starlost had made these kinds of contemporary references before, in Circuit of Death a scientist had been named Sakharov, after a famous dissident Soviet nuclear scientist of the time. More than once, the Starlost has skimmed images and ideas transparently from popular culture, often with very little mediation.

In fact, the visual and dramatic core of this episode, literally taking up twenty-seven of the forty-eight minute running time, is an almost unmediated borrowing from contemporary science fact of the day: The extended spacewalk drama, where Devon risks his life to go outside the Ark to conduct repairs.

Now, of course, this seems trite and worse, it's long and boring. But again, you have to go back to the times. This was the early 70s. I remember during those days, as a child, I would be glued to the black and white television set all day, breathlessly watching live television of men walking on the moon. Like many other kids my age, I kept a scrap book full of newspaper clippings, of a Russian robot lunar module that looked like a bathtub with wheels, of flyby probes with new images of Mars and Venus, of the Skylab and Soyuz space stations.

Spacewalks, going outside the modules, those were events reported on front pages or in science sections of newspapers and magazines. The first spacewalk had only taken place on March 18, 1965, by Alexei Leonov of the Soviet Union, for ten minutes. This was followed a few months later on June 3 by Ed White for the U.S. for 23 minutes. This had been only eight years before the show. By 1973 you could literally count the entire number of accomplished spacewalks on one hand. It was a huge thing.

The space age was real then, new, indisputably romantic, genuinely dangerous, and presented to the public in an almost plodding fashion, the newspaper reports earnest, the television coverage documentary verite, as indeed it was.

This was well before the days of hyperkinetic video games, or the sizzle and flash of Star Wars. In comparison, the earnest plodding drama of the repair mission in Farthing's Comet looks dated now.

But in this episode it builds on and captures the genuine documentary verite feel of actual space missions that were going on at the time, and it did so in a way that even Star Trek and certainly Lost in Space never accomplished. Indeed, to add to the verite feel and add drama, most of Devon's spacewalk takes place in real time, with the mission counting down and the clock ticking away.

Ed Richardson, the Associate Producer and episode Director, related a memory to Phillips and Garcia – *"The scenes of Keir floating around in space were accomplished by putting Keir in a black chair against a blue-screen and moving the chair around with little rods. When we keyed in the star background, it looked like he was floating in space. The meteors were little pieces of Styrofoam that we threw past the camera lens."*

Talk about low-fi.

Dullea had worked with state of the art special effects and wire work playing an astronaut in 2001: A Space Odyssey. Now he was sitting on a black chair in some half-assed version of a space suit, getting pushed around by rods. I'm sure the contrast wasn't lost to him.

On the other hand, Robin Ward remembers the episode with some embarrassment for the slack attitude of the Director.

"I remember a shot where I was tethered outside the mother ship. Fixing something or other and there was an obvious space between my helmet and my suit. I pointed this out to the director of that episode who said "Don't worry, it will never read on air "Of course later when I watched the episode you could clearly see that the helmet was not connected to the suit. It was that kind of incompetence which gradually eroded our initial enthusiasm and caused us to become jaded about the show and

our work in it. But that all took time and in the beginning, even after we lost Trumbull, we still felt hopeful and enthusiastic."

Ward's memory may be a little off here. There are only two episodes where he wears a space suit, the first is The Alien Oro, the seventh episode, where he wears the helmet, there is an obvious space between the helmet and the suit, but it's simply a walk through a depressurized section of the Ark, not a tether outside the ship.

In Farthing's Comet, Ward's character is in a space suit again, but not wearing a helmet – he's simply piloting a shuttle. It's Dullea's character who is tethered outside the mothership. Although it could just as easily be Ward inside the suit at least some of the time – a lot of the shots you don't see a face. It's a small mystery.

Nevertheless, we should be prepared to forgive what modern viewers may not. It worked for its time and the resources available.

It's really just a 'spacewalk' episode, nothing more, nothing less. There's no subtext, no politics, there's no character study, there's nothing deeper to it.

And frankly, there is much more to be genuinely unhappy about with the episode. The budget allowed for only two guest stars and no extras, which is reminiscent of all those Gerry Anderson puppet series in which endless numbers of alien races, lost civilizations and hidden conspiracies were uncovered, always consisting of only two individuals. Usually both male, which makes one wonder just how viable these alien races were.

Where are the other people? Doctor Farthing may well be the last survivor of the Astronomy Module, but where did he come from? McBride, an engineer and programmer, talks about going back to her people, but if she indeed comes from a sophisticated Ark society, why aren't they occupying the Astronomy Module? Where are they?

This is yet another occasion where we run into evidence of a society or group on the Ark with knowledge of the impending disaster and at least the capacity to acquire the technical skill or resources to save the Ark... and no one does anything. It's just fatalism.

There are also huge issues with specific motivation. The whole problem comes about because Doctor Farthing has altered the entire

Ark's course to cruise into the comet. He explains that this is because he knows they're doomed to fall into a star.

But if he can alter the course to get a better look at the comet, why can't he arrange to avoid the star? Farthing admits to firing the navigational engines, the implications of that are obvious to Devon and his friends.

"The search is over," Rachel exults. She has a point. If Farthing can change the trajectory of the Ark to get a better look at the comet, why can't its course change to avoid doom?

Why are he and McBride so fatalistic about the Ark's fate? If McBride is from a sophisticated society, then her people should know about the danger as well. Again, where are they? And why was Farthing allowed to do this?

Farthing's character comes across as bluff and avuncular. He seems content to bicker away with McBride. There's no sign of the sort of obsession, or the kind of personality that might put everyone's lives at risk.

Indeed, once Devon and friends show up he his character shifts around erratically immediately. At first he's obnoxious, trying to shoo them off. Then he's condescending, but oddly eager to explain what's going on. When Devon figures out that he's responsible, he denies it at first, but almost immediately confesses. He just wanted to get a close look at the comet, and spent years figuring out how to change course into the comet's path. The Ark is being battered, domes are being cracked, but he shows no concern or remorse over the damage done or imminent destruction of the Ark. There's something deeply wrong with him.

Eventually, under Devon's relentless questioning, he agrees to help them make repairs to outside the Ark to take it out of the comet path. Farthing summons McBride to help plan out the repair, and together, they willingly assist Devon and the others in going on a repair mission.

"I got tired of arguing with them," Farthing explains to McBride.

Moments later he cheerfully says of people he met literally moments before, *"I'm beginning to care about those three."*

When a couple of domes receive critical knowledge, he displays no concern, simply saying, *"The Ark is holding together better than I thought... now to see about our friends."*

Still later, in the middle of acting as ground support for the spacewalk, he seems to forget about it and instead gets into an angry, pointless argument with McBride.

His emotions and attitudes are utterly fluid. He seems unable to maintain focus in the face of distraction, simply reacting to whatever he is dealing with at the moment. Seriously, what is wrong with this guy?

The other sub-plot is Farthing's thorny relationship with McBride, which finds renewal through the episode. The pair bicker like an old married couple, which is essentially what they are. McBride, feeling isolated, wants to leave and go back to her family and community. Farthing finally finds enough within himself to reach out to her and replenish their relationship.

There's an issue here. What the hell is going on with McBride? This is worse than Tabor in Only Man is Vile. In this episode, Farthing is putting everyone's life at risk, he might well destroy the Ark and everyone on it. Why is McBride working with him? Why is she helping him? Why isn't McBride stopping him? Why doesn't she talk him out of it? Hit him with a lead pipe and tie him to a chair?

Apparently, she's been working with him on this little project for years. What's wrong with her that she just seems to accept his demented nonsense?

During the spacewalk mission, McBride becomes frightened and flees, and has to be coaxed back by calls from Devon and Rachel, which suggests she's only a little more stable than Farthing, but not much more.

Still, McBride's relationship with Farthing forms the B plot of the episode. It's nice, it's interesting, and it could have been played out around a coffee table in a suburb of Chicago. The Farthing/McBride dynamic is obviously filler, meant to kill time and give us something to watch through the slow spots of the episode's spacewalk. It's not bad, but it does highlight for us how thin this episode actually is.

Finally, the episode never really addresses the consequences. Devon's quest is to restore the Ark and save it from a plunge into the sun. But at the end of the episode, there's no real conclusion.

The Ark is saved from the comet, the final scenes are the trio silently returning to the Astronomy Module in their space suits, where Farthing and McBride are waiting for them. Even that final shot feels like something out of that era's NASA.

But that's it, the closing shot. There's no follow up within the episode, no standard denouement, where the protagonists head out to the road, ready for their next adventure. Possibly, because that simply wouldn't work here.

As Rachel says, 'the search is over.' They've repaired a firing module and steered the Ark, even in a small way, that's the point of the quest. The star is still months away, even a small nudge would save them.

We don't know what they say or what happens after that. Would they really just move along and leave a man who has already nearly wrecked the Ark alone to be free to do it again?

Do they ignore as well, Farthing and McBride's wealth of technical and astronomical knowledge? Ignore the possibilities offered by McBride's unseen people? Ignore the fact that the Astronomy Module actually offers a degree of genuine control over the Ark?

It seems that, as at the end of The Return of Oro, Devon had found a great deal of what he was looking for to save the Ark. With this episode, in every practical way, once again, Devon has accomplished his mission.

This episode, plus the Return of Oro, and the contributions of a few others like 'Children of Methuselah' basically mean Devon has the support and resources to save the Ark.

In a sense, the dramatic narrative arc is completed, the story is told. The Return of Oro completes the arc, and now Farthing completes it again, it's like a hat on a hat.

So what is Farthing's Comet, following immediately after The Return of Oro? Is it just a reset to zero, forgetting what has gone before? Is the intention simply to ignore The Return of Oro, despite the opening hints of external alien attack? Or is it post-Oro troubleshooting and another step on the journey to repairing and controlling the Ark.?

The 'reset button' is a function of episodic television, where literally, every episode starts at the beginning without consciousness of what has gone before. It works somewhat in Star Trek, where each planet they visit is a brand new world, unconnected to any other.

In the Starlost, it doesn't quite work as well because every world is connected. The whole Ark is connected, it is all the same ship and one intrinsically expects that there might be some accumulation, rather than starting over from scratch each time.

Still, the episode remains thin and badly flawed. Farthing's conduct doesn't make sense, his attitude changes are too fluid. The character is either unrealistic or clinically insane. And McBride may not be too far behind. The episode doesn't really grasp the implications of these characters. Nor does it really follow through on the consequences of its premise.

Simply, the script calls for the Ark to be in danger and Devon having to go out on a protracted spacewalk to fix it, and literally, that's all there is to it. The entire episode revolves around getting the characters into, and then through, this situation intended to mimic the real space program.

Despite its shortcomings there was a real attempt to capture an audience here. This is the last genuine gasp of the Starlost. They're attempting to dress up sets, do locations, costumes, and special-effects shots.

Despite the wonky plot set up and character shifts, which clearly don't matter, there's an effort at spectacle, with a dramatic opening, allusions to alien attack and ongoing crisis, an extended space mission literally ripped from newspaper headlines, and the promise of genuine immediate and long term stakes.

Creatives

This is the final of the four episodes Ed Richardson directed. In addition to directing, Richardson was also the associate producer for the entire series and probably one of the core creative people.

This episode is attributed to Doug Hall, and is his single IMDB credit. It's likely that he was actually Douglas Hall, credited with Lazarus from the Mist. We have no other information on him. Presumably, he was a Canadian content hire.

The IMDB lists Klenman as the unattributed writer. Klenman, in addition to four credited episodes, also performed uncredited major rewrites on four other episodes, including this one. In practical terms, he wrote eight of the sixteen, and is credited as story consultant/script editor for the entire series.

Backstory and Continuity

It's amusing to watch the trio's interactions with the William Osler's sphere projector. The trio have become quite good at interrogating an Artificial Intelligence which seems bent on not giving a straight answer. It's funnier than it has a right to be, and Osler manages to be fussy in a weird bureaucratic way.

"Chief of Ark Security is by appointment only," Osler's Sphere Projector tells them. The reference by the Sphere Projector to the Security Chief may be a deliberate foreshadowing of Space Precinct.

Dr. Farthing's conduct is so reckless and he's so indifferent to consequences, that I find myself wondering if he has some mild form of dementia, perhaps a mild touch of the 'space senility' referred to in the episode Pisces. And perhaps McBride as well.

Speaking of which, through the episode, we are hear that at least three of the biosphere domes sustain major damage, including cracks or ruptures in their outer shells. It appears the damage was contained by back-ups secondary shielding, so no apparent loss of life. But the damage is massive. Dr. Farthing and McBride appears to have only escaped being a mass murderers by sheer luck, even with Devon's intervention. They've done more damage to the Ark than anything in the last 400 years, and perhaps more than the great disaster itself. One wonders if there would be consequences for them. At the least, the repairs required have increased exponentially.

One strange thing is a throwaway comment by McBride that she helped to design the space suits life support packs. But if the Ark has been travelling for five hundred years, and derelict for four hundred, how is that possible? Unless she is like the Children of Methuselah, and is functionally ageless, or at least long lived. The Ark might well be sprinkled with near immortals.

One of the cool elements of the episode's production, is that they've placed the actual Ark model in the set, so the characters are actually walking around it. They miss out on a full loving shot of this remarkable prop, but we do manage to glimpse it. Don't miss the recycled Astrogation Console set-component, which shows up several times through the series.

Once again, Garth demonstrates a much higher degree of technical knowledge than you'd expect from a 19th century level Mennonite blacksmith. This reinforces the notion that at least some people in Cypress Corners were privy to sophisticated technical training. Garth may have pounded horseshoes, but the dome also required someone who could rewire a circuit when needed.

Creators and Cast

Directed by Ed Richardson
Written by Doug Hall and Norman Klenman
&&&
Devon: Keir Dullea
Rachel: Gay Rowan
Garth: Robin Ward
Sphere Projection: William Osler
Dr. Linus Farthing: Edward Andrews
Dr. McBride: Linda Sorensen
Earthship Ark Computer: Allen Stewart Coates
&&&
Original Airdate: December 22, 1973

THE BEEHIVE – EPISODE FIFTEEN

Our heroes investigate an alarm and find giant mutant bees.

What to say about this one? It's almost certain that the genesis of this entire episode was that someone found some National Film Board stock footage of bees and decided to build an episode around it. Honestly it's probably not more complicated than that.

It would certainly explain the endless gratuitous shots of bees in close up, swarming, crawling around, and doing 'bee things' that the episode constantly cuts to. There seems to be little narrative purpose to most of these cuts, except to remind us again and again that the episode is about bees.

Yes. We get that. It's about bees. Got it.

There are only one or two shots where they even bother to project the stock footage onto blue-screen, so that Rachel and Garth can gawk at 'giant bees on the other side of the window.

That's as far as it goes, there are no super-sized bee puppets or props or even pieces of props. I suppose the budget and schedule simply didn't allow it.

It's just playing a lot of stock footage of bees, mostly intercut straight in, with some minimal composites inserted, and a lot of buzzing on the audio track. But then again, take out those stock footage inserts, and there's just damned little to the episode

The story: There are zoological stations on the Ark, one of which is devoted to bees. The idea is that in addition to preserving humanity, they're also preserving a multitude of other species to build or rebuild ecologies on alien worlds.

Looking over the beehives are a quartet, a cantankerous scientist, Doctor Pete Marshall played by William Hutt who we will call Doctor Pete, his wife, Doctor Heather Marshall, played by Antoinette Bower and an animal communication expert, Ron Callisher and some middle aged beekeeper, Harry Keeble.

Doctor Pete is wandering around being a dick to people when Garth, Devon and Rachel show up wearing Ark crew uniforms. For some unexplained reason, they've changed out of their Cypress Corners garb.

They explain the module is setting off alarms all over the place and they've come to investigate. Doctor Pete tells them to piss off but they won't leave.

Although it's never explicitly spelled out, it seems that our trio's role and mission may have shifted after the Return of Oro. Devon and crew are no longer dressed in homespun Cypress Corners outfits, bumbling around looking for help or trying to find a Bridge. Instead, they're wearing uniforms, responding to 'Danger' alerts, tracking down and stubbornly investigating problems. They aren't wanderers, they're trouble-shooters.

Or at least, that's my interpretation from some of the dialogue and the uniforms. The Ark uniforms are intriguing. We've only seen Devon and company wear them once before, in the Gallery of Fear episode, where they turned out to be hallucinations. This is the first episode where they're actually in uniform. Normally, you'd presume that the shift to Ark uniforms represents some kind of narrative shift – that in putting on the uniform and acting as investigators, Devon, Rachel and Garth's adventures have turned a corner.

In terms of a changed role, moving from searchers to trouble shooters, we kind of get a similar vibe from them in the preceding episode, Farthing's Comet. They've got a plan now, and they're out fixing things.

Of course, in both Farthing's Comet and Space Precinct, episodes before and after the Beehive, they're back in Cypress Corners duds, so it's unclear how much we should make of the costume change. Given the exigencies of television production, the breakneck pace, it could have been as simple as the regular costumes all being at the dry cleaners.

Anyway, it turns there's something wrong with the bees, they're invading adjacent corridors. Garth and Rachel spot giant mutant bees on the other side of a window. It seems that four of the bees have mutated, and now these giant mutant super bees are controlling the hives. There's apparently a giant mutant queen, but we only hear about her. If she's shown, she's not distinguished in any visible way from her giant workers.

As we go further into the episode, our heroes figure out that the mutant bees are intelligent and are using sub-sonic frequencies to control the hives and hypnotize Doctor Pete. His personality doesn't change, he's apparently aggressive and obnoxious as always, but he does their bidding, mostly without realizing it. We never hear them speaking to him, just buzzing around. Because of his connection, they can also apparently read his mind, and he relays on their behalf.

Again, this is a handicap. It's like the absence of physical giant bee props to interact directly with the actors. Without the audience actually hearing the bees speaking or participating in dialogue, Doctor Pete just seems cranky. It puts distance between the audience and the story, it's difficult to engage.

There's a nice shot where Keeble gets overcome by fumes when they're trying to kill the bees, and when they unzip his tunic, his insides are a mass of bees. That's a hell of a money shot. But then cut to commercial and after that it's never so much as mentioned. So apparently, it was just a teaser.

That's a shame, because the episode is almost entirely people talking to each other, it would have been effective to see some actual direct interaction from the bees. As it is, they're an almost completely abstract menace.

Anyway, Devon and the scientists have to fight the mutant bees. The Bees survive the poison, manage to frustrate the attempt to freeze them and slowly take over the exterior corridors, trapping the humans in the lab.

But a sense of urgency and drama is lacking. Doctor Pete gives it his scene chewing all, but the other characters, particularly Doctor Heather, just don't step up.

In the end, Devon is trapped by Doctor Cranky while the mutant super bees try to dictate terms. Luckily, Garth rushes in in and manages to stop the mutant super-bees plans to take over the Ark by freezing them directly with a cryogenic spray.

Once they're dead, Doctor Pete is himself again, all the rest of the hives go back to normal, and we're on to the next adventure. It's a little underwhelming, to say the least.

So the entire episode is: Show some stock footage, then cut away to have characters figure out the plot to each other, then show some more stock footage, then back to the characters explaining the plot to each other.

Eight to twelve year olds might have been enthralled. They'd get right into the stock footage of bees, there's nothing too scary, and kids are good at filling in the gaps between the monsters and the rest of the footage.

This is a quixotically cerebral episode. It's basically all 'tell don't show.' But stock footage doesn't make for a subtle acting partner, and it's notoriously resistant to direction.

It's an extremely talky episode, so much so it would actually work better as a radio play. For all we know, it may have been adapted from a radio play, the sound cues are strong. The characters don't so much deal directly with the menace as explain it to each other. Pretty much everything that happens, the back and forth contest between the bees and the humans is described and seldom shown, it's all dialogue with a few sound effects.

There are a few kind things that I can say. One is that Doctor Pete, when hypnotised and doing the bidding of the mutant bees, is basically the same guy he is when he's not hypnotised.

There's none of that zombie-eyed 'yes master' shtick that's so cliché. He's basically a dick, same personality, it's just that his priorities have been rearranged without him noticing. It's a small thing, but I'll take what I can get. It's a subtle thing though, and I'm not sure how apparent it is to the audience. Given the abstract nature of the conflict, it might not be all that noticeable.

Robin Ward came away with strongly positive impression of Doctor Peter, aka, William Hutt. *"In the last episode the great Shakespearean actor William Hutt made an appearance and never was there a more pleasant and down to earth guest, far from being the rather grand and condescending man that one might expect when a great actor is given material like this to work with. And by this point the writing was appalling and we would regularly get the giggles at the dreck we were forced to speak."*

So this seems to have been a genuine, even sophisticated acting choice. It would have been easy to just phone it in, but Hutt seems to have given some genuine thought to the performance, based on Ward's assessment.

Rachel Ward also had clear memories of the episode and was less impressed: *"I remember the makeshift beehives and having to act as if there were bees all around. William Hutt, he was a very Shakespearean actor. They cast people, I guess they just didn't have the right people to cast."*

Or then again, maybe he just went the opposite way and put in no effort at all.

Ward also noted, *"There weren't that many women guest stars... Antoinette Bower, she dressed very provocatively. I'm not a prude. But for that time, she kind of wore her sexuality like it was a tool."*

The other redeeming feature is that the characters actually do figure things out and work their way through the story. There's no big dump of information to the audience. Rather, the story unfolds with information carefully managed to try to build tension. It's not effective, but you can see what they're doing.

So we aren't shown the mutant bees plotting to take over the hive. There are just bees, being a little weird. The danger is slowly revealed. We aren't shown Doctor Cranky being a zombie slave of the bees, he's just being his dick self. Instead, there's a story that's being unravelled bit by bit.

As the protagonists slowly come to grips with the problem, they try various strategies to deal with the bees, and in turn, the bees counter, until they have our heroes trapped, in a chess-like sequence of move and countermove.

Still, this feels like digging deep to justify a dull episode. Any cleverness to the script and narrative structure is undermined by the sparse production values, and the actors can't really save it.

As with all of the Starlost episodes, it's rather stage oriented. In this case, perhaps beyond stage, all the way to radio drama oriented. Most of the 'action' takes place on a single set dressed up as a lab, complete with Bunsen burners and beakers. There's a few shots and scenes with the doorway set dressed up. There's plastic looking 'garden of beehives' set that's blue-screened in, and there's the stock footage of bees. That's it.

The Starlost production team was never working with a lot of money, and it showed. But this close to the end of the season, most of the budget had clearly been spent and the cupboards were bare. Earlier episodes had gone over budget and this episode was likely shortchanged to pay for that. That almost certainly handicapped the episode. They were basically making it with leftover spare change.

It might have been more effective if they had at least one mutant bee prop or costume to interact with the cast, or if the bees directly communicated with the cast members in some effective overt way.

It would have been more effective if we'd been shown the bees attacking or sealing off corridors or reacting to attacks – some physical going-ons separate from blue-screen projection of stock footage. But that's simply not in the budget apparently, no physical models, no props, no set dressing, no interactions or significant effects. Without any of that, a few blue-screen projections just can't carry the story.

Simply having cast members going 'the bees are saying' or 'the bees are doing' makes things remote and removes any sense of immediacy or tension.

It's not a great episode by any means, it is silly and insubstantial, and as hard as the actors try, there's just not enough to really carry it off.

It might have had the potential to be gripping, if there had been the time or resources to depict the threat beyond some stock footage. Instead it's just talk, it might have worked for radio, but it made for dire television.

Even the music, taken from a recently concluded soap opera called Strange Paradise, feels under-used, playing almost randomly in the background. Sometimes the music, with its haunting qualities is effective, but in this case, it fails to add to proceedings.

A likely factor was the hellish production schedule. Everyone had been running flat out for months, putting in eighteen hour days at every level of production, just desperately getting episodes in the can days ahead of broadcast. It's likely by this time, everyone connected with the show was burned out.

As it turned out, the cancellation notice came in during this episode, guaranteeing that no one involved in production would put any extra effort into this or the next episode.

Earlier, I called the episode quixotically cerebral, but bottom line this is an episode about bees. It isn't deeper than that. There's no subtext, there's no topical or thematic concerns. What you see is what you get: It's about bees.

Go figure.

I wondered, were killer bee movies some big thing back in the 1970s? Was Starlost tapping into some zeitgeist going around at the time?

Oddly, although there were a lot of killer bee movies, most were well after this episode aired in 1973. There was Killer Bees in 1974, Savage Bees in 1976, The Bees, Terror Out of the Sky and the embarrassing Irwin Allen/Michael Caine disaster, The Swarm all in 1978. Only the Deadly Bees, an English potboiler from 1966 precedes this episode.

A related movie, Phase IV about ants gaining sentience and confronting human scientists studying them, was released in 1974. It's very reminiscent of this episode, albeit far better made, and if the timelines were different, I'd have suggested this episode was inspired by that movie.

Empire of the Ants and Kingdom of the Spiders were both 1977. The 70s seem to have been an era of ecological horror - spiders, ants, frogs, you name it.

Part of eco-horror or 'bugs/nature strikes back' may have been the exhaustion by that time of the conventional horror tropes. Vampires, Werewolves, Frankenstein, had all been played out.

Part of it may have been an awareness of ecological issues, and attempting to capitalize on these concerns. But honestly, the episode doesn't address any ecological concerns and seems to lack any subtext. Perhaps all it really amounted to was the availability of stock footage.

There actually was a flurry of media coverage of 'Killer bees' however. In 1956 African bees were introduced into Brazil and hybridised with local South American bees. This Africanized species was extremely aggressive and began spreading north. By the late 70s, American media was agog. But again, most of the media attention was long after Starlost.

On this one, Starlost was weirdly, pointlessly a few years ahead of its time.

Interestingly, in Harlan Ellison's series bible, he offers a series of story ideas for stories they'd like to tell. In his list are mutated animals who evolved to dominate their domes – perhaps intelligent apes or dogs, or even intelligent insects.

The episode aired Saturday, December 29, 1973, following Farthing's Comet and just before Space Precinct. The final three episodes were airing literally around Christmas and New Year's, which were probably pretty brutal in terms of television audiences.

This is the period of seasonal programming, preferably low cost or public domain 'It's a Wonderful Life.' This would have been the period where Starlost's ratings were at their lowest ebb. This may have contributed to the cancellation decision.

Had the series launched earlier in the year and built more of an audience, perhaps the December ratings dip might not have been fatal. As it was, the decision to pull the plug was made while this episode was in production.

Creatives

Bill Davis the credited director was born and died in Belleville, Ontario. He was a successful television director, accumulating over forty series credits between 1959 and 1990. Like many of his peers, after starting off in Canada, he went to the US to seek his fortune. He was unusual in that most of his career seemed to revolve around musical and variety specials and comedies, rather than the usual television dramas.

George McGowan is also listed as director in IMDB but not on the series credits. McGowan was another Canadian director, born in Paris, Ontario, whose career seemed to move back and forth between Canada and the US. He also directed the Astro-Medics. Interestingly, he directed the 1972 ecological horror film, Frogs, about nature striking back.

The episode is credited to Norman Klenman, the story consultant for the series. According to Klenman, when the cancellation notice came in, he volunteered to resign early to save money, and departed the show.

Backstory and Continuity

This episode takes place in one of a series of zoological station, presumably a subsection of one of the modules. There's a reference to the place being a shambles twenty years before. But there are also records going back two hundred years. It's also a site of active research.

This implies some sort of active societies operating zoological stations in the Ark. As it appears that significant parts of Ark infrastructure have continued to operate, more or less, since the disaster. In addition to Zoological stations, there are functioning Medical and Police services, and even the Astronomy module is in service after a fashion.

There do appear to be breakdowns, the Bee Zoology station was more or less abandoned for centuries, the Astronomy module is down to Doctor Farthing, and the Institute for Re-Education seems to be completely disconnected. The best evaluation is that many of the Ark-wide systems and specialties are still functioning, but not necessarily co-operating or supporting each other.

Sharp eyed viewers will note that the Astrogation Console, usually scene on episodes in the Bridge, and most recently observed in Farthing's Comet, has migrated once again, where it pretends to be some sort of different machine.

Finally, although it's likely coincidental, Harlan Ellison's bible does vaguely suggest an episode where they find mutant animals evolved to a dominant life form, a society of intelligent apes, dogs or even insects.

Creators and Cast

Directed by Bill Davis
Written by Norman Klenman
&&&
Devon: Keir Dullea
Rachel: Gay Rowan
Garth: Robin Ward
Sphere Projection: William Osler
Dr. Peter Marshall: William Hutt
Dr. Heather Marshall: Antoinette Bower
Harry Keeble: John Friesen
Ron Callisher: Alan McRae
&&&
Original Airdate: December 29, 1973

SPACE PRECINCT – EPISODE SIXTEEN

Garth gets enlisted into the Ark's police force, while conspiracies abound.

The final episode of Starlost. Space Precinct. What is there to say?

They decided to do a cop show in space... and failed utterly. You'd think that would be hard to do, but there you go. It's hard to describe how completely and profoundly this episode misfires.

We open up with Garth deciding to go home. The trio are back in their country clothes, not their Ark uniforms, which implies a breakdown in continuity. And Devon is still trying to find the Bridge of the Ark.

Which is weird because all that got sorted out at the end of Return of Oro. But this isn't the only point at which the episode violates the show's continuity and premise. Perhaps by this time the writing was on the wall and no one cared very much anymore.

Although this time, he wants to visit an agricultural dome. That doesn't seem on mission, so maybe he's just being a tourist, or again, maybe the writer had lost the plot.

Anyway, Garth is cranky and decides to quit the mission, he's tired of wandering around trying to save the Ark, so the trio part company. The rest of the episode belongs to Garth.

Devon and Rachel are barely in it. In a few cutaways they make their way to a freight elevator, put on spacesuits and then get trapped, where they proceed to slowly suffocate. That's it. Seriously, all of their scenes could have been shot in about half an hour, with so few lines they could have been written on the back of an envelope.

My best guess is that given that the show was cancelled with episode fifteen, Keir Dullea and Rachel Ward might have decided to depart early after shooting a few second unit shots, leaving Robin Ward as the last man standing, and that's how they wrote the script.

According to Robin Ward, "*Keir rejoiced, Gay seemed to have mixed feelings while I had the sudden realization that I would soon be unemployed and possibly unemployable.*"

That's understandable. Dullea was mainly a film or stage actor where the pace and structure of work is very different. He'd put in regular sixteen or eighteen hour days for months on end, with scripts and shots constantly compromised by the need to get episodes finished and in the can. It must have been like living in a cement mixer, and we can imagine he was exhausted. Everyone was exhausted.

Anyway, after Garth departs, he wanders around the corridors, gets lost, and then gets arrested by some old geezer named Rathe Masters. It turns out he's the Chief of Inter-Ark Police.

Rathe takes him back to Space Police headquarters, which consists of two other people, his secretary Tech, and a shuttle pilot, although there are apparently many others out on missions somewhere.

Rathe runs Garth's tissue sample and downloads all the biographical information on him - who he is, where he's from, who his parents were and what he and Devon have been doing. The Space Police have been keeping tabs on them apparently.

Garth is pretty astonished by this. And to tell you the truth, so are we. So the omniscient, Orwellian, Space Police have been monitoring Devon and the gang as they stumbled around the Ark... and they never did or said anything? Presumably they know what's going on in the various domes... and they never did or said anything?

They knew about Oro and his effort to take over the Ark? They knew about the toxic nightmare festering in Manchester? The situations in other domes? They knew about Doctor Asgard's shenanigans? They knew that Farthing tried to pilot the Ark into a comet nucleus? They knew the Ark was drifting into a sun... and they've been sitting there doing nothing the whole time?

What's wrong with these fuckers?

To recap: The Ark is rudderless, leaderless, the Bridge crew is dead and it's heading for a sun. Meanwhile, these chowderheads are keeping tabs and surveillance on everyone on the Ark. Presumably they know everything. But they can't be bothered to do anything about anything?

What the hell are they thinking? It's heading into a sun! Why aren't they doing something? Why didn't they do it long ago? Centuries ago? Why have they just sat there and watched Devon and his friends wander around aimlessly?

The very existence of the Space Police makes the entire series pointless. It invalidates the premise of the show.

We've encountered this problem before through several episodes - people or entities that are aware of the danger – the Astro Medics, the AIs, Farthing and the Astronomy Module, all of whom you'd think should be a bit more pro-active about not falling into a star and being incinerated. But this time it's the worst, it just rubs our nose in it.

Somehow Rathe talks Garth into joining the Space Police as his assistant on a case. Well, so much for going back to Cypress Corners.

But considering everything else, that's trivial. We've previously seen that Garth tends to defer to authority – in both Pisces and Circuit of Death, an authority figure commands Garth to load boxes and he just does it. At least Rathe seems to offer some purpose.

At this point, we are let in on the plot. It seems the Space Police are leaving. Rathe is apparently tired of being the Chief of Police for the Ark. He wants to decamp and join the Federation.

The Federation you ask?

Yes. The Federation. It seems for the last five years, possibly six, Rathe and the Space Police have been in contact with his counterparts in a federation of worlds in a nearby solar system, ten planets, nine supporting life, with two of them currently in a dispute.

This seems weirdly consequential. The doomed Ark is passing close to an interstellar federation, and apparently, some of the Ark folk have been in regular contact for the last five or six years.

Maybe they could have helped us out with that whole 'crashing into a sun' kind of thing that everyone else on the Ark seems to know about?

Maybe they could have intervened? Changed the Ark's course? Evacuated people?

I know I sound like a broken record, but Christ on a crutch! It's a plot issue the size of the Hindenburg, and it's just bursting into flame, taking the whole show with it.

There's an urgent police matter. Apparently two of the Federation members are in a dispute over ore mining on an uninhabited moon. But the shipments are being hijacked. One world is blaming the other, and the two are on the verge of war. Rathe suspects, without any apparent cause, a criminal conspiracy at work. A crime in which the fate of worlds hangs in the balance that he must solve.

Not that we are shown any of this. It's just not in the budget. What we get are a few shots of a toroid (wheel shaped) space station, and a few onscreen shots of Rathe's Federation counterpart, Rena, literally phoning it in. For some inexplicable reason, Rena is wearing an Ark uniform, go figure.

The space station, by the way, was built from a standard Pilgrim Observe Space Station plastic model kit, with a life-saver ring attached. I'm not slagging it, it's a nice space station, looks good. I just figured you'd be interested in knowing.

I'm thinking an interplanetary conspiracy light years away might not be the most dramatically effective pathway for a story, any kind of story.

It would be like an episode of some New York-based sitcom, where the plot revolved around shoplifters at a Bazaar in Afghanistan, with no Afghan scenes, just the occasional phone report. It's all taking place far away and off camera.

Mixed in with this is Rathe's plan to take off on the Space-Patrol shuttle and relocate to the Federation to expose the conspiracy, solve the crime and give them the benefit of his amazing police skills. Skills which he is confident of, but are never actually in evidence. He's been waiting for five years, the launch window is coming up soon.

The Ark Police shuttle, by the way, is our friend the Pisces, last seen repainted as the Astro-Medic shuttle, now repainted gold for one last appearance.

I've got a problem with Rathe's motivation here. I mean setting aside this whole 'Ark crashing into a sun thing' which doesn't seem to be on his radar, he seems really enthusiastic about jumping ship.

It would actually make more sense if he was going *"the Ark is doomed so we're getting out of Dodge."*

But that would make him a bad guy, or at least a coward. And apparently we can't have that.

So instead, apparently, his motivation is to conquer new worlds by becoming the 'Super-Detective' of the Federation. He talks about that a lot. But he's the head of the Ark police...so what happens after he leaves? Any way you slice it, it feels like he's deserting. Frankly, his 'new worlds to conquer' shtick is a little creepy.

It would almost be more acceptable if he was doing it for love - Romeo and Juliet, star crossing lovers. Middle aged to older lovers, but still, you could do something with that. That's just barely vaguely slightly hinted at. But it would get in the way of the whole police procedural shtick they want to do, so you can't have that.

And of course, he needs to be over in the Federation to stop the impending space war. But that doesn't make sense, since by the time he flies over, it'll be too late. And anyway, it gets solved without him.

In any case, he can't leave because the Space Patrol Shuttle's computers are being jammed! And according to Tek, his other assistant, the jamming is coming from the Federation. This makes no sense whatsoever.

Actually, it's Tek herself doing the jamming. We're shown that when she pulls out a button and presses it. There's no actual mystery here, the omniscient camera just shows us. The characters still have to figure it out. Tek turns on the jammer, she turns it off, she turns it on again... for fun, I guess. Meanwhile, she keeps reporting it coming from more and more precise locations, eventually from Rena's, the Federation Security Commander, own personal office.

Garth finds out about Tek, by virtue of accidentally overhearing Tek scheming. Unfortunately, this turns out to be useless. Tek gets the drop on him, marches him into an airlock and stuns him, leaving him there to die.

Rathe never figures it out, he's that kind of brilliant detective. Through the whole episode, Rathe comes across as deeply stupid and self-absorbed. The man is impossibly thick. Given an opportunity to reach a conclusion, he makes the wrong one, blaming Garth.

Meanwhile Rathe other assistant blames Garth. Rena from the Federation blames Garth. Everyone blames Garth. Tek ups the ante by blaming both Garth and Rena. Red herrings abound.

Then on their own, literally everyone separately assembles their own clues, and independently figures out it's not Garth but Tek. This is clinched with an off-screen confession from some bad guy in the Federation. Apparently, the plan was to steal shipments, hide them, start a war and then... profit!

Garth has nothing to do with any of this. He doesn't prove his innocence. He never even knew he was a suspect. He's accused in his absence.

So you have this situation of the wrongly accused innocent man, the noose tightening around his neck... He has to prove his innocence. There's some dramatic possibility there.

Except that he's off stage, has no idea he's being accused, no idea the noose is tightening, never realizes he has to prove his innocence, never actually does anything to prove his innocence, that's all done for him without his ever knowing.

What the hell?

Some other time and place, in the hands of people who were cannier, I'd assume that this was some kind of subversive meta-deconstruction of the genre. But probably this really is, is someone trying to reproduce the form of a mystery or police show without any actual idea of what that is.

Garth shows up for the climax. That death trap he got locked in? He just walked out apparently, offstage. So if there was some kind of dramatic tension they were working towards there... they just kind of forgot about it.

Tek is caught and disarmed. Interplanetary war averted.

The audience is just sent a post it note on the plot developments, as characters explain things to each other. Almost all the plot developments take place off screen, it's not like any of it was so important it needed to be shown to us.

Nothing makes any sense. In the final showdown, Tek is trying to abort the launch and stop Rathe from leaving, even though he's in the room with her. Why?

We never get a window into Tek's motivations. Why is she doing this? At one point, for no apparent reason, she cancels a rescue mission to save Rachel and Devon from their elevator. Just because... Then later, she tells Garth they're dead. Again, just because...

What does she get out of screwing with the launch even after she's exposed? Or trying to kill Garth? Presumably not money, there's no way for her to profit.

Does she love Rathe and not want him to leave? Does she hate Rathe and want him to fail? Does she have her own plan to escape the Ark and needs to screw with Rathe? We never know.

Allegedly, it's all part of a scheme for her to take Rena's job and run the Federation police, in a year's time when the next launch window is open. But even that makes no sense.

Tek is just bad, that's it. She's in it for the villainy.

The launch window for Rathe to go to the Federation has closed. He's stuck on the Ark for a year until the next window opens.

Wait, what?

Is the Ark in orbit now? It's not crashing into a sun? Was the Ark actually saved? The course changed because of the Return of Oro or Farthing's Comet? And nobody bothered to tell the audience? Otherwise, how can there be another launch window in a year's time?

Oh but apparently, the Ark's Bridge is back in action. Rathe goes up there. So much for Devon's search for the Bridge, or back up Bridge. Apparently, it's found and operational. Maybe the Ark really was saved and they didn't think to mention it.

Or maybe it was just the Bridge of the space police shuttle? That's probably it.

Rathe invites Garth to continue on as his assistant. The closing shot, is Garth cheerfully saying he'll think about it - the end.

Devon and Rachel are still stuck in the service elevator by the way. But we're told that everything worked out fine for them. We don't actually see them get rescued.

For an episode which showcases Robin Ward's Garth, he comes across as rudderless and somewhat inept. He leaves Devon and Rachel to go home, but he's easily derailed. He joins the Space Police but he contributes nothing material to the story, Tek gets the drop on him. He just kind of bumbles through. The story largely takes place around him.

It's honestly hard to find something positive to say. Sad way to end a series. What went wrong with this episode?

It's most likely they just gave up. The word had come down during the production of the fifteenth episode, The Beehive, that the series was cancelled. Everyone working on this episode knew it was over.

That may have been a pervasive sense for everyone in the production crew – 'we're done for, there's no reason to work hard. Let's just put in the minimum and go home.'

Some had already left, Norman Klenman had resigned as of the fifteenth episode, so there wasn't a story consultant or a script editor for this one, and perhaps that absence has a lot to do with the complete failure of the script. There was no one at the wheel to fix the script's massive problems. And probably, no one even cared.

I've noted that Dullea's and Ward's scenes are extremely brief. It's possible that they simply chose to leave early, as Klenman did.

Towards the end of the season, you just run out of money. All the overages and extra expenses of all the previous episodes come due, the piggy bank is empty, and you're just trying to shoot with whatever spare change you find in the seat cushions. If the show had been extended, CTV might have pulled some bridge financing to sustain the production. But end of the road? There was no reason to spend an extra dime.

A winding down episode, going through the motions, filling a remaining contractual or scheduling commitment, with no money, no time, people departing and no one caring.

Space Precinct fails in literally every single thing it sets out to do. A high stakes mystery to solve? Interplanetary politics? Mysterious sabotage? False accusations? Deathtrap? Dramatic countdown?

They raise these things, and then they just bungle them one after the other. The narrative progress of the previous fifteen episodes is simply abandoned, the distinctive themes and subtexts that made so many episodes interesting are completely absent.

Annoyingly, everything about the episode, from the omniscient omnipresence of the police, to the Federation, to the references to the Bridge, to the false drama of the launch window, undermine the very concepts of the series.

I will confess, I have never seen an episode of a series so completely and violently repudiate and invalidate the premise for the entire series. How do you do that? Why would you want to?

And that's it, the Starlost ends, not with a whimper, but with a violent implosion, as if a donkey somehow managed to suck a giant fart back into its anus.

It deserved better, but by this point, everyone was too exhausted and demoralized to care.

Creatives

Last of the six episodes directed by American Joseph L. Scanlon.

Last of the four episodes written by Canadian Martin Lager.

And the weakest for each.

Backstory and Continuity

This has the same problem as the Astro-Medics. Apparently, there is an Ark wide organization with enough manpower or access to records that they know exactly who Garth, Rachel and Devon are, what they've been up to, and are capable of rescuing them when they get into trouble. But they're also not concerned that the Ark is heading for a star? What's wrong with these people?

Rathe is more interested in ditching the Ark and starting a new career as Federation Policeman, than in asking them for help with their 'falling into a star problem' or even trying to arrange a rescue or evacuation? What's wrong with him? It feels like he has the same narrow minded obsession verging on dementia that we've seen with Farthing.

Regarding the Federation, the space around the Ark sure is crowded. In addition to the Federation and its nine worlds, space stations and mining colony, there's also the Exar from the Oro episodes, and that passing spaceship of reptilian aliens. How do they all fit together in this relatively tiny volume of space?

In particular, I'm intrigued by the fact that two civilizations – Exar and the Federation appear to be practically sitting in each other's laps, cosmically speaking. From the Ark, both can be reached by relatively small craft, either Oro's scout or Rathe's Police Patrol ship. Even if they are on opposite sides of the Ark, they can't be more than three light years apart, and likely much, much closer to each other. It's possible they may even be orbiting the same star. What are the odds?

Moreover, the Federation has been communicating with the Ark for at least five years. Oro's people have detected the Ark on long range micro-sensors for well over a year, minimum. There's zero chance these two civilizations haven't detected and aren't aware of each other. Are they communicating? What's their relationship to each other? Are they related to each other? Is one the descendant of the other? Do they have a common source or ancestor?

I'm deeply underwhelmed by the Federation. Despite being an interstellar or interplanetary multi-world civilization, they're apparently unable to reach the Ark on their own – Rathe must travel to them. He's also offering advanced Ark police methods, which seems odd in a Federation of nine worlds – how is it that their own police aren't up to snuff.

Finally, I should have mentioned this before, but in the Oro episodes, the Astro-Medics and now this, it turns out that communication with distant aliens all takes place in real time – that is, you ask them something, they hear right away, and reply instantly.

But wait, this is a show with somewhat grounded science (artificial gravity aside) there is no FTL People talk about 'launch windows' in order to reach their targets. The aliens would have to be within a million miles to have a fast conversation. Even as close as Mars to Earth, there would be a sixteen minute delay. If they're only a tenth of a light year away, that's' an almost two and a half months lag.

So either they're impossibly close, or everyone has some kind of subspace radio that works at very short distances (say a fraction of a light year) that's almost instantaneous and gets around the problem.

Or everyone turned out to be impossibly close.

Or the script just requires it, so... Shut up, Nerd!

Creators and Cast

Directed by Joseph L. Scanlon
Written by Martin Lager
&&&
Devon: Keir Dullea
Rachel: Gay Rowan
Garth: Robin Ward
Sphere Projections: William Osler
Chief Rathe Masters: Ivor Barry
Tek the Technician: Diane Dewey
Mike: Richard Alden
Reena: Nuala Fitzgerald
&&&
Original Airdate: January 5, 1974

PART FOUR - CREATION

STARLOST GENESIS AND THE CORDWAINER BIRD STORY

For most Sci-Fi fans, what they know of Starlost, if they know of it at all, tends to come down to Harlan Ellison's vivid hatchet job.

Mainly, Harlan Ellison had the story to himself and perhaps was more passionate than accurate.

None of the other people involved offered any kind of systematic rebuttal, or told their own story in any detailed way. So perhaps in examining the genesis of the series, we should scrutinise Ellison's account carefully. He had many opportunities to have his say, and he was not shy.

The Starlost was one of Canada's only bona fide Sci-Fi series. But as we've noted, it wasn't originally Canadian. Allegedly it wasn't even intended to be produced in Canada. Canada wasn't even on the radar. Somehow, it just ended up here.

The most detailed account of how the Starlost came into existence is from Harlan Ellison, who is hardly unbiased. Ellison gave a number of accounts, including a CBC interview, a two hour lecture in Bowling Green, Ohio, an extended taped interview chronicling his experiences in late 1973, a 7100 word essay, titled: Somehow, I don't think We're in Kansas, Toto, among others. He also told or retold the story many times in interviews and in person.

According to Ellison, the story begins in February of 1973, when his Agent sends him to meet with a 20th Century Fox executive named Robert Kline. Apparently Fox was negotiating with the BBC to co-produce a series of mini-series, or short run television programs.

When he attends, he finds Kline is working on a number of projects, but wants to do a Sci-Fi series. Kline's idea is: 'The Fugitive in Space.'

We'll accept that as accurate. In the 1970s 'The Fugitive' premise was all over the place, particularly in science fiction television. The idea was that the protagonist were being hunted, and with their pursuer nipping at their heels, had to keep moving on to their next exotic adventure. This was used earlier in The Invaders and later in both the Logan's Run and Planet of the Apes television series. This is the original premise, and it would make it at least as far as Harlan Ellison's series bible from April, 11, 1973, and perhaps to Ellison's version of the pilot, from August, 1973.

But there might be something that precedes this original concept. Around this time, Douglas Trumbull and his partner, Howard Zeitman, were trying to develop a new Special Effects technology, Magicam, which promised bigger, bolder effects.

This isn't something you just pull out of a hat, it's likely that Trumbull, fresh off Silent Running and 2001: A Space Odyssey, had been actively pitching Magicam, and that may have been known to Kline. Conceivably, Trumbull may have pitched directly to Kline, and that may have been the starting point. Ellison would not have known. We don't know one way or the other.

But there was another 2001: A Space Odyssey connection that may have been in the works. Kline was working closely with a New York associate, Preston Fischer, and Preston Fischer was apparently close friends with Keir Dullea, the star of 2001. Kline and Fisher identified Dullea as a science fiction star based on 2001, A Space Odyssey, so it's possible that they already had him in mind, or were talking to him, for a Sci-Fi premise along the lines of 'Fugitive in Space' even before Ellison sits down with Kline. The 'Fugitive in Space' concept really does feel like its tailor made as a starring character vehicle. But again, we don't know, we can only speculate.

To be fair, if the idea was to build a series around Dullea or Trumbull's Magicam, Ellison wasn't aware of it, and Kline certainly wasn't mentioning it. It's only much later, but still extremely early in the process, within days or weeks, that their names are mentioned to Ellison.

Both Trumbull and Dullea were closely identified with science fiction at that time, from Stanley Kubrick's seminal 2001: A Space Odyssey, released in 1968. Both were extremely reputable as artists and most importantly both were bankable. Either man's name attached to a project might have been enough make it viable. Their connection on 2001, even suggests that one might have brought the other in, but again, that's speculation. So it's possible that, one or both may have actually been attached to the project before Harlan Ellison. Most of the participants are passed away now, or retired so this is speculative.

But Ellison, when he walks into Kline's office in February, 1973, isn't in a position to know, and certainly isn't told, whether Kline has been involved or engaging with either of these men. As far as Ellison is concerned, he's the start of the journey.

Harlan Ellison isn't all that interested in Kline's idea. Instead, he pitches a larger premise – A generation ship whose inhabitants have forgotten they're on a spaceship.

It's unlikely that he came up with that out of the blue. Ellison seems to present this as an 'off the cuff' inspiration, but he also reels off various precedents, which suggests he'd done some thinking or planning. It's not unusual for a good writer to have some pitches ready to go when they walk into a producer's office. He's going in to pitch to a television guy, he's probably developed some ideas in advance. So likely he walked into the offices with Starlost and a few other pitches in his back pocket. Ellison mentions that Kline rejected another one of his proposals as too expensive, which adds to the likelihood he wasn't making it up on the spot.

A Generation ship is not actually a new idea. Even a Generation ship whose occupants have forgotten they're on a ship is not new. The concept had been used in Star Trek a couple of years earlier, in an episode titled For the World is Hollow and I have Touched the Sky. But it goes back much much earlier to the 1930s pulps. Robert

Heinlein, Alexei Panshin, Harry Harrison and Brian Aldiss had all written stories or novels around the concept.

Robert Kline likes the idea. Allegedly, the intention was to do a limited run co-production with the BBC. But I'm skeptical of this. Not necessarily that Kline said it, it's likely that he did – Ellison has no need to make that detail up.

But I am skeptical that the BBC was a serious plan. That doesn't seem to accord with the way the BBC was operating at the time. It was a public programming corporation funded by license fees and catering to the British audience. Some of its productions were sold or marketed to other countries, particularly commonwealth countries.

In 1970 the BBC had switched over to color, and were flush with cash through the first half of the 70s. There was no financial or commercial need to do co-productions. All of their programming was in house. It wasn't until the Thatcher era, that they were pushed into commercial partnerships and co-productions. So the BBC feels like a nonstarter.

ITV the private British television network did do such partnerships. Ellison in his interview does mention Lew Grade Studios, which is ITV not BBC. But during this time frame, ITV was committed to a second series of the live action Gerry Anderson show, UFO, which eventually morphed into Space 1999. And their plate was pretty full. It's not clear that Kline had ever talked to them, or that they were ever in the picture.

It's possible that there may have been discussions between Fox and ITV or the BBC that didn't go anywhere. In Hollywood, all sorts of things are talked about that never get past the talking stage.

It's possible that both Kline and Ellison knew the Writer's Strike was just around the corner, Ellison was worried, and Kline simply pulled the BBC option out of a hat to allay those worries. Ellison would know that a British production wouldn't be derailed by an American writer's strike and he'd be free to work on it.

Keir Dullea is living in England at this time, and seemed to prefer working there. Given that this is the only concrete connection to the U.K., then possibly, if Dullea was in mind or even in discussions prior to Ellison, this might have something to do with Kline's proposing a series in England. Perhaps the project was being tentatively shaped around him?

It is peculiar though, the BBC reference is both oddly specific, and peculiarly infeasible.

Kline was receptive, but there was no money. Ellison wouldn't write without money. They agreed to an audio tape. Harlan Ellison fleshed out his sparse verbal premise of a generation ship fallen into chaos into the elements of the Starlost concept in a twelve minute free-associating monologue delivered into a tape recorder.

At this point, Ellison had his friend Walter Koenig, Chekov from Star Trek, in mind to star as the protagonist, Rick, who would eventually be renamed Devon. I'm not sure if Kline or Fischer ever seriously considered that. Koenig wasn't really a big name, or any kind of name. Certainly he wasn't on the level of Dullea.

According to Ellison, Kline had this monologue typed up without his consent, and went further, having additional material written by Preston Fisher, and even some artwork commissioned.

Ellison correctly saw this as a major ethical breach. He was a screenwriter, there were rules and union contracts. He wasn't going to write without getting paid.

At the same time, what exactly did he think was going to happen? You dictate a premise, and then what? Did he think Kline was going to play it over the radio? In boardrooms? Over the phone? Was Kline supposed to make and distribute audiotape-copies? What exactly did Harlan Ellison expect or intend to happen to his taped dictation?

Ellison had been in the business for a decade, dealing with Hollywood types, he's not a babe in the woods. It seems disingenuous to claim naiveté. The best construction is that both Kline and Ellison were deliberately skirting the rules with a wink and a nod.

This audio recording and transcript became the foundation of the series, with Ellison to be credited as creator and head writer. This is what Kline took around to sell the series. Assuming that all you needed to sell a television series was a transcript of a sloppy twelve minute Harlan Ellison monologue running a thousand words, tops.

Ellison was a major genre writer. But this seems like a thin reed to sell a series on.

According to Ellison in March or April, Doug Trumbull, his partner Howard Zeitman and their Magicam system come in. Ellison hints that he was working with Trumbull on a fantasy series around that time and that this might be how the effects technician got involved.

This isn't verified, and it's unlikely, since according to Ellison, he didn't have regular communications with Kline. Except sometimes there's hints that he did. Ellison's role in the actual creation of the deal and marketing is often erratic.

Ellison claims Trumbull is in by March or April. But given that the Writer's strike starts March 6, and Ellison would have been required to stop working and cease involvement, Ellison's timeline starts to seem a little suspect.

Ellison talks about a delay where he doesn't hear from Kline for a while. He phoned his agent, and then suddenly he gets a call from Kline. At that point, the BBC or ITV dropped out, if they were ever involved, and suddenly the project is in Canada, with CTV. At that time, or shortly after, NBC has signed on as s syndicator. Presumably according Ellison, this must happen even later in March or April, but again, that puts him well into the Writer's strike, which is a contradiction.

Ellison correctly points out that this is fairly dicey conduct by Kline. There's no contracts anywhere, and if things are happening after March 6, Ellison can't sign a contract. Ellison claims he refused to do anything after the Writer's Strike, but this seems to imply he was still somewhat involved. Nevertheless, without contracts Kline, and CTV are flying by the seat of their pants.

After that, according to Ellison, Dullea comes into the picture. Ellison is told about this in an elevator on the way to meet with NBC brass and he goes ballistic. Keir Dullea is 'wrapped in saran wrap' Ellison claims, he doesn't want him.

But there is a contradiction here, William Davidson, the producer of Starlost for CTV/Glen Warren Productions, is very definite that Keir Dullea was already attached to the project, before they came on board.

"Arthur Weinthal of CTV and Ted Delaney of CFTO-Glen Warren called me in to discuss producing The Starlost," Davidson told Mark Phillips and Frank Garcia, as recorded in their book, Science Fiction Television. *"...Keir Dullea had been contracted before I signed on. I had a high regard for his acting skills. He was a nice, enthusiastic person. He was very intense, and intrigued by the character of Devon."*

We will accept Davidson's claim that Dullea was already attached to the project when it came to CTV. But this suggests that Kline and Fischer delayed avoided telling Ellison that Dullea was involved, possibly because Ellison was pushing for Walter Koenig. At the least, Dullea was involved much earlier than Ellison knew.

Ed Richardson confirms that Dullea, Ellison and Trumbull were all attached to the project before it ended up in Canada. Certainly when budgets for the series were being drawn up and studio space was being reserved, the promises of Trumbull's Magicam were driving decisions.

Now according to Ellison, he claims that he found out that Dullea was involved, and meets the NBC executives in April or May. He notes that the Writer's Strike is about to take place. Around this time, not only is it backed by NBC but it's been sold to the Westinghouse Network and forty-eight NBC affiliates.

Ellison's timeline doesn't work. He claims all of this takes place before the Writer's strike. But the Writer's Strike commenced March 6, and lasted 112 days until June 24. Ellison also claims he basically froze up during the Writer's strike. If Trumbull, CTV, Dullea and NBC were all lined up before the Writer's strike, then it had to be before March 6t, and not April or May. There are contradictions.

If we accept that Ellison's initial meeting is February, 1973, then, working backwards, literally, everything that Ellison describes in the early phases – the meeting with Kline, the tape recording, Doug Trumbull and Magicam, Keir Dullea, and CTV must have all literally fell together in the space of a few weeks in February and early March, 1973, before the strike. That seems extraordinarily fast.

Ellison claims it took three months for the parties Trumbull, Dullea, CTV and the Syndication package to come together before the strike happens, the only way that works is if his meeting with Kline actually happens sometime November/December 1972, not February of 1973.

But Ellison in his radio interview, available on Youtube, dating from late in 1973, is absolutely firm on February, 1973. If this interview had been years later, being fuzzy on the timelines would be excusable, but it's the same year.

The other possibility is that Ellison remained actively involved with the show to some extent while the strike is going on, and was reluctant to admit it because he might have been skirting the rules.

No matter how it's sliced, Ellison's timeline is unreliable, and that goes to his credibility. His story is being massaged.

Following the start of Writer's strike, which Ellison places following the NBC meeting in April or May, but which must be the period from, March 6 to April 10, he describes a campaign of harassment, attempted bribery, subterfuges, even hiring a scab writer to create a series bible. A lot must have happened.

During this period, Ellison wasn't satisfied by assurances, and demands a credible confirmation that the series is a Canadian and not an American production, which is a legitimate position.

Harlan Ellison eventually wrote a series bible, dated April 10, 1973, with the assistance of Ben Bova as technical writer, and Tim Kirk doing concept drawings. This was right in the middle of the Writer's Strike.

Notably, this bible lists both Gay Rowan and Robin Ward as Rachel and Garth, and the behind the scenes CTV crew – Klenman, Davidson, Richardson, Rochon, Weinthall, etc., so all of these people were nailed down and in place apparently before April 10.

The grounds for him agreeing to do this, was a ruling by ACTRA, then representing both Canadian writers and actors, that Starlost was considered a Canadian production, and therefore exempt from the strike.

Writing the bible resulted in a complaint against him by the Screen Writers Guild, but this was eventually dismissed.

Ellison reported almost nonstop harassment and badgering from Kline and others on the project, from the start of the writer's strike, literally up to the date production. And in fact, the badgering continued even after he delivered the bible.

There's no reason to doubt him, and the harassment and tactics reported were inexcusable. But there may be another side to the story.

Assuming the project was put together as quickly as it seems, all the players were in place by March, and the series was already sold in syndication, then there were contracts signed, and schedules confirmed for the fall. Kline was probably behind the eight ball, trying to make something work.

Basically, Kline had a live series – A bankable star, the special effects technology in place, syndication and marketing, and deadlines for pre-production and broadcast, and what was holding everything up and putting the whole thing at risk was one temperamental, capricious, notoriously litigious writer.

At this point, Harlan Ellison's name was attached, he's acknowledged as the creator of the concepts. Making the audio recording is sufficient to create copyright for Ellison. But there's no contract, he hasn't even paid a dime, which means Ellison had sole copyright.

Ellison is notoriously litigious. Kline's over a barrel. He couldn't get rid of Ellison or he would sue and without a contract, Kline wouldn't have a leg to stand on. The lesson, we suppose, is always get a contract.

Kline couldn't even ditch Ellison's entire premise and sell a new concept, because it's already sold into syndication. It's too late to come up with anything else. They can't work with Ellison, but they can't work without him. Meanwhile, Ellison refuses to work, initially due to the writer's strike, but later on, as a matter of procrastination and perhaps having other priorities.

But there are deadlines and the clock is constantly running down. Kline likely didn't had the option of waiting. Given that Ellison was dragging his feet, Kline probably felt that simply waiting on him might be a suicidal risk. There were broadcast deadlines. So there had to be production deadlines and pre-production deadlines. If you missed those, you might not make the broadcast dates. Miss the broadcast dates and game over, as would be Kline's career, to say nothing of the backlash and potential lawsuits from all quarters. None of this was Ellison's problem. But it was a huge problem for Kline.

On the other hand, Harlan Ellison's notorious idiosyncrasies, his procrastination, his schedule, none of that was Kline's fault.

Kline certainly didn't create the writers' strike.

If there was ever a serious proposal to take the project to England, Kline had no control over that outcome.

He certainly didn't invent the Canadian content rules that he had to contend with, or the fact that Canada was going through a period of nationalism, that Canadian producers and artists were literally creating their industry from the ground up.

There was no way for him to predict or have any control over any of these things.

He was just a man trying to put a deal together, put people together, and overcome obstacles as they came up. All of these things were just things happening to the project that he had to cope with, and Ellison was simply part of the one damned thing after the other.

This doesn't excuse the shenanigans described in Ellison's interviews and essays, the bizarre and sneaky maneuverings that Kline was pulling, apparently attempting to seduce or intimidate or bribe Ellison into completing his work. But it may explain them.

It's just not as evil or toxic as Ellison makes it out to be. It may come down to desperation. And there may be some element of exaggeration, there are, after all, holes in Ellison's narrative. Not everything he says is absolutely accurate.

We certainly don't condone these actions. But by this time, it's clear that reports of Ellison's work on Star Trek or the Outer Limits indicated he could be more than a little hard to get along with himself. He appears to have developed a reputation as a passionate but quirky and cantankerous writer. He would also develop a reputation as a procrastinator, which seems well earned.

Most damningly, Ellison doesn't seem to have understood or cared about the production process or production deadlines.

After writing the bible, delivered April 10, Harlan Ellison apparently did no further work on the project for the next few months. The Writers' strike ends on June 6, he still did nothing.

Instead, in June and July, he spent six weeks at a Conference in Michigan, probably Clarion. This may have been a prior commitment. But in his account, he noted that Kline and company are desperate for him to get to the project, literally calling up people and trying to send them into the woods to hunt him down. That desperation is understandable.

The first episode of Starlost, Voyage of Discovery, aired September 22, 1973.

Let's work backwards: Before that September 22, airdate, you need to shoot the episode, edit, do the sound, add music and effects. All this takes time.

But before you can shoot, you need a budget, studio space reserved, sets built, costumes sewn, effects commissioned, actors hired, a director assigned. All this pre-production needs to take place. All of that takes even more time, before production and post-production.

For the first episode of a series, even more pre-production time is needed. You need to nail down your principal cast. You need to identify, commission and build your principal sets and costumes, the ones you'll use over and over again. You need a series budget, studio space, crew, the whole nine yards. Basically, for a series, you have construct or organize the framework and schedules that episodes will take place in.

But to do that, you need to know what the series is, what the requirements are, the main characters, the main locations, etc. The series bible will give you some of that, perhaps a lot. But it will only get you so far. You need scripts, especially the pilot script, well in advance. Again, more time required.

But that's the shooting script. It's a first episode, so from the original version of the script, there has to be a period between the first draft which is almost abstract, and all the compromises and accommodations that are necessary to make it a practical working document. Add more time.

Typically, the production process, from commissioning a script to getting the episode in the can, takes weeks, potentially months.

Ideally, for Starlost, for an airdate of September, you might prefer to see the pilot script in June or July to start the process. If it shows up in August that's bad. If it shows up in September, that's a nightmare.

But that's only the pilot episode. A television show is not a single episode, it's an assembly line with a train of episodes each going through the production process, and a set of schedules for each episode, all of them culminating in a succession of broadcast dates that cannot be missed or contracts are breached. You can't miss a few weeks and catch up later, because other programs are already scheduled for that slot. You have to be on time.

Ideally, you need at least a handful of scripts ready to go, in order to build, budget and cast the show's episodes in advance for the opening phases. The further ahead you can plan or line up, the more effective and efficient the production is. You can work towards savings, you can avoid disasters or unplanned events. The bible is only half of the details necessary for production.

Admittedly, it's not unusual that over time series move along and deadlines tighten, scripts come in later and later, and everyone starts running ahead of the tidal wave. That's life. Often that results in expenses, weaker writing, less polished performances, shortcuts and poorer results, the show declines.

But late or absent scripts at the beginning, that's a recipe for crisis.

In particular, if you're doing a complicated show with action set pieces, or complex special effects, calls for new sets or locations, you need more lead time.

There's a big difference between a sitcom where every episode takes place in the same living room set, with the same cast and a narrow range of camera set ups and a space opera which takes place on a different planet every time, with new sets, new costumes, new props, casts and effects.

Time, particularly lead time, was absolutely critical. Despite this, Ellison did almost nothing. Even with a union dispensation which allowed him to write the bible, Ellison did nothing in the weeks after. Even after the Writer's Strike ends in June he does nothing. Through June and July he didn't seem to do anything.

Kline and others were tearing their hair out, there are deadlines bearing down. You can't just throw the whole thing together at the last minute, and Ellison was proving ... unreliable.

It is not until late July/August sometime, literally weeks before the first episode's airdate that he came up to Toronto with Ben Bova. His role there was to write the pilot, and to prepare and guide Canadian writers to work on the series.

William Davidson recalls recruiting as many as thirty-five writers to meet with Ellison, almost none with the necessary experience or familiarity with science fiction.

Ellison winnowed it down to a half dozen, accepting or generating story ideas and trying to flesh them out on audiotapes with Ben Bova. These tapes were transcribed and given to the writers.

According to Ellison, they opted for giving biblical mythological titles. He mentions three: Lazarus from the Mists, Children of Methuselah, Goddess of Double X. Clearly, he had some influence on at least these three. It's not clear what the other three script ideas were, or if they made it to completion – it would be a guessing game. In addition, it's not clear what Ellison's influence was in each case. Did he come up with the ideas? Were they pitched to him? How involved or detailed was he in working out the stories and plots? We can only say he had some role.

In Canada, Ellison made very little progress on the pilot script, about six pages. After about a week, he left, pleading that his mother was on her deathbed, without a completed script, either by himself, or by any other writer. Ellison's mother lived several more years, she may have actually been ill, but she wasn't dying.

Ellison made it very clear that the writers needed a lot of hands on help. But after returning to Los Angeles he seems to have done no further work with the Canadian writers or their scripts.

All of this amounts to a pretty lackadaisical approach, while deadlines and airdates are bearing down like a runaway express train.

But whether it's being stretched thin, procrastination, obstinacy or some degree of ignorance or indifference to the requirements of an impending production, there is a genuine likelihood that Ellison's conduct harmed the production.

Harlan Ellison eventually delivered a script, Phoenix Without Ashes. This is either late in August or September, literally on the eve of production. The window is literally bare days.

Remember Klenman's story of being called out of the blue by a desperate Davidson.

According to the Producer, William Davidson, as reported by Phillips and Garcia, *"He made no attempt whatsoever to understand our budget and production problems. He wrote scripts and story ideas that called for Spielberg-like production budgets."*

Ellison had always been at the front end of the process, he'd never actually worked in production, and we don't think he fully understood the requirements or the full role of a script editor, or the rigors and demands of a production process.

The script that he turned in, according to Norman Klenman, was unworkable, impossible to film with the budgets, sets and time frames available. We'll credit this, in part because we saw similar complaints on his Outer Limits and Star Trek scripts.

Even revised, the pilot episode, Voyage of Discovery, ended up at least 50% over budget, an overage which would have to be made back from the budgets of later episodes.

Ellison threw one of his infamous tantrums at this rewrite, of course.

That was the end of Harlan Ellison's involvement, he exercised his right to have his name taken off, and replaced with his 'FU' pseudonym – Cordwainer Bird and ended his involvement.

That was it for Harlan Ellison, except for the lawyers, and the settlement.

He submitted his original script to the Writers Guild, and won the award for best Screenplay.

In 1975 Ed Bryant would write his novelization of that script: Phoenix Without Ashes.

According to Norman Klenman, as late as the 1990s, the subject still rankled with Ellison.

As to the Starlost itself, Harlan Ellison's incessant delays and furious departure left the production completely in the lurch. Apart from the unshootable pilot, there were no other completed scripts. Norman Klenman had to step in as script editor and writer.

With short time frames, there was no time for rewrites, no time for rehearsals or to fix problems or lines. People were literally working with first drafts at times, running as they went.

Robin Ward, along with his co-stars complained bitterly about the quality of the scripts. Gay Rowan noted that sometimes they'd get pages the day of shooting. This created innumerable problems for the show, which arguably, were never fully resolved.

Many things went wrong in producing Starlost; Magicam for instance. It's true that the production crew was inexperienced, particularly for a show like this. The budgets and money were inadequate. There are all kinds of problems and legitimate criticisms of the series. There are various reasons why things went wrong or failed to go as planned. Things always go wrong.

But at least some of the show's problems have to come down to Harlan Ellison half-assing his way through.

To put this in perspective, We'll quote Jeff Hirschfield, one of the creators and principle writers for the LEXX television series, 1996-2001.

"None of the scripts end up the way you wrote them. There's always 28 million reasons why. Oh yeah, it was the call at eight in the morning going, 'this scene's not working' and this happened or that. There was a million reasons. No show is any different. We'd lose the actor, he was sick. Things just changed. There was a lot of stuff on the fly."

"It's the nature of production, you write a scene where the hero comes bounding out of the jungle, but by the time you have to produce it, he's just rubbing up against a potted fern. There's always compromise. I was happy to do my drafts. Lex (Gigeroff) did the hard stuff. I stayed out of it."

He procrastinated and delayed far longer than he had any justifiable reason. He failed or refused to understand the realities of the production process and mocked producers as they struggled with unfamiliar material. He delivered an unfilmable script at the last minute. And he utterly failed to shepherd other writers or the writing process even to completed scripts, much less through the production process.

Other people, particularly Norman Klenman, were left to clean up messes that he left behind because he simply couldn't be bothered.

We acknowledge Ellison's talent as a writer. He was a giant in the field of science fiction and talented as a screenwriter. He was idealistic, passionate and stubborn. He was also an enfante terrible, with an oversized ego, a bad temper, a penchant for drama, and lazy streak.

Although he was the creator of the show, his commitment to his role was limited – the Pitch, the Bible and somewhat the Pilot. He seemed barely involved and barely interested in most of the actual work of deals and development, he wasn't a producer or interested in production at any level, and shirked much of his role.

For all his protests of playing the victim, Harlan Ellison's version has discrepancies, the timelines don't work, some of his details are untrue or nakedly self-serving, his protests of naiveté ring false, and he had only his own limited perspective. His descriptions are colourful, but sometimes come across as self-serving, and he likely exaggerated.

Unfortunately, most of the other characters in the story never got to tell their side, or at least, not as publicly as Ellison did. At best, there are a few snippets from Klenman, Davidson and Richardson. But the little there is suggests another side to the story.

The story he tells is engaging and passionate, and his anger and outrage is genuine. But it's not without its flaws.

Ellison is a gifted storyteller, but perhaps an unreliable narrator.

SPECIAL EFFECTS AND THE FAILURE OF MAGICAM

The foundation that the series was supposed to stand on was Doug Trumbull and his new Magicam system. It failed.

In a very real sense, the whole series had been premised on Magicam and what it promised to do – Magicam shaped the budgets, the studio spaces, the sets, it offered the equivalent of film quality visuals for dimes.

It just didn't work out, that's all.

Douglas Trumbull's father had helped work on the special effects for Wizard of Oz. With that kind of background, it's inevitable that the son, born in Los Angeles, would follow in his father's footsteps. He started out doing short films for NASA and the Air Force in the early 1960s. His big break came working on Kubrick's 2001: A Space Odyssey, where he quickly rose through the ranks to become head of special effects.

After a falling out with Kubrick, he returned to the United States, where he directed a film, Silent Running in 1971. After that, his story is fairly typical, he kicked around Hollywood, looking for work, and trying to get various projects going.

One of these projects was a new special effects format he called Magicam. The idea of Magicam was to shoot with two cameras, a live action camera against a blue-screen, and a secondary tracking camera, locked into the same movements on a reduced scale for miniature sets. The system was designed to track and coordinate these two cameras.

"We were to employ on the show," Robin Ward recalls, *"a marvellous new process called 'Magicam' developed by Doug Trumbull the genius who had been the tech creator of '2001-A Space Odyssey" His Magicam invention would revolutionize the use of imposing the actor's images into elaborate miniature sets including its ability to cast appropriate shadows."*

Magicam would then composite the two coordinated camera images together, and voila, you'd have live action characters seamlessly integrated into miniature tabletop landscapes, the camera moving fluidly throughout, rather than fixed in place.

Basically, it was touted as a superior form of blue-screen or blue-screen compositing, which could seamlessly integrate actors into backgrounds. With Magicam you could literally get away with miniature sets, and simply post the actors in.

Result: You didn't need big sets or sound stages, you didn't need complex builds, matte paintings or any of that expensive stuff. You'd just build a miniature on a tabletop and insert the actors. The potential was huge. Big effects and visuals done dirt cheap, savings everywhere and spectacular production values.

You could do the equivalent of a sprawling cinematic outdoor location shoot inside a small studio for a fraction of the cost. You could create the illusion of elaborate gigantic sets, epic scale, and impossible vistas. You could give your television show big budget movie quality scenes with breathtaking images, panoramas, vast horizons, open spaces. You could create any kind of environment or location, all through shooting models and integrating them seamlessly with live actors, and it would look great.

You could save on full sized sets, opting for miniatures instead. You could save on studio space. You could do otherwise nigh impossible or hideously expensive special effects, easily and cheaply. Magicam offered spectacular potential.

Did we mention it was comparatively cheap? With Magicam, Starlost could be made for far less than normal, with fewer actual sets, smaller studios, and deliver feature film results.

The problem was that it didn't work. Or it didn't work reliably. It certainly didn't work as quickly as hoped, the first attempt at a magicam shot on Starlost required endless tinkering and consumed twenty hours.

And it definitely didn't work cheaply.

"It was supposed to be this amazing production, you know," Gay Rowan recalls. *"Doug Trumbull was the special effects guy, he was really well known through the industry and we were really excited about his vision and what it was going to be. He was a very humble guy, he was very excited about what he was doing, and excited to talk to us about what he was doing."*

"He was very disappointed that his vision was never realized. I think he was pretty upset that his vision was taken away from him. We called the producers the 'White Shoe Guys' - they'd come in and make decisions about what was going on. One of the things that Doug felt was that they were taking away his right to choice. They were taking away the choice part from Trumbull. I think that was unfortunate that happened."

It appears though, that the level of technology for motion control simply wasn't quite there. It would take a few more years until Star Wars, and more years until we had computer controlled camera motors to achieve that level of precise coordination.

It's not discussed, but another issue was the premise of miniatures for sets. That might work some of the time for simplified miniatures. But there are things like texture and feel. It can be difficult for miniatures, particularly complex ones, to reproduce the right texture. The more complex a landscape is, the harder it is to reproduce accurately, and the feel is subtly different.

Premised on Magicam, several sets, notably the Ark corridors and Bridge were originally miniatures. The corridor miniature was twelve and a half feet long and a foot and a half high, divided down the middle, so that technicians could shoot either side. It had its own functioning miniature door. If a long tracking shot for a corridor was needed, the opposite side could be used to extend the model set.

The Ark Bridge miniature was six feet long and a foot and a half tall, composed of three walls and a functioning miniature door. The windows were divided into five removable sections, to allow for shooting at different angles.

All of the miniatures were vacuum formed plastic panels, glued to clear acrylic with wooden bases, and panels, modules, and transparencies added for complexity and texture. The doors were removable, and made of acrylic sheet plastic, and opened with the aid of a hidden wire cable and 12 volt motor. Closing was accomplished with rubber bands or springs.

A good miniature can be a difficult proposition itself. We can see the effort put into the Bridge and corridors. But often, the vacuum formed plastic looked a lot like Lego, it has that sort of feel and texture. The Ark's support craft also had that Lego feel. You could sort of get away with that because it was Sci-Fi, but honestly, it was likely that the miniatures concept was inherently difficult.

Other locations, particularly 'natural' locations inside domes were likely to be challenging. Just look at the 'outdoor' scenes in the Voyage of Discovery or Goddess Calabra. I suspect that they hoped to get around that by stressing the alien-ness of science fiction locations. But that could be difficult. A chase scene in the pilot episode ends up looking uncanny. Tabletop models used through the series look like tabletop models.

Ultimately, Magicam was only used for a small handful of shots in the first episode. It became clear that the technology wasn't viable, and couldn't deliver on its promises.

Once that was off the table everything had to be rethought and revised literally from the first episode onwards. That's challenging to do on the fly under the best of circumstances.

Robin Ward recalls, *"Problem was, it became quickly obvious that setting up the required precision for this to work was going to be prohibitively expensive.*

"We used it once in the first episode to great effect. But it took twenty- two hours and a small fortune to set up the first shot, so the 'Suits' as we scathingly referred to the powers that were, decided to scrap the whole thing. Trumbull fled and we were stuck with a less than convincing set and special effects that were almost ludicrous." Ward recalled.

Budgets were already tight and the production was operating on shoestrings. Planning the show around the untried, untested Magicam system resulted in massive problems down the line, for budgets, sets, schedules and shooting.

Ultimately, with almost no time left to adapt or plan effectively, the production had to fall back on static chromakey blue-screen effects.

Meanwhile, the production was forced to shoot scenes in too cramped studios, build full sized sets that they hadn't budgeted or had adequate space for and use passive shots of plastic tabletop models to try and establish setting.

"Once the powers decided that the Doug Trumbull designed 'Magicam' was too expensive to use in the production, we were stuck with primitive special effects, barely more sophisticated than the old Flash Gordon movies of the forties." Robin Ward recalled.

It didn't go over well. It looked terrible at the time, and the cast, particularly Ward and Dullea hated it.

Miniatures continued to be used. In The Alien Oro, the protagonists in space suits pass through a shattered corridor, looking at a massive hole in the upper section. That's visibly a miniature composited in blue screen. Again, it has that Lego feel.

Beyond that though, the sets and studios had been commissioned based on Magicam working, and were too small and deeply inadequate. You could spend more on sets, but you were stuck with a small studio, too small for requirements. A show that wanted to be large and expansive often looked cramped and confined.

On the other hand, shots of the Ark itself, and its support vehicles, the Pisces and Medical shuttle were filmed more conventionally.

The Ark model itself was roughly twelve feet long and five feet wide and carried thirty-six biospheres, represented by domes a foot in diameter each. The frame and dome bases were wood, covered with vacuum formed plastic, model parts and bits of metal.

The Ark was supposed to be two hundred and fifty miles long and eighty miles wide in some accounts. The earliest original production concept was supposed to be a thousand miles long with hundreds of biospheres. But clearly, that wasn't a buildable model. Bova's concept in the April 10 bible placed the Ark as two hundred miles long, with fifty-mile domes clustered around it like grapes in various sizes, as opposed to the final appearance. As it is, the existing prop probably approached the limits of what was viable under the circumstances.

The support ships – the Pisces initially, was constructed of wood, covered with putty, and finished with vacuum formed plastic and model parts. After that they were repainted as required to serve as the Astro-Medic and Space Precinct ships.

Since there was no human interaction or integration, Magicam wasn't required. Instead, the models were simply hung or mounted stationary against blue-screens and the camera was moved around it to make it look as if the ships were moving through space. Star fields were inserted in post-production. For sufficient coverage, a number of camera passages were used at different angles and perspectives.

Because the camera was taking multiple passes from different angles, the Ark had to be lit so that it looked identical from every angle, which required careful intense lighting. To ensure adequate detailing, and to avoid shadows on the models or blue screen, heavy lights were used to illuminate the props.

This is where there seemed to be some incidents of bright lights melting the props. This is attributed to the inexperience of the lighting crew. The story is that they were used to lighting sports like Hockey Night in Canada, so they poured on the lights until the models started to melt.

But it's also true that the Ark was a very large model with a lot of complex surface area which had to be lit uniformly. That was going to call for a lot of separate lights and lighting, which was going to produce heat.

To make it worse, the model was covered with vacuum formed plastic with a low melting temperature. It had a huge number of secondary components with different heat resistances and conductivities, in particular, metal bits got hot easily and conducted heat quickly. Most of the components were glued on, with the glue itself at risk of melting.

So basically, you had a very large, incredibly complicated prop which needed to be lit simultaneously from a multitude of angles, for which you were going to be doing several passes. The result was a lot of light and a lot of heat on a very delicate structure for a long period of time.

Melting or burning was an inherent risk and difficult to avoid, particularly as time went on in the shoot. This was always going to be a challenge. Canadian crews were inexperienced, but not incompetent.

On Starlost, Trumbull, for his part, probably had some honest grievances with the medium of video as a format. The money, the time, the luxury to make Magicam work was simply not there. Enthusiasm does not substitute for results.

That early experience was the end of Trumbull's and Zeitman's association with the show. Once Magicam failed to prove out and was abandoned, they went back to Hollywood and left Starlost behind.

The Magicam system continued to be tinkered with and promoted as a special effects tool. A Magicam corporation was established in 1974 and at one point was going to be used as the effects foundation for the Star Trek: Phase Two series which never got off the ground.

Magicam may or may not have eventually solved its problems, but the technology never really caught on and was abandoned by 1980. It was superseded by more advanced computerized motion control systems, and ultimately by emerging CGI.

The Starlost production never fully recovered from the failure of Magicam. The entire production, the stories, the visual sense, the special effects, the sets, studios, budget and schedule had been premised around it.

When it failed, that failure rippled across every aspect of production and those effects carried across the entire span of the series.

The production crew, could only adapt, working ceaselessly to adjust, to accommodate, to abandon what was impossible, and to find new solutions, to work within what could be done and achieve what they could.

THE LOOK, SETS AND COSTUMES WITHOUT A DIME

"A thousand spray painted Javex bottles do not a set make,"

a comment attributed to Keir Dullea,

It's a fair comment, Starlost came in for legitimate criticism for its decidedly unimpressive sets and costumes. They were often clunky, empty and in some cases a little too recognizable.

The grim task of designing and building sets fell to Gordon White and Jack McAdam, the production designer and art director. Why grim? Well, late scripts meant short notice to build, and the failure of Magicam meant that they had inadequate studio space and inadequate budgets to build with. It's the classic story: No time, no space, no money.

Which explains why, in Implant People, Queen Serena's offices have been decorated with Sears catalogue office furnishings, complete with plastic tropical plants. In Circuit of Death, Devon and Richards lounge on leather Easy-chairs from Woolworths. The modish 70s office chair shows up on the Bridge, on the Pisces, at the Projector Sphere, the Federation, in Oro's ship, in random offices and laps – they may have only had two of these chairs for all I know, and just re-used them for everything.

Attempts at set pieces were occasionally dire. When Garth and Rachel pilot a repair shuttle in Farthing's Comet, you can tell the windows are empty, there's nothing there. The shuttle is a shell, with almost no interior. It's like that scene in Plan 9 From Outer Space where an airline cockpit amounts to two lawn chairs, a curtain and a lot of pretending.

The laboratory in the Beehive is out of a 1920s mad scientist lair, with a table full of glass tubes and beakers and funny coloured liquids in flasks. It's deeply superficial and cliché.

Some of it was wrongheaded. For instance, Oro's ship was an impressive build. It was a prop that was literally a set in itself. You could shoot in and out of it, put a camera up against one of the windows to look in, or walk completely around. It was even a functional prop with working lights and a door that could open and close. It just looked ugly as a boot and was nakedly made of plywood.

Frankly, it is what it is, with no time and money, with no warehouses of props or costumes to raid, you improvised and did the best you could with what you had. Sometimes that meant shopping from the Sears catalogue and getting out the spray paint, or just kind of sketching out the vibe of a set piece in plywood and hoping that audience will just focus on the actors and the action. I'll acknowledge it, but I won't bust them for it.

No time, no space, no money.

Having said that, faced with those challenges, McAdam, White and their crew did better than one might expect.

In some cases, such as the art gallery in Gallery of Fear, the warehouse in Mr. Smith of Manchester, or the docking bay in Pisces, sets were extended quite effectively with blue screen chromakey, giving it a sense of vastness and perspective. Despite cheapness, inexperience and primitive technology, there are shots that still look decent today and probably worked quite well on 1973 era cathode tube television sets with their lower resolution.

Space was at a premium, and a relatively small studio held up to six cramped sets. Sometimes it was visibly cramped. In only Man is Vile, Doctors Asgard and Tabor look like they're working in a broom closet. But in that same episode there are tracking shots of Devon and Garth wandering around large rooms and corridors with genuine depth, the sparse basement gives an impression of space.

Starlost sets were always modest, they tended to be plain and utilitarian, gray and bright pastel colours predominated, and there was a visual sameness. But perhaps it was better than you'd think initially, and better than it had a right to be.

One advantage that they had was the design philosophy. No matter where Devon and company were, it was all part of the Ark. If you look at any town or village, there's a lot of diversity – different buildings built by different persons for different purposes and over a period of time. It all has a cluttered accumulated look.

That wasn't the Ark, it was a single unified structure built all at once. It stood to reason that it's physical design, its structure and visual elements would be uniform. The relentless underlying consistency, in part forced by the budget, actually does well to convey the sense that no matter where they go and what they are doing, they're still inside the same uniform structure – the Ark.

That made sense, no matter where you went on the Ark, a sphere projector was always going to look the same. Doorways were going to look the same. The black half sphere module could show up all kinds of places.

Set pieces – chairs, beds, gurneys, consoles, tables and instrument panels could simply be repurposed, recycled, re-positioned, depending on the purpose of the set and how you wanted to shoot.

A cryogenic tube, became a medical gurney, or a sleeping platform. Desks, tables, chairs, platforms, control panels, it could all be moved around. Even small set pieces were re-used. The amber computer slides that Devon tears out to destroy Magnus in Gallery of Fear were also used in Pisces and Only Man is Vile as set dressing.

The distinctive Astrogation Module on the Bridge, for instance, shows up times on the show, on the Bridge of course through several episodes, but also in Farthing's Comet in the Astronomy section, and even in the Beehive.

Unlike Star Trek where most of the action takes place on the Bridge, Starlost didn't have a main set. Devon Garth and Rachel were exploring the Ark, constantly on the move. The closest they came to a permanent main set was the Bridge, which shows up in at least four episodes.

Mostly, rooms were allowed to look similar, and simply be dressed or utilized differently. Instead of continually designing new sets, the designers just kept repurposing.

They also tended to try and shoot around sets. If sets were cramped and bare bones, sometimes it was more the suggestion or an idea or vibe of a set than anything realistic. You tried not to dwell on it, and put the camera on the actors or whatever it was they were doing or saying. There aren't a lot of points in Starlost, if at all, where you could look at a set and say *"Yes, this definitely a hospital room / factory / warehouse / workplace etc."*

Compare it to its contemporary show, Space 1999. In that show, it looked like the technology worked, that controls actually did things, that props functioned and that cockpits and workstations felt like they were operational. Space 1999 was very good at feeling authentic. In contrast, Starlost often feels sparse and oddly bare and unadorned, instead of feeling authentic, it often feels... representational, as if their sets and props are signifying the thing so we know what something is, rather than actually being the thing.

It was always verging towards something like abstraction, the idea of these things, rather than the things themselves. I think that often gave the show a theatrical, where the stage is sparse and minimal, than a cinematic quality. I'm sure that they would have gone Technotopia if they could have, the style of the era, from Kubrick's 2001, to Space 1999, to later Alien and Star Wars was to represent a Sci-Fi setting in the grittiest, most textured, most real feeling fashion possible.

Starlost, I'm sure, would have done that. They just couldn't, they didn't have the budget. So they opted instead for spray painting a thousand Javex bottles and just moving along. It was definitely out of step with the American audience, and it was honestly forced by circumstances.

But it's not the first movie or television show to take this sparse abstract approach. In many stage plays where there's no time or storage space to shlep thousands of pounds and hundreds of items of set pieces between scenes, that's an approach forced by necessity which has become a style.

Still, there may be an element of some national aesthetic at work. If you look at American and English productions, it was all Technotopia, machines as gritty and realistic as they could get away with. But over in Europe in the 60s and 70s, the aesthetic is bright and colourful, full of glorious, even ridiculous excess, of comic books come to life. Starlost avoids both poles, consistently its visuals were muted and abstract, Spartan and sparse, with a formal minimalism. When it did vistas they were stark and empty. Maybe that was us, our sensibility, careful, formal, restrained and distant.

The ultimate setting was a gigantic spaceship, so it had to be technological and futurish. There were a lot of grays in the motifs. To suggest the feel of the interior of a vast craft, there were endless plastic panels, with doodads and projections – that 'thousand Javex bottle' look that Dullea accurately skewers. Instead of plain featureless surfaces, these uniform plates, identical, would cover walls.

Overall, this made for a very consistent visual style through many of the episodes and formed a kind of pallet which actually had a quiet charm to it. Partly it was poverty, and partly inbuilt limitations, but also partly an artistic choice. That bland pallet, unassuming and inoffensive, provided a visual foundation and allowed the production to build oddly thoughtful stories in many episodes. Through the series, the mechanical utilitarian corridors, the distinctive 70s futurism, with its sweeping curves, flat surfaces and bright pastel colours has grown on me.

As to wardrobe, Shirley Mann was in charge. The Starlost probably goes down in history as some of the most unflattering costumes ever worn by a pair of leads. Devon, Rachel and Garth spend most of the series wandering around in their Cypress Corners clothes, sticking out like a sore thumb everywhere they go. Robin Ward's Garth does all right, but Keir Dullea's Devon and Gay Rowan's Rachel outfits are dull coloured, baggy and shapeless, and don't seem to offer much at all. Would a vest have killed them? Accessories? Contrasts? Colour? A better fit? A little bit of style? I hope they were at least comfortable. But still, I think it dragged the show down a touch, it made it the show look like "Hippies in space!" They could have been more dashing and effective.

Occasionally their costumes did change up. In The Alien Oro, Farthing's Comet and Space Precinct, they expressly change their clothes for silver jumpsuits, which, with the addition of helmets are the space-suits. There's something about them, they're more flattering, but look more uncomfortable. They're wearing these suits without explanation in a fourth episode, Circuit of Death, which might indicate this episode was intended to follow on Oro. Finally, in two episodes, Gallery of Fear and Beehive, they wear gold Ark Bridge uniforms. The first time, it's a hallucination of Magnus, when the spell is broken, they're in their regular clothes. No explanation for why they wear them in Beehive, but it may have signified a change of mission.

Moving away from the main cast, the low points of costumes were probably the Goddess Calabra, way too much skin tight athletic wear, capped by obviously plastic Roman soldier helmets that looked like they'd been bought from a Halloween store. Special attention goes to the Elvis impersonator look of the soldiers in Manchester. Overall, the 1970s were a bad time for fashion and wardrobe in general, and that sometimes went double for Starlost.

Oddly, once you get away from the appalling Cypress Corners look, and the most blatant misfires, the costumes are often quite serviceable.

Ark uniforms seemed to be simple with bright pastel colours, colour coded by status. Or at least that was probably the thinking. The Bridge uniforms worn by various characters are gold with white highlights for instance. Security wears red, or wore it, judging by the tube dwellers in Lazarus. The Astro-Medics wear white jumpsuits. Shuttle pilots for the Astro-Medics and Space Precinct wear green.

That breaks down a bit towards the end, in Space Precinct, the Ark police are wearing recycled Astro-Medic whites, and the Federation representative is wearing an Ark uniform. It was the last episode, so probably they just didn't care.

As a general rule, costumes seemed strongly influenced by 70s sensibilities, and were fairly decent. Almost everything looked better than Cypress Corners.

Women's wardrobes tended to be more flattering. In several episodes, costumes emphasized sexuality, although cleavage was never a thing, several women wore short skirts and gauze layers, although cleavage was never a thing. Alexandra Bastedo in Return of Oro, Angel Tompkins in Gallery of Fear, Pattie Elsasser in Manchester and even Diane Dewey in Space Precinct all had attractive costumes that showed a fair bit of care and thought going into them.

Oddly, the cinematography never really dwelt on these costumes, they tended to be shot very casually without any special emphasis as simply regular clothes. I don't think there was ever a 'fashion model' shot in the series. Perhaps an element of Canadian prudishness was at work. On the whole, women were dressed better than the men, even women who weren't supplying cheesecake tended to be well dressed.

In contrast, men's wardrobes were often hit or miss. Ed Ames white jumpsuit in Manchester is distinctly unflattering, showing the beginnings of a pot belly, but that actually worked for the character. In Implant People Roloff and the resistance costumes are uninspired to the point of being lazy. The rags of the tube dwellers in Lazarus are simply silly. A lot is just average, lab coats, overalls, etc.

Some of this came down to choices, but as always time and money was an issue. Shortcuts were taken. There was no time to think everything through, to get everything right. There were good choices, bad choices and sometimes it was just working with circumstance.

PRODUCTION – RUNNING AHEAD OF THE TIDAL WAVE

Television production, like gravity, is a cruel mistress.

There was no shortage of compromises demanded by the series. The first problem, and one which dominates any production, is money.

Starlost was not a network production, rather, it's financing seems to have been a shaky house of cards, partly funded by Fox and NBC syndication, partly funded by CTV and its affiliates and partly funded by Canadian cultural subsidies.

Despite syndication, it remained very much a shoestring production. The budget averaged about $100,000 to $125,000 per episode, which was low for television, even then, and incredibly low given the production demands of a science fiction series.

Star Trek's first season in 1966, had averaged $190,000 per episode. Adjusted for inflation that would have been $265,000 per episode in 1973. But even that doesn't tell the full story. Star Trek had the benefit of a massive pre-established infrastructure – studio lots were already built, paid for and waiting. Star Trek episodes could take place in the old west, gangland Chicago, in Nazi Germany or Roman forums, because those sets were already built and available cheaply. There were warehouses of costumes of every kind that could be had for rental. Even location shooting in the desert was cheap because literally hundreds of films or television shows had already shot there, and all the challenges had been solved, the equipment was paid for and available to requisition. So that $190,000 (or $265,000 adjusted) went a lot further. There was at least another $100,000 in these hidden advantages.

For Starlost, literally everything, every prop, every model, every costume and set, had to be built from the ground up, and often for the first time. There were no short cuts or economies. There was no warehouse of costumes to rent, no pre-existing sets to take advantage of, there were no established facilities to requisition. Many of the things that Star Trek could have cheaply or at no real cost had to be commissioned and paid for at full price. In practical terms, Starlost's resources were probably less than a third of Star Trek's.

That tight budget was premised in part on Magicam and savings that never materialized. In turn that meant you had to save costs wherever you could. Ambitious stories had to be reconceived or abandoned, the scripts that were written had to take account of physical and financial limitations.

But it can also be seen in the visible poverty of the sets and production design. Partly this was the failure of Magicam, they hadn't expected to need as many sets, they hadn't booked studio space. Now they had to bite the bullet, crowding as many as six small set into a small studio, with little time or money to build.

As a result, the sets and models are frequently threadbare, in some episodes sets are dressed with 1970's office furniture straight out of a Sear's showroom.

There were other examples: The robot in Return of Oro was rumoured to be borrowed from a shampoo company's promotional campaign. The explorer ship in The Alien Oro has a lot of obvious plywood in its DNA. Oro's 'space suit' is partially sourced from Woolworth's department store. You can see cost cutting everywhere, particularly in the continual re-use of props and set pieces.

There were other problems. Video was at the time a cheap and largely inferior medium, not quite perfected. It was perhaps not up to the job it was being asked to do. This had been an early decision.

The production crew and supporting actors, mostly Canadian, were fairly inexperienced and unused to a production of this sort. This was a new thing, and an order of magnitude more ambitious than almost anyone involved was experienced with.

Added to all this were the rigours of shooting episodic television.

A movie is a thing in and of itself. Generally, a movie is a one off project, not bound to a demanding schedule, but rather, at Dullea and Trumbull's usual levels at least, there was a certain luxury of time.

One might take an extended period for pre-production, twenty or thirty days for principal photography for a man like Stanley Kubrick, weeks for second unit photography, more weeks or months in editing and post production. There was the luxury of specific set ups for scenes, and the luxury of taking time to light and shoot a scene.

Sometimes you had a release date that you had to make, but that was often months away, in many cases, you took the time you needed and if you missed the release date, you'd just reschedule to the next.

In contrast, television worked to a weekly delivery schedule, and the demands of television required that episodes basically be shot in a week to ten days. You would be shooting several pages of script a day, often brutal twelve or sixteen hour days, with simplified camera set ups and lighting, limited sets and locations and only a few takes allowed.

Editing, sound and everything else would be on a tight schedule. Television production was a factory assembly-line. An episode might air only a few days or a few weeks after it was shot, and it had to meet that deadline. There was no rescheduling, no extra time. Your episode had to be ready for airing on the designated day, and that was it.

The production schedule of Starlost was particularly brutal. Ellison dithered and procrastinated, a lot of time got eaten up between the bible and his visit to Canada to try to work with writers and develop story ideas. And more time got eaten up between his visit and turning in his pilot.

This cut deeply into pre-production. Generally, the more lead time you can get, the more time you have to build sets and costumes, retain crew, hire actors, fix scripts and generally plan the production and solve problems. The shorter the lead time, the harder it is to plan, to get things right, the easier it is to make mistakes, to have problems and encounter costs.

The pace of production was demanding. Before production could start, you needed a script. So writers had to be engaged, they had to make pitches, and get hired, scripts need to be commissioned, revised and edited.

Preferably you wanted a backlog of scripts, say two or three or a half dozen, so that you that you can plan more effectively across the season.

The scripts had to be dissected and used to prepare shooting schedules in order to use studio time effectively. Props, costumes even sets arising from those scripts had to be commissioned and built. Special effects had to be commissioned and designed.

A Director had to be retained, guest stars and supporting actors needed to be hired. The Director had to figure out how to shoot the script with the sets and actors and time allowed. There had to be read-throughs and rehearsals with the actors.

Except that there was only Harlan Ellison's Phoenix Without Ashes pilot, turned in late, which was deemed unshootable with the sets and resources that they had available, and which ended up being heavily rewritten.

Beyond that, there were no scripts at all, just a half dozen or so story ideas or outlines worked out between Ellison, Bova and the writers, with Ellison's comments on drafts recorded on audio tape and transcribed. This literally seems to have been on the eve of production, sometime in August.

Absent, last minute, late or heavily reworked scripts were a major blow to the production process. Late scripts, even if there were outlines to work from, made casting tricky, made commissioning props or sets difficult, and made scheduling impossible.

It was difficult to fix problems with logic or dialogue in last minute scripts. Both Robin Ward and Gay Rowan complained about the quality of some scripts, and Rowan noted pages arriving on the day of shooting. The actors would often try to amend or fix dialogue on the fly, sometimes successfully, sometimes not so much, depending on the director.

So without scripts, Starlost started off handicapped, literally running in front the tidal wave that was the production process. This may well have continued on through the series, as timelines were incredibly short and money started running low.

Principal photography was only four days. That was almost insane for a show of this sort. The Starlost tended to very talky episodes, so the scripts were probably long, forty-five to fifty pages or more.

"Eighteen or twenty hours in a shoot. Ten to fifteen pages of script in a day. It was insane. We'd have a lot of pages of script. They would change the script in the middle of the day. It was exciting and thrilling, in a way, but it was also very very difficult. We were shooting some nights until two or three in the morning, and we'd have to be back on set at eight am. Everyone was doing the best we could, but oh boy." Gay Rowan recalls

It's not clear if this was a factor of scripts being delayed or last minute, or if it was incredibly, ludicrously optimistic scheduling by the producers. Four days is an incredibly punishing pace that doesn't allow for a lot of camera set ups, or a lot of takes, or a lot of anything. There's simply the need to get shot after shot in the can, get this page of dialogue down, and move onto the next. And science fiction drama, by nature, is unusually technically demanding.

Both Robin Ward and Gay Rowan remember extremely long hours and sheer exhaustion, and a relentless grind that just wore on and on. Gay Rowan talks about regularly working until two or three in the morning. Their descriptions are reminiscent of a death march, a relentless marathon of exhaustion that wore their spirits down.

"As time went on, it lost its shine," Gay Rowan said. *"It was along the same feeling as when the show was cancelled. We felt like we were on a dying ship, the Titanic. It felt sort of like that. We lost what seemed to be such an amazing thing."*

Four days shooting was followed by three days for complex editing, laying in music and special effects. In particular, even without Magicam, on a show like this, the effects work, both in camera and post production, the second unit model shoots, and the optical effects would be seriously challenging.

Finally, everything was assembled and a two inch master videotape was delivered literally three days before airdate.

This amounted to an incredibly punishing schedule, with absolutely no wiggle room. Everything had to be completed in time for broadcast, with no cushion at all. The schedule was so tight that even a single day missed was potential disaster.

"The completion schedule was frightening," William Davidson, the show's producer, recalls in Phillips and Garcia's book 'Science Fiction Television. *"We knew we would be working twenty-four hours a day, seven days a week. The lights never went out in the Starlost Offices."*

Part of this brutal pace may have simply been that they didn't know what they were letting themselves in for – planning may have been fundamentally naïve and unrealistic. CTV had very little experience doing hour-long dramas, and none doing science fiction.

Part of it, as we've noted, was likely inflated expectations of what Magicam was supposed to accomplish, as well as the time and cost savings it promised, none of which materialized. They had to do things the hard way, without time, money or experience.

But regardless, you didn't go through this ordeal just once. You did it script after script, week after week, for months on end. The actors, the writers, the production crew were working this brutalizing pace from August 1973 into January, 1974. That's at least five months of punishing work, eighteen and twenty-four hour days, constantly, over and over.

In this harsh environment, this death march through fire, Dullea, Rowan and Ward had nothing but each other. They were the only constants in a continually shifting whirlwind of dreadful scripts, directors, guest stars, extras and set builds and dressing.

Robin Ward relates the experience:

"Up and running, we rehearsed Starlost at a Unitarian church in Toronto before moving out to the wilds of Scarborough where Agincourt productions could be found and where the show was taped."

"(We) gradually became jaded about the show and our work in it. But that all took time and in the beginning, even after we lost Trumbull, we still felt hopeful and enthusiastic.

"As for the cast, we became great friends, socializing with each other on our days off, and getting to know each other's families.

"For a big star Keir was modest and unpretentious and a wonderfully witty friend. Gay was a smart and perceptive woman with a great sense of humour and a wry take on life. I loved them both. I was grateful to be working and with various directors and a motley assortment of fellow Ark travellers. We were actually naive enough to think we might be onto something with the show.

"In the studios at CFTO where we shot the series we worked very long hours as I mentioned and spent a lot of time when we weren't on set, living in our tiny depressing dressing rooms, and in those sad little rooms the cycle of our lives played out. Love affairs began and ended, marriages were compromised and occasionally the smell of ganja would waft through the halls (we explained when asked that we were fond of Gitanes cigarettes).

"We invariably complained about the scripts, even at that stage, the writing was pretty bad, but little was done to improve them. I was happy to be there though, and still entertained the quaint notion that we were in something special, although with bad writing and laughable special effects, by episode two, small cracks were beginning to appear.

"Over the months we found a way of working long tedious hours together, mainly because of a shared sense of humour (When any of us would get a bit irritable one of us would say primly "Well there's no need to get testy")

"We three amigos continued to get along famously in spite of long days and a growing unease about the kind of show we were making. It was a joy to work with two people I loved. There was much hilarity on the set in spite of the obscenely long hours and discomfort. And in hindsight perhaps there was even some worth in the stories we created.

"The surreality of our work environment was in some ways a perfect metaphor for the surreality of drifting through space to an unknown destination and with no guarantee that we would ever get there."

The only other constant for the trio of actors were the remote producers and management staff, who were the authors of their torture, endlessly demanding, always inflexible.

Robin Ward called them the 'Suits,' Gay Rowan referred to them as the 'White Shoes Guys' – the people who sent them awful scripts, who refused to allow changes, who forced eighteen hour days, and mandated a hellish pace. There was a sense of 'us versus them' to the production, the trio of actors on one side, and the 'suits' on the other.

Dullea, Rowan and Ward were practically the three musketeers. They found much in common with their characters, literally alone together, bound by friendship and loyalty, the world changing every week, the challenges insurmountable, the landscape daunting and indifferent, and yet they pressed on.

POST-SCRIPT

There were at least a couple of other episodes somewhere in production when the hammer came down, and apparently two completed scripts.

The God that Died

People in the Dark

There is little more information about these scripts, beyond the titles and bare synopsis. Due to the nature and frantic pace of the production, there is no chance that any pre-production work or shooting was done. All that would exist of these lost episodes are the scripts themselves. If they're still out there, they're not in wide circulation.

Most of the sets and gear for the show were torn down or discarded, but a few props and items found their way into the hands of collectors.

The model Earthship Ark, a massive prop a dozen feet long and at least five feet wide ended up in the hands of a fan named Kevin Atkins, of Rochester New York, who worked at a Planetarium. He kept it in his garage and slowly restored it. Later Atkins moved to Denver, Colorado, taking the Ark with him. He was an active member of local science fiction communities and popular at conventions. He passed away on May 25, 2021, and is survived by his wife, Carole. I received information from Steve Behrends, the current owner of one of the domes, that sometime between ten and six years ago, the Ark was dismantled, or partially dismantled, and components were sold to collectors. Occasionally pieces will show up on eBay.

Atkins also obtained some of the miniature sets, notably the corridor and Bridge miniatures. These were passed to Allie C. Peed, who rebuilt them. Their ultimate fate is unknown.

The series was re-broadcast on television in 1978 and 1982.

Sometime in the 1980s, the series was reconfigured, ten episodes were selected, and packaged together, as a series of five 'movies' – two episodes per movie, to sell to Cable television. The same thing was done with the Planet of the Apes television series, so it was a relatively common thing.

The episodes were not otherwise altered or edited, simply run back to back, out of order, based on some notion of apparent linkage – as an example the Alien Oro and Return of Oro were packaged together. The movies were:

The Beginning (The Voyage of Discovery/The Goddess Calabra)

The Return (The Pisces/Farthing's Comet)

Deception (Mr. Smith of Manchester/Gallery of Fear)

The Alien Oro (The Alien Oro/The Return of Oro)

Invasion (Astro-Medics/Implant People)

Subsequently, the five movies were released on VHS to home video, and eventually released on DVD, dates unknown.

Apparently, the entire series was later released on VHS as a box set, date unknown.

In 2008 the entire series, plus the promo video was released on DVD.

In 2019, the entire series, including the promo video, became available as a dedicated Roku Channel.

PART FIVE - NERD STUFF

This section represents my speculations and efforts to hammer the Starlost Universe into some coherent shape. I'm just having fun.

I rely on various sources for background and content – Harlan Ellison's series bible, which is available online; his descriptions of his travails, also available online; the seven minute promo video, and especially, of course, the sixteen episodes of the series itself.

I draw upon and try to sort the information from different sources and attempt to fit it into a rational framework, interpolating my own speculations, extrapolations and guesses, and sometimes arguing openly with some of the source material, either rejecting suggestions or offering varying interpretations.

I hope that you will read it in the spirit of fun, and that it may somehow, in some way, possibly add to your enjoyment of the series or of this book.

THE ARK – HISTORY AND DESCRIPTION

The giant Earthship Ark, drifting through deep space over eight hundred years into the far future, its passengers descendants of the last survivors of the dead planet earth, locked in separate worlds heading for destruction...

The concept for the Ark, based on Harlan Ellison's original ten minute dictation, and as revealed in the Promo, was for a single colossal ship, fifty miles wide, with a hundred habitats or levels, all stacked on top of one another like a layer cake.

The protagonists would then proceed in a linear fashion, up one level after another, in an effort to reach the top and the ship's Bridge, which would be the final layer. In between, there would be no avoiding trouble. They'd have to go through each layer to get to the next.

Or perhaps not. Ellison seems to have repudiated the 'layer cake' and claimed that was an interpolation by Kline or Kline's artists and publicists. Ellison apparently commissioned his own production drawings for his bible and described it as resembling a cluster of grapes. These drawings are lost to us.

Regardless, the layer cake concept, wherever it came from, seems to have given way early, by March or early April, 1973, with the switch is modular domes. Possibly by Ellison.

Or his might well have been a decision driven by the March, 1973, Promo. Because the Ark wasn't built yet, Trumbull used footage from his previous film, Silent Running, featuring a spaceship composed of a series of domed habitats, and this may have driven a shift in design choice. Or perhaps, given Silent Running, that was where Trumbull would have gone anyway. Certainly, the domed habitats concept was probably more visually interesting than a giant layer cake.

When you think about it, a dome probably isn't the most efficient shape for a habitat. It seems like there's inevitably a lot of wasted space at the top end that you have to fill, maintain and heat.

But domed habitats have been a staple of science fiction since the 1930s. So there may have been no avoiding them. The ideas of Buckminster Fuller, regarding the structural strength and stability of geodesic domes may also have been influential during this period. In 1967 at the Montreal Expo in Canada, Fuller's ideas were expressed in a huge geodesic dome or globe titled Man and His World, which remains a world famous landmark to this day.

Ben Bova, brought on board as technical advisor conceived the Ark as a modular structure, with domes capable of detaching in order to seed habitable worlds along the way.

Bova wrote his own technical bible for the series. A hard science fiction writer, Bova's vision was of a massive vehicle moving at 30% of the speed of light, using 'reactionless drives, powered by magnetic funnels scooping up interstellar hydrogen and feeding it into a series of CTR (Controlled Thermonuclear Reactor) reactors which would supply power for a 'field drive' which converts power directly to acceleration and motion – so no rockets (magic).

The final build of the prop was likely by or under the supervision of Doug Trumbull. The prop itself was a monster, as much as 12 feet long, and as much as 6 feet wide.

&&&

Within the series, the Ark is a massive construction, 200 hundred miles (325 kilometers) long, over 50 miles (80 kilometers) wide, as per Bova's bible.

It is composed of a series of eight physically separate modules, connected to each other in a train, forming the central core. Around this shaft are 36 domed habitats, in two layers of branches, as many as three to a branch, most of them on a plane with each other. The components of the Ark, both the modules and habitats are connected by a network of struts, braces and tubes.

Travel through the tubes was accomplished by zero gravity 'bounces' – conceived initially by Ben Bova in the April 11 bible and shown only in the first episode. Thereafter it was avoided probably because it looked stupid, visually.

The Ark's, according to Ellison's bible, was built for half a million people. But in the series the population was initially given as three million.

Just for the record: As a general rule, where there's a discrepancy between the series bible and the actual series episodes, I'll go with the television version. At times, the bible is internally inconsistent.

Three million would have been the launch population, but the Ark has been through hard times and it's not clear what the population is during time frame of the series.

The construction of the Ark was an Odyssey in itself. Humanity was largely confined to the Solar System, with most of the population on Earth and a handful of research and industrial bases scattered here and there on other planets, satellites, asteroids and space stations. The solar system had mostly proven uninhabitable, or at least not habitable on a cost-effective basis.

Between 2080 and 2200 there had been a series of twenty interstellar expeditions, all of which had mysteriously failed. The program was discontinued. The technology was mothballed.

In 2261 the approaching 'Disaster of Galactic Proportions' was identified. We never get to know what this is, although there were speculations and conjectures. Ellison offers hints, but these are unverified. Regardless, Earth and the Solar System was doomed. The only hope was an interstellar ark, despite the failure or disappearance of every previous expedition.

Construction on the Ark initially began in 2273 and was completed in 2285, an incredibly short span of time for a project this colossal.

Presumably, administrative planning and project design was taking place between 2261 and 2272. The design and engineering specifications were by computers built by other computers built by computers. No human understood the entire design.

Given the scale and resources required to construct it, it must have consumed a large share of the natural resources and industrial production of humanity.

There would be no time to develop, test, refine and implement any new technologies. So the Ark was constructed based on and using existing 'off the shelf' technologies.

The domed habitats were likely based on at least one or more prior 'space dome' projects built to house whole sustainable ecosystems in place. Something equivalent to the 'Valley Forge' in Silent Running, or perhaps, actually that, depending on approach to continuity.

The propulsion, power, engineering and other life support systems were almost certainly taken from the accumulated information and technology developed for the Interstellar expeditions from 2080 to 2200. It's likely that the Expeditions were increasingly complex and ambitious as time went on, but the scale of the Ark dwarfed everything that had come before.

Accompanying or supplementary to the Ark were a variety of smaller secondary craft. Shuttles and short and medium range craft were found all over, these included a swarm of short range Medic ships, meant to accompany the Ark, security patrol ships, repair craft, shuttles etc.

These secondary craft had varying capacities. The Medic shuttles for instance were capable of travelling to distant targets but had no more than a few weeks' food and oxygen. On the other hand, the long range scout, Pisces, was built and equipped to journey for years.

According to the series bible, the underside of each dome contained a large number of shuttlecraft to transport to planetary surfaces, since the fifty-mile domes themselves were incapable of landing on a planet. But there are no signs of these craft in views of the undersides of the domes, so they were either lost, or more likely inside hangars.

Given its mass and manner of construction, the Ark was incapable of sharp maneuver. Scout-ships like the Pisces were constructed to look for hazards and evaluate stars in the travel cone of the Ark in order to help plot courses and identify habitable worlds. For this reason, the scout ships were equipped for long term travel, despite small crews. The Scout ships were also required to travel much faster than the Ark, likely as much as three times faster or more, otherwise effective scouting ahead, or return to the Ark would be impossible. The Ark was likely traveling at 30% light speed, while the Scout ships were travelling in excess of 95%.

It is not known whether there were other Scout-ships apart from the Pisces. The fact that it was named after a zodiac sign suggests other Zodiacs, and therefore as many as twelve. The fate of the other Scouts, if any existed, are not known.

The Ark is lopsided. There are twenty domes on one side, and sixteen on the other. No explanation is on offer. It is possible that this was the original design.

It's also possible that the Ark was launched prematurely, before all the planned domes were complete – suggesting that the catastrophe might have been imminent. There is some support for this notion in in Children of Methuselah: Tutoring on the immortal children began on Earth, but continued on the Ark after departure. There is also evidence of ongoing social experiments, as in Only Man is Vile, and other active research, which suggest that the Ark was an ongoing 'work in progress' when it was launched. Or to put it another way, they launched before it was quite finished.

Two other possibilities present themselves. One is that the Ark was designed to shed habitats as it went, and may actually have been doing so. In which case, the number of habitats is uneven and lopsided because some habitats and possibly even modules have been dropped away around one or more habitable solar systems.

The other, less happy possibility, is that when the Disaster of 2385 struck the Ark, some of the modules were destroyed and either broke off or were jettisoned. In the episode Pisces, Rachel refers to seeing a dome that was visibly shattered from the Bridge, and seeing a shattered dome when touring the Ark from space. While no visibly shattered domes are apparent on the model, this does suggest that domes could have been lost.

It is clear that the Ark was designed for maximum survivability. Hence the physically separated modules and domes, presumably self-sufficient, held together by a variety of tubes, struts and pylons. The design means that if any section or sections are destroyed, then the unaffected ones will survive.

The Ark was built to be a series of independent self-contained systems, hence a high degree of technological, functional and social segregation. Functional and social segregation was also likely indoctrinated in an attempt to ensure social stability.

Obviously, this was intentional. Leaving an alternative to the command structure in place, or allowing for alternatives or competitors to arise could have led to power struggles which would be disastrous on the Ark.

This seems to have worked better in the modules and crew than the domes themselves. Despite efforts, this did not prevent the dome wars. It's likely that segregation resulted in resource demand issues that eventually lead to the dome wars.

However, it appears that in using social engineering to make the Command structure irreplaceable, once that Command structure was destroyed, there was no way to replace it. This appears to have been a calculated risk.

More critically, although technological and functional segregation allowed the Ark to survive the disaster of 2385, the institutional functional and social segregation has made it impossible to re-establish a command structure since then, despite large parts of the Ark, like medic or security maintaining their function.

It is possible that inbuilt or automatic running indoctrination programs are preventing agencies or domes that would normally be in a position or inclined to take control from stepping up.

Or it's possible, given the size and complexity of the Ark that it really is beyond repair and doomed. However, the Ark's community of artificial intelligences, clearly do not believe this, even if they appear unable to take action themselves.

The best hope for the Ark might be an occupant from one of the primitive domes who is outside the indoctrination structure and social limitations.

Finally, so far as we know, the Ark is the last refuge of humanity. But there are other possibilities.

Given the behaviour of officers of the Pisces, they seemed to believe that the Earth or some remnant of humanity in the Solar System survived until at least 2385 and perhaps to the present. They may well have been delusional, but this at least holds out a hint that the great Cataclysm had not taken place by 2385, or that somehow if it had, that there were survivors.

Depending on when the Cataclysm took place, there may have been other Arks launched. This would have been a factor of how much time was left, incorporating the time needed to get away.

The Ark took twelve years to construct. Presumably a second or third or further arks could have been constructed on consecutive twelve to fifteen year intervals.

Or perhaps less immense craft could be constructed more quickly. An unknown number of smaller escape ships could have been built.

The key would have been not just building another Ark but getting it a safe distance away. If for instance, thirty or more light years was necessary to reach a safe distance, there would be no point in building another Ark ten years ahead of disaster. They'd have never made it to a safe distance.

But if the disaster was sixty years away, that would be time to build and launch at least two more arks before it arrived with some hope of them getting far enough away to survive.

On the other hand, if the disaster that struck the Ark was from the same source that struck Earth, as Ellison hints in his bible, then a hypothetical second or third Ark would have been much closer to the wave front. Even at a century's distance the Ark was badly damaged. A hypothetical second or third ark, much closer might not have survived.

Of course, a second or third Ark, or smaller but still massive craft, might well be moving faster than the Ark, say 50% to 75% light speed.

Of course, if there was a second or third Ark built, there'd be no way to ever know. We leave that possibility to the hopeful.

Finally, while all of Earth's Interstellar expeditions vanished, that doesn't mean that every single one of them was destroyed.

Some of them, particularly if sufficiently ambitious and adequately equipped and provisioned, might have been able to survive and establish colonies of their own. Again, we leave that possibility to the hopeful.

INTERSTELLAR EXPEDITIONS BEFORE THE ARK

Around 2080, the first manned interstellar voyages, the XR projects, go into space. In 2200 the last.

The Interstellar ships are tiny by the standards of Earthship Ark, but prior to the Ark are among humanity's crowning technological achievements.

Designed to travel at relativistic velocities for years and decades, perhaps even centuries, and to be self-sustaining maintaining life support and function through that time, it necessarily follows that the ships are comparatively immense. Tiny compared to the Ark, but definitely larger than terrestrial cruise ships or ocean liners. Crews number in the hundreds or thousands, with multiple redundancies of skills, mixed populations, and provision for multiple generations. The ships themselves are stocked and built with multiple redundancies and could sustain two or three times their initial populations.

In this universe without Faster Than Light Travel, even voyages to the nearest stars will take decades, even at near light speed. Travel time extended because they must accelerate to reach near light speed, and then decelerate when reaching their destination, and do it all over again for the voyage home. Hence, for the first few decades, no one really realizes that the ships are disappearing.

In the meantime, Interstellar voyages continue to be launched. Over time, it becomes increasingly clear that they are vanishing. None of them are reporting back. This is a mystery. For a time, this leads to the voyages increasing in size and complexity, with larger populations, more resources, and more elaborate preparations to compensate for unexpected hazards.

2200 After twenty expeditions are lost, the XR project is suspended. We assume that the abandonment of the XR program took place long before the discovery of the coming disaster. The question comes up, what happened to these expeditions, and was it connected to the disaster.

Harlan Ellison in his bible says that the cause of the interstellar expeditions' disappearances is the same as the catastrophe that afflicts the Ark and probably the Pisces. Ellison drops hints that the cause is a black hole or quantum singularity, potentially a gigantic galaxy sized one with an event horizon thousands of miles across.

There are some problems with this. First, there's no evidence of such a gigantic singularity within a thousand light years of Earth. If there had been, it would have been known from stars perturbed in their orbits. The gamma ray flash of matter disappearing over the event horizon would have been another giveaway, though Ellison may not have known that then.

Second, the idea that twenty two expeditions all were lost to close encounters to the same admittedly massive object seems ridiculous. Right now, our best guess is that the Ark was about 30 light years out from Earth when it had its cataclysm.

It's likely that the earliest expeditions were to nearby stars much less than 30 light years away. It's also likely that not all of the expeditions took off in the same direction, quite the opposite. Different stars were undoubtedly targeted all over the northern and southern hemisphere. Thus it seems unlikely that all twenty XR expeditions, plus the Ark, plus the Pisces would have stumbled onto the same black hole, not unless it's a very mobile black hole.

Even if it were some other stellar event, such as a supernova in the neighborhood, only the expeditions heading towards it would have been lost. A Supernova would produce a devastating wave front hundreds of light years in diameter. But that's only a danger if you were heading towards or at angles to it. Expeditions heading in the opposite direction from the Supernova would have gained several years more grace.

What does that leave us? Some less dramatic possibilities. First, mechanical breakdown or other failure might have led to the loss of the earlier expeditions. After all, if you blow a fusion reactor out towards Alpha Centauri, there's no place to get spares. Internal problems, like mutiny, social disruption, inadequate supplies, mechanical failure and even normal but unforeseen circumstances might have destroyed some of the expeditions.

Over time, all of these possibilities would have been examined and the risks ironed out. The obvious response to mechanical or social breakdown theories would be to increase the size of the expeditions, their social and psychological engineering, their levels of preparedness, their redundancy, etc. In short, to build better and better expeditions. And still they were being lost.

What else could have been happening? Space senility. Experiments on humans experiencing strong relativistic time dilation effects confirm the existence of a 'space senility' syndrome. The symptoms identified include narcolepsy, spells of disorientation and euphoria similar to intoxication, autism-like behaviour, neurodivergent affliction, difficulty integrating or responding appropriately to stimulus, delusions, mood swings, and memory impairment among other symptoms.

The syndrome appears progressive, triggered by relativistic changes, and incurable. Expeditions launched at high relativistic velocities, inside 98% light speed or better probably were afflicted by and fell victim to space senility. Some may have survived, lost and adrift,

This phenomena was well documented and well described even before the Ark was launched. It may have been the reason the Ark's speed is limited to 30% of light speed.

The remaining interstellar expeditions are launched at much lower relativistic velocities to avoid 'space senility' but these ships too are lost.

It's possible that even at lower velocities there's a risk of mild dementia. Indeed, it's possible that some of the stranger behaviour Devon and Company see on the Ark may be mild 'space senility' – or relativistic impairment.

Alternatively maybe there was something more out there? Was deep space more heavily occupied than we thought? Were all the expeditions lost to micro meteors or meteors?

Perhaps it was something a little more esoteric. Ellison speculated about a giant quantum singularity. Perhaps the real culprit were micro singularities, miniature black holes the size of a pinprick but of thousands of tons of mass.

That might not be so farfetched. If the ships were moving at appreciable fractions of the speed of light, and using magnetic scoops to collect interstellar hydrogen for reactors, they may have distorted time and space to act like a kind of funnel or magnet for these sorts of singularities. The magnetic collecting fields that swept interstellar hydrogen to power its engines might well funnel a micro-singularity right into its CTR (Controlled Thermonuclear Reactor) reactors.

Magnetic shields might have served to deflect most conventional meteors, but nothing could stop one of these objects. A ship that encountered a micro-singularity might not be destroyed, but it would almost certainly be crippled. Even if you survived the experience, you might well find yourself a derelict, drifting uncontrollably at near light speeds. In space, there's no such thing as slowing down or losing momentum, there's no atmosphere or road to steal your inherent energy, once you achieve a velocity, you'll keep it, until you do something to slow down, or hit something.

Ellison in his bible says that whatever it is that happened to the XR expeditions was connected to what happened to the Ark, same cause. He's cagey about what that is.

But if micro-singularities are a thing in this universe, then that may be what happened to the Ark. In the Pisces episode see that one of the CTR reactors, #11, on the Ark has been exploded. This is not necessarily inconsistent with the 'Wave Front' hypothesis, since a wave front may well generate or carry micro-singularities.

The Pisces itself may have almost met this fate, its CTR reactors weren't damaged, but its crew may have spotted the singularity and evaded it somehow, perhaps a dangerous course deflection, perhaps by shutting off the magnetic hydrogen collectors and CTR reactors temporarily. Whatever they did, it killed half the crew.

This raises the spectre of crippled XR expeditions. In some cases ghost ships flying endlessly with their crew dead. In other cases, the crews still alive and due to time dilation, barely aging over centuries, coursing along at near light speeds.

Or how about this, an XR ship in permanent flight, endlessly fleeing a swarm of micro-singularities drawn into its magnetic funnel, unable to ever stop or slow because that would allow the micro-singularities to catch up.

By the way, we reject the suggestion Ellison made of alien invasions. Aliens who were good enough to snuff twenty interstellar expeditions in all directions over a hundred and fifty years or so? The Ark would have never made it out of the solar system. Hell, we'd never have had a chance to build it.

Ellison suggests that the disaster that overtook Earth was related to the fate of the interstellar expeditions, so we're ruling out alien invasion as a red herring.

Oddly, though, as we see, the Ark does indeed encounter aliens, at least three times. This bears examination.

ALIENS IN THE STARLOST UNIVERSE

It's peculiar that for a series whose premise was that the whole thing was intended to be set on the many landscapes of a generation ship, aliens featured prominently in four of the episodes

It sort of undermines the whole premise, doesn't it?

To be fair, it's not handled recklessly. The aliens in Space Precinct and Astro-Medics only communicate, they don't visit the Ark, and the Ark inhabitants don't visit them. In the Oro episodes, the aliens have a single representative, Oro himself.

But still, it's a bit questionable. All three groups of aliens speak conventional English, which is very convenient. And two of the groups are unquestionably and thoroughly human.

Maybe this is simply television convenience. It doesn't make for good drama when your alien is a cuttlefish costume spouting gibberish. You're trying to tell a story, not extrapolate plausible first contact, so you make the aliens human, or human-ish, and with or without explanation, you make them human because that's a lot more relatable than a cuttlefish costume.

And honestly, the production crew is just trying to get episodes in the can, and it's not more complicated than that. Continuity is not that big a deal. As one of Doctor Who's showrunners once said, *"Canon is what we could remember that week."*

But having said that, there's an opportunity here to explore and develop the backstory and world of the Starlost universe. None of this is something that Harlan Ellison suggested, or likely that anyone thought of, but let's give it a shot.

We know that the Ark is moving relatively slowly, 30% of light speed. Assuming that the entire series takes place over a year to a year and a half. That means that the Ark has travelled no more than a third to a half a light year.

That's a vast distance, but out here in our part of the spiral arm, most stars or double/triple star systems are typically several light years from their nearest neighbors. Alpha Centauri is over four. Barnard's star is almost six, and Sirius is nearly nine light years. The Ark is at best only roughly a hundred and fifty light years away, which means it's still in the same general area of the galaxy. We can generally assume similar distances between stars for wherever the Ark is. Even in a star cluster there aren't likely to be a lot of stars only a third or a half light year apart. The Ark is likely proximate to only one star during this period, two at most.

Encountering three civilizations almost simultaneously, literally on top of one another in a fraction of a light year seems like a stretch. But not as much as you might think.

In his bible Ellison writes that the first manned Interstellar expedition took place in 2080, and that over the next century or so, by 2200, there had been twenty expeditions, all of which were lost without a trace.

That's a terrible record, by the way.

But if Earth is sending out twenty expeditions over a hundred and twenty years, we can make some guesses. These ships were likely designed to travel at relativistic velocities. If the Ark is moving at 30% light speed, these expeditions were probably travelling well over 90% or much higher.

Even at relativistic velocities, a round trip to the nearest stars would be a minimum of a decade, and likely several decades. So the ships and their crews would be designed for long term sustainability. You would expect huge ships, capable of maintaining long term self-sustaining life support, crews of hundreds or even thousands, multiple redundancies of skills, mixed populations, provisions for multiple generations. The later expeditions would become increasingly elaborate and complex –

after all, they keep not coming back, so you'd want to keep building bigger and better.

Now, according to Ellison, we don't know what happened to any of these expeditions. They just never came back.

But we do have a clue in the episode Pisces, where the crew of an Ark scout-ship returns after what is to them a ten year voyage, but is over four hundred years on the Ark, with the trio suffering varying degrees of 'space senility.'

Basically, travelling at high relativistic velocities does something to the human neural structure, creating an incurable degeneration when things move back to non-relativistic velocities.

This implies that perhaps this was a problem with the expeditions, and a lot of them travelled a lot farther than intended. They may have found that slowing down to brake and return to Earth was a bad idea, or that in slowing down, they lost the ability to return.

When Oro says he is from Exar, perhaps he's really referring to XR? Possibly, his civilization are the deep space descendants of one of Earth's interstellar expeditions.

How viable is this? Well, we can work backwards a couple of ways. We know that Starlost takes place in 2790. And we can calculate that the Ark is roughly 150 light years away from Earth.

If Oro really is the descendant of an XR expedition, then it took off somewhere between 2080 and 2200. Likely, it was one of the later expeditions, since they would have kept building them bigger to try and improve survival, and the bigger they were, the more likely they would be to found a sustainable colony. So assuming that the XR were hitting over 90% light speed and starting between 2080 and 2200, they'd have reached the area the Ark arrives at as early as 2230 and no later 2365. Even if we add a few decades for braking, it's likely not later than 2260 to 2395.

So Oro's XR expedition would have had four or five centuries to settle into their new home, forget about Earth, and build their own civilization. It's feasible.

Is there anything to support that, apart from the fact that Oro looks human, speaks English and gets jiggy with Idona?

Well, there is the fact that Oro seems able to utilize the Ark's technology for spare parts to repair his scout-ship, and to communicate with the Ark's systems. Think about that. Nowadays, American and German or Japanese cars parts aren't interchangeable. A completely independent alien technology shouldn't be compatible with the Ark at all. Unless Oro's technology originates from the same place the Ark did – so basic units of measurement, all kinds of basic uniform standards, must have been in place. The Ark is likely more advanced technology than Oro's ship or civilization – the XR were working from a much smaller population base since then. But there's likely an underlying compatibility.

There are other pieces of evidence. Oro's world is poor, too far out from the sun, with low temperatures and low oxygen content permitting human existence only at subhuman levels. That doesn't sound like a place humans would evolve. Yet Oro seems perfectly happy and well adapted for the Ark.

We know from the Pisces episode that space senility is a thing. By the time the XR Interstellar Expedition reached this point in space a large proportion of the crew would be experiencing or at risk of 'space senility' and mortality rates would be high.

At the limits of their ship's capacity, with the crew in a desperate situation, they decided to stop there. Over time, the colonists or their descendants physically adapt to the harsh environment, but their culture is tainted by the long isolation, harsh conditions and the space senility of their ancestors to create a nearly autistic society. They call their world Exar.

This may explain Oro, and his odd manners, and the apparently ruthless predatory culture he hails from. They're descendants of the damaged survivors of an XR expedition.

But what about the aliens of Space Precinct, and their Federation of nine worlds plus mining colonies? Who are they, and what's their relationship to Exar? Interestingly, in Space Precinct, Exar is never referenced, either by the Ark police or the Federation.

Are they even aware of Exar? They must be. At the very least, they'd pick up each other's radio transmissions, at the absolute most, they're likely less than a light year away from each other, possibly much closer.

Perhaps there's a rivalry – this may be one of the reasons why Exar was so eager to obtain the Ark. Because possibly, the other guys could get it. There might be some tension, even a cold war, between the two cultures.

On the other hand, the Federation, despite being a multitude of worlds, apparently lacks the technology or resources to reach the Ark. Exar is only able to send one lousy scout, but the Federation can't do it at all, instead, Ark inhabitants are supposed to travel to the Federation on their own.

That itself is a paradox, presumably a federation of a nine worlds would have the manpower and industrial resources to dramatically outmatch Exar. They should have been the ones sending probes. But they're not. This implies that the Federation is significantly smaller or less robust than Exar, despite consisting of several worlds.

Like Exar, there are other indications of limited technology or resources – both show very narrow windows where the Ark will be in range to visitors. Both Exar and the Federation are sub-liminal societies, no FTL for either of them. Both have 'launch windows' after which the Ark will be out of range.

Bizarrely, in Space Precinct, Rathe notes that another launch window will open in a year to the Federation. That makes absolutely no sense, unless we assume some very strange fast orbits, or that the Ark is expected to swing around the sun. Who knows?

But interestingly, the discussion with the Federation is to recruit the Ark's police chief, so that he can bring modern, Ark era methods and technology to law enforcement in the Federation. If they're headhunting individuals, that may imply a less than overwhelming population. If the Ark police's skills or technology is sufficiently unique or advanced that the Federation can't simply do it on their own, then that suggests they have severe limitations.

Again, human appearing, English speaking, and their technology is at least relatively congruent with that of the Ark. Their basic furnishings and wardrobe is also pretty similar. They're humans.

Here's an interesting thing, we don't actually see the Federation worlds, they're not really depicted. We do see some interiors in a

Federation complex. There's a reference to a mining world or mining colony.

Most tellingly, we see a wheeled space station. Our guess is that the worlds of the Federation are not actual full planets. It's more likely that they're a culture based on a loose cluster of Asteroids and Space-wheels. Possibly the cast-offs or components of a decommissioned XR, or some later build.

How do they relate to Oro's Exar? Two possibilities.

One is that they may be a second XR Interstellar Expedition sent after the first one. They found it and determined it was unwelcoming, and so they established their own long term outpost in the neighborhood, later and on less welcoming territory.

That's vaguely possible. It's not impossible or completely unlikely that some of the expeditions would have expressly been sent after previous expeditions, especially early on, before they realized that no one was coming back.

That may explain their relative friendliness and lack of apparent sociopathy, and being a younger society with less access to resources, their relative limitations. They're a different culture with a different history.

The other is that they're simply an offshoot of Exar during its 400 year history. Perhaps a crew faction decided not to go down to their cold, low-oxygen planet and took their chances building a society in space. Or perhaps they're the escapees, rebels or revolutionaries from some conflict on Exar. Or maybe simply a coalition of orbital stations/colonies that broke away and took themselves to the Oort cloud.

It's possible it's the other way around, Exar is a colony that broke from the Federation. There's plenty of time for shenanigans in four or five hundred years. I doubt it, Exar appears to take its name from the original XR expedition so it likely was the first settlement.

Either way, when the Ark comes through, it encounters two distinct, independent, human-alien civilizations, estranged from one another, possibly for centuries, culturally and politically distinctive, both ultimately originated from Earth, still speaking English, and still using the same basic technologies and standards.

One random thought regarding the history of Exar and the Federation. We estimate, loosely, that these civilizations are about 150 light years from Earth. We don't know for sure if the disaster that struck the Ark in 2385 is related to the Cataclysm that was going to destroy Earth.

If it is related however, we estimate that the disaster was moving no faster than the speed of light. Which means that it would have hit Earth in 2355, the Ark in 2385, and continued moving out at light speed. So it would have hit the vicinity of Exar and the Federation somewhere around 2505 give or take. So they may have experienced a disruptive catastrophe around then too. We don't know the history of either society.

Of course, if it is the same Catastrophe, then something that destroyed Earth in 2355 and shook up the Ark 30 light years out, may have been much more attenuated. Again, we don't know. Oro does mention that they recorded the event.

So what about the reptoid Rillians?

They're the wild cards here. The reptoids are definitely truly alien. They're a cold blooded intelligent, space faring species. What are they doing in the neighborhood? That seems like a really huge coincidence.

Except that it's not actually. You see, Exar and the Federation have been pumping out radio traffic for as much as four hundred years. They've been making themselves known. So if the Rillians are somewhere within a couple of hundred light years, they might receive signals and decide to come and say hello.

Like everyone else, the Rillians are sub-liminal. No FTL for them. So if we assume that they picked up on significant radio traffic, it would take time for that traffic to reach them. Then once it did, probably time for them to decipher it and decide to build a ship. T

Assuming that the Exar have been broadcasting for four hundred years, the Rillians are probably within a maximum of a hundred and fifty light years away – or somewhere within a bubble a maximum of three hundred light years in diameter. They're probably on the further side of that bubble from Earth.

Probably they are actually much closer. Depending on whether they initially had the capacity to build an interstellar vehicle initially or had to create that ability, whether they communicated back and forth, and how fast or slow their ship was. They might be as little as a dozen light years away.

So somewhere within a bubble twenty-five to three hundred light years. That's a lot of potential space.

The reason that the Rillians can communicate with the Ark – using English and compatible radio/electronic protocols - is that they may have spent decades or even a century listening to and deciphering Exar's and the Federation's radio traffic. Possibly, they've even exchanged messages.

This is why the Rillians are in the neighborhood. They're not cruising around randomly in space. They're on an expedition to Exar or the Federation, possibly both.

The Ark just happens to be passing by at the right time. The Rillians may not even be distinguishing the Ark from the Exar society, or distinguishing Exar from the Federation. It's all monkeys to them.

This may explain Oro. Perhaps Oro's original mission as a lone scout was to meet the Rillians in space and reconnoiter and investigate before they got too close? The Ark, when it appeared, silent and derelict, changed the mission parameters, and Oro was sent there instead. He crashed because he wasn't properly equipped or trained for the Ark mission?

Overall, the Rillians technology seems less sophisticated. Their computers are top notch. Their ship appears to be a huge drum with projections and panels, including large solar panels. The central drum looks like a massive centrifugal wheel, they may not have artificial gravity and simply mimic it with centrifugal force. They're also caught by surprise by the heat-plague which suggests that they're not experienced interstellar or even space travellers.

That ship would probably travel anywhere from say 5% to 90% light speed. The Rillian ship is not darting around the Ark, however. It has a rotating drum and what looks like solar panels, it's likely less sophisticated than the Ark, so it's likely on the lower end, arbitrarily, let's assume 20% to 25% light speed.

Why is it coincidentally happening to them now, when presumably they crossed light years safely? Easy answer, because now they're braking. They got up to some fraction of the speed of light, probably slowly and safely, and now they're having to brake and slow down, and that means that they have to shed a lot of inertial energy, and that leads them to heat problems they never expected.

Again, this suggests that the Rillians are deliberately in the neighborhood, likely to visit one or both human civilizations.

Why don't they visit the Ark? I suspect that they've already committed their deceleration to one or the other, possibly both. They don't have the power or technology for major last minute maneuvers.

STARLOST - A FUTURE HISTORY TIMELINE

Making sense of the history...

2050 Silent Running. Although not formally part of Starlost continuity, I've decided to throw it in as a starting point, because of use of the footage in the Starlost Promo, and because the design and structure of the movie's ship, Valley Forge, resembles an earlier prototype of Earthship Ark of Starlost.

No surprise since both were designed and built by Doug Trumbull, and one may have genuinely inspired the design of the other.

Thematically, the film also plays as a forerunner to Starlost, with an ark containing the remnants of Earth's biosphere lifted into space to preserve it, and a man committed to saving that biosphere.

(Look, just get over it. I'm a Nerd. This is my book. If I say Silent Running is in continuity with Starlost, then it is. If you don't like it, write your own book.)

Moon base established and becomes a semi-permanent research installation. Sparse colonies established on Mars and Venus. These remain small and relatively unimportant. Solar system explored, as per Ellison's bible.

2080 First Interstellar Expedition – XR 1.

2200 – Final Interstellar Expedition XR 20.

2260 Or thereabouts – possibly a century later. An early XR Interstellar Transport ship, possibly crippled and derelict, reaches a barely habitable world 150 light years out from Earth. The world is cold and bleak, with low oxygen, but the expedition survives and builds the Exar civilization of Oro.

2261 News of a coming disaster of 'galactic proportions' is discovered. The nature of the disaster is unknown, but it will make the solar system uninhabitable for centuries. The population of Earth as well as the Lunar and Martian colonies are doomed. Most of humanity experiences functional madness. Ellison's bible: *"We'd had Space travel for three hundred years."* I assume he's counting all the way back to the early manned space program, and I'm also assuming that he was referring to the discovery of the disaster. Honestly though, Ellison is very imprecise and the three hundred year benchmark is loose.

2273 The Earthship Ark project is commenced. The goal of the project is to create a gigantic interstellar transport to preserve a representative spectrum of terrestrial cultures and ecologies. Ellison's bible refers to the construction of the Ark, 'All of this happened three hundred years from today {1973}' which seems a much more precise reference than his other, broader discussions.

2285 Earthship Ark completed. Ship launched and *leaves solar system*. The Ark starts from a stationary position at zero light years from Earth, but over time accelerates up to 30% of the speed of light, or three light years per decade.

It's not clear how long it takes the Ark to reach its maximum of 30% of light speed. Arbitrarily, we'll estimate ten years, so that in the first decade, it travels 1.5 rather than 3 light years from earth, and base our estimates on that.

Note that Ellison's bible suggests the Ark is travelling just under light speed. Ben Bova's portion says 30% light speed. There's some inference that it may still have been accelerating, but given that a century has passed, we assume it's reached its intended 'cruising speed.' We prefer Bova over Ellison on this point.

Magnus, the greatest AI on the ship goes rogue. Instead of turning off or destroying it, the AI is simply isolated.

2300 Ark has passed beyond Alpha Centauri, the nearest star system to Earth. It is roughly *five light years beyond Earth. Apparently, the* magnitude of the coming disasters is so immense that not even nearby stars are safe. Or perhaps the nearby stars are not appealing.

Missing Modules? Ben Bova writes in his section of the bible that the domes can detach from the Ark and be parked in orbit. It's likely that the Ark was designed to spread humanity's eggs from one basket, and might offload domes and modules around several worlds.

When we see the Ark there are 36 domes, but the arrangement or pattern of them is odd, as if some of them are missing. This suggests that either some of the domes have already been placed in orbit around likely star systems, or that the Ark had been launched before all the domes and modules were complete.

If the Ark was launched as an unfinished work or a work in progress, this supports two further inferences. 1) The disaster was imminent and the Ark was being launched at literally the last safe moment. Note: the last safe launch date might have still left years or decades before the Cataclysm. Or 2) Some of the domes may have been more highly industrialized than originally planned, in order to facilitate completion of rough work on the Ark.

2340 Some of the dome populations expand to the limits of their dome to support them, even with trade and intercourse between the domes the ultimate fact is that resources are finite. *Seventeen light years out.*

2345 The redistribution movement starts among some domes. Reaching the limits of their allocated resources, some domes are seeking to stave off disaster by seeking reallocation of resources from other domes. Political conflict begins. *Eighteen and a half light years out.*

GREAT DISASTER STRIKES EARTH... sometime. Contact with Solar System is lost. We don't know when the disaster took place exactly, nor do we know for sure what it was or if it was connected with the disaster that overtook the Ark or the Pisces, or caused the loss of the XR expeditions. Ellison in his bible posts many possibilities, including solar flare, giant meteor, war or alien invasion. He hints that the culprit is a galaxy sized black hole, but it's never conclusively answered.

Ellison's bible offered some cryptic hints:

"Something dreadful and apocalyptic has happened to Earth... we will find out much later..."

"Whatever strange and final fate had befallen the twenty deep space ships that an adventurous Earth had sent out to find new world... now befell the Ark. ..."

And he suggests a *"smashing secret ending of the series... a startling conclusion to the series and ties it all up..." which seems to connect the fate of the Earth, the loss of the previous expeditions, and the disaster on the Ark."*

On the other hand, I tend to connect Earth's disaster with the Ark's disaster, partially supported by references within the series in the Pisces and Alien Oro. But this would exclude the Interstellar expeditions.

Of course, I've also speculated on an alternative hypothesis that connects the Ark's disaster to the Expeditions' loss.

But I can't connect all three, I'm obviously not as smart as Harlan Ellison.

2350 Possible date for the 'Disaster of Galactic Proportions' which wipes out Earth, assuming that this same disaster was responsible for the cataclysm on the Ark (see later notes) we don't know what the disaster was, the spectacular description and need to abandon the solar system entirely suggests a stellar event. Earth's or a neighboring sun going nova, or perhaps a black hole impinging on Earth's or a nearby system, which might also trigger a nova or even Supernova event.

Assuming it was identified as coming from a discernable direction, we can assume that the builders would have sent the Ark in an opposite direction, to gain as much time and distance as possible. If the event was truly stellar, then it would have occurred at Earth or reached earth at this time.

Because the shockwave or cataclysm would have been moving at light speed, or near light speed, it would take a little over thirty more years to hit the Ark, at around 2385.

2350 Dome Wars break out. Manchester quarantined. Other domes isolated. Eventually, domes are locked down and travel is minimal to nonexistent. Each dome is left to fend for itself on its own resources. Or perhaps only certain domes are isolated. Twenty light years out.

The crew become a separate self-sustaining community, occupying the modules of the central train, as well as the various tubes and gantries. Different departments and functions become increasingly isolated from each other.

No date is given for this, but the Dome Wars are referred to, directly or indirectly, in several episodes, notably Pisces and Manchester.

The most interesting reference comes from Pisces, where the Colonel Garoway makes a disparaging comment 'don't treat me like an old veteran of the Dome Wars, I can walk.' This implies two things: 1) The Dome Wars had taken place in the Garoway's lifetime or immediately prior. 2) That they had taken place so long ago that the veterans were retired and many were disabled, given that the reference was one of contempt, it's unlikely many veterans were still active in the command structure. Garoway's age is given as forty four years.

Based on this, we'd hazard a guess that the Dome Wars occurred thirty to forty years before Pisces left.

We also speculate that the Dome Wars were not a single conflict, but more likely a series of conflicts and may have taken place over a period of years.

2381 Scoutship Pisces leaves with a six person crew, on a ten year mission to scout habitable worlds. The Ark is over twenty-nine light years from Earth.

This suggests that there was some consideration of parking the Ark or at least detaching some of the domes in orbit around potential worlds.

Two further inferences may be drawn 1) that the Ark crew felt that they were safe at almost 30 light years from the disaster of galactic proportions, and 2) that they may have already offloaded domes.

Earthship Ark under command of Admiral Baines and Captain Rogers.

2382 Scoutship Pisces loses radio contact with Earthship Ark. Crew affected by space senility at some stage. *Approximately twenty-nine and a half years out.*

2385 Great disaster strikes the ship. Bridge is destroyed, although physically intact the electronics are fried and crew members killed. At least one Dome's outer shell is ruptured. Fusion Reactor 11 appears to be exploded. Radiation contamination is reported in the tubes. The range of impacts suggests a shipwide disaster. *Thirty and a half light years out.*

An apparently related development, several of the medical transports are lost, with only five surviving.

Scoutship Pisces loses half its crew, including Captain Armstrong. Technician Janus receives a field promotion to Captain. Possibly this is connected to the disaster striking the ship. If so, this suggests that a simultaneous space disaster hit the Ark, Medical Transports and Pisces all around roughly the same time.

Given that Pisces at least, must have been billions or even trillions of miles away, a disaster or event with that wide a wave front may well be the same disaster that struck Earth, finally catching up to the Ark at light or sub-light speeds.

Security measures lock down Domes permanently, but many or all have already been locked out already as a result of the Dome Wars, this possibly saves them. Manchester is unware of the Disaster due to quarantine.

The Disaster is acknowledged in many places, but as a result of the existing isolation of surviving departments and possibly as a result of widespread contamination, there is no effort mounted to regain control of the ship.

The Bridge / Navigation crew population is almost entirely wiped out, suggesting either fatal and rapid depressurization, hard radiation or sudden contamination of life support. Only small pockets remain, such as Astronomy, the Training Bridge and Security forces isolated in shielded compartments.

Ark drifts off course, heading towards a G type star similar to Sol.

Over the ensuing centuries, artificial intelligences maintain life support and ship integrity, but appear to be locked out of navigation. Navigation is reserved to the human Bridge crew, with a backup in reserve.

Damaged sections of living areas are repaired, cleansed and repressurized by auto-repair functions.

Survivors of the crew or explorers from some of the domes begin to repopulate the ship module areas. The population is thin and appears to be primitive.

2505 Assuming the disaster that strikes the Ark was the same that struck the Earth thirty light years back, then the wave front will hit the region occupied by Exar around this time. Possibly with major consequences. But also possibly highly attenuated.

Civilization on Exar has rebuilt to the point where the Exar are now able to send manned probes to explore their immediate vicinity. The probes are generally small single person ships utilizing an unknown drive system.

A rival culture, the Federation, emerges in the Exar system. Either from an earlier XR rescue mission, or the Exar themselves dividing into factions. The Federation organizes itself among relatively nine worlds/asteroids/space stations.

Sometime in this era, Rillium, a reptilian civilization becomes aware of a technological civilisation broadcasting from the vicinity of Exar and/or the Federation.

Around 2750 A prototype Rillium space ship is built and begins its journey to this neighboring civilization(s).

The Reptilians are clearly not experienced in space travel, or they wouldn't encounter the problems the eventually do. The ship features a rotating cylinder suggesting that they don't have artificial gravity control. It too is moving at a fraction of light speed.

Time estimate is relatively arbitrary. We assume that the Rillium may have been affected by the Disaster of Galactic proportions as well, roughly on the same scale as Exar.

Their space travel would be after recovering from that. A period of time for the Rillium to receive and pinpoint signals and commit to building a ship would be required.

The Rillium ship is likely less technologically advanced than the Ark, so almost certainly sub-luminal. Likely travelling somewhere between 5% and 50% of light speed, probably in the lower range – 20% to 25%.

Based on this we arbitrarily assume that Rillium may be *twenty light years or less distant* from the Ark, possibly in the same star cluster.

After 2785 Exar sends out a one man probe ship, manned by Oro, possibly to meet the Rillium in space and investigate.

This is an extrapolation, Oro's scout ship is already in deep space when it is assigned to investigate the Ark. What is it doing out there? The Federation and the Rillium are in the neighborhood, and of the two, the Rillium are approaching. So this seems to be Oro's most likely mission.

Around 2789 Exar detects an anomalous massive object approaching their area of space. They divert the scout probe manned by Oro, to investigate, even though it is not equipped for the mission.

2790 April 3. Oro of Exar crashes into the Ark. Meets up with Idona of Egrek. The Ark is about *one hundred and fifty-two light years* out from earth, ballpark.

Where is the Ark precisely? Obviously, neither the series nor the bible give any indication. But clearly, it is near one or more stars.

Space is mostly empty, estimating approximately one hundred and fifty two light years from Earth, then the most region is the Hyades Star Cluster, visible in the constellation Taurus of the zodiac, with over a hundred stars packed relatively close.

2790 Devon of Cypress Corners is banished and leaves his dome for the first time. He is joined by Rachel and Garth. The Ark, drifting at 30% light speed is roughly *one hundred and fifty-two light years* out.

Voyage of Discovery (1)

Lazarus From the Mist (2

The Goddess Calabra (3)

The Pisces (4).

Children of Methuselah (5)

Only Man is Vile (6)

Circuit of Death (7)

Gallery of Fear (8).

Mr. Smith of Manchester (9)

2791 The Alien Oro (10). Almost a year after the Oro's crash. The Ark is slowly moving out of range of Exar.

Astro-Medics (11)

Implant People (12)

Return of Oro. (13) Exar is now about half a parsec away. The Ark is skirting the outer fringes of Exar's Oort cloud, which contains cometary bodies. Devon becomes admiral.

Farthing's Comet (14) Achieves partial control of the ship, enough to get it out of cometary swarm.

Beehive (15)

Space Precinct (16) – Contact with the Federation, narrow window to reach it.

God that Died

People of the Dark

PART SIX – A FEW WORDS FROM THE AUTHOR

Thanks for Reading or How I Wrote this Book

When I started this project, I was dead certain that there was no market for it.

I couldn't imagine a single other human being than myself who might want to read this book.

A fifty year old failed television show, cancelled in sixteen episodes? A television show widely accorded, thanks to Harlan Ellison, as the worst Sci-Fi series ever?

And my take on it, a singular period in national history? Canadian national history?

Canada???

God frigging help me.

But here I am, I had to write the book that I wanted to read. And apparently, other people believed in it too, enough to contribute to it on Kickstarter.

If by any chance, you've read it all the way here... all I can say is: Thank you!

I wrote my first version of the Starlost essay that would form the core of this book, probably fifteen years ago, probably more. I didn't think that anyone would care much. But I like to write, I like to think, and I wanted to put my thoughts down on paper to organize and develop them.

And it sold! Sort of. A fellow named Edo Von Belkam was doing a book on Canadian Speculative fiction film and television for McFarland Press. I was flattered. He sent me the contract, I signed and sent it back, and then didn't hear from him for a year.

Eventually, I got around to asking him what was up. It turns out, the anthology was cancelled, and McFarlane had pulled the plug. Edo apologized for not notifying me, he'd sent the message to everyone else months ago.

He enclosed the cancellation letter from McFarland. Among the issues they'd cited, was the Starlost essay. My little essay had killed his book deal! It wasn't the only thing, but it was pretty front and center. Which was why he'd never notified me.

I suspect he felt bad for me that the Starlost piece was singled out. He didn't want me to feel bad. I don't think he even intended to provide the cancellation letter to me. He just got caught by surprise when I wrote to him.

I've always felt a little bad about that, I killed his book. As writers we all get rejections, it comes with the territory. You get face in the pavement. You're supposed to take it. But, killing someone's book on them, wow, that's harsh. I have a mental promise, someday, that if we ever meet up in person, I'll buy him dinner or something.

Anyway, I forgot about it for a while. The essay must have floated around, because Norman Klenman ended up reading it, and he was motivated to track me down. We had a brief, pleasant exchange. Sadly, I wasn't in a good place in my life. A different time, a different place, I'd have loved to conduct a much more thorough interview.

In hindsight, perhaps I should have picked up on that and started writing this book a decade or more ago, when more people were alive and accessible.

I eventually picked up all the episodes on DVD, and for my own entertainment, I started writing reviews and analysis of different episodes, delving into and deconstructing the Starlost universe.

Eventually, I decided to turn it into something, posting a revised version of my essay on my website, kicking ideas around, writing bits and pieces off and on, until I realized I kind of had the makings of a book.

Regrettably, so many people have passed, so many of their stories are lost. Even ten or fifteen years ago, there would have been so much to learn.

But there are still the episodes, there's an amazing amount written on it, in part because of its infamy.

I like to think I've found something new and unique to say about it. Anyway, if you're here, thank you for reading and accompanying me on this long journey. And if I'm talking to myself, that's fine.

I want to thank Norman Klenman who was kind enough to like my take and to talk to me, and Ben Bova and Ed Bryant, who I met and chatted briefly about the show a long time ago. I thank Harlan Ellison, invective and all, who probably kept the show alive albeit ignominious, Robert Kline, Doug Trumbull, Keir Dullea, William Davidson, Ed Richardson and everyone connected with the show, and everyone who wrote about it, good and bad.

No one sets out to make something terrible, but sometimes that happens.

But everyone sets out to say something that's important to them, and for a group of people, for a particular moment in time, for a nation, that's Starlost. Maybe it says something interesting.

Finally, I'm sure that there are errors, there always are. For now, I'm going to live with them. They're mine and I accept the blame.

Have a great day.

...

Oh, and if you liked this, how about you leave a good review? Tell your friends? Buy an extra copy as a gift?

...

Still here?

Well, let me do some acknowledgments, and then I can I tell you about some of my other books?

ACKNOWLEDGMENTS

Without venturing into the tasteless, I prefer the 'Author is Dead' approach.

I just want to evaluate and write about the work itself. That's what matters. I don't want to know what the writer thinks of their work. I believe that if if they've done their job, then everything is in the work. If they have to explain, it's like an unfunny comedian painstakingly explain why their failed joke is actually hilarious.

As such, the first and foremost reference source in writing this book were the sixteen episodes of Starlost itself, the performances, the dialogue, the stories and ideas. That's where I went. That's where I wanted to stay.

A good rule of life is, never meet your heroes. It's always disappointing.

But background and context does sneak in after a while. You learn about things, you talk to people. Things you picked up along the way become relevant to thinking about the show. You end up reading, discussing, interviewing.

So I should acknowledge, even in a cursory and incomplete way, the sources I drew on to write this book.

Harlan Ellison's essay on his travails, 'Somehow I don't think we're in Kansas, Toto.' Ed Bryant's novel, Phoenix Without Ashes. I have read and remember the essay vividly. I have the novel somewhere and must have read it, but have no particular recollection.

There are various YouTube videos on the show, including two half hour segments of a 1973 audio recording interview of Ellison discussing the show.

The Series Bible, written by Harlan Ellison, and supplemented by Ben Bova, is available online, and was used as a resource. You can look it up easily enough.

Other potential documents – the transcript of his original pitch, the so -called scab bible, or other records were not found or used. CTV and/or Glen Warren productions had substantial documents and records, including the unproduced scripts. But I doubted that these would have been retained for over fifty years, and did not seek them out.

No surprise, many of the people associated with the production, including Harlan Ellison, Doug Trumbull, William Davidson, Norman Klenman and likely Ed Richardson have all passed away.

In particular, I am saddened by the passing of Norman Klenman. I am grateful for the opportunity to correspond with Klenman years ago, it was inspirational and I should have done more.

A few persons connected to the show appear to still be around, notably Keir Dullea, Robin Ward and Gay Rowan. Both Gay Rowan and Robin Ward appear to be active to this day. They were kind enough to cooperate and participate in this project.

Keir Dullea is still active, and I contacted his agent with various inquiries. I respect that he opted for privacy.

Robert Kline still seems to be around, but despite a number of attempts, I was never able to contact him.

I wish them all well, and if any of them or their heirs feel mistreated by this book, I offer my apologies.

Regarding other sources, I have already mentioned Harlan Ellison's essay and audio interview. I have to acknowledge Mark Phillips and Frank Garcia's landmark work, Science Fiction Television, (1996) chronicling predominantly American television from 1959 to 1989. It had a comprehensive section on Starlost, with interviews with Klenman, Davidson and Richardson, and was an invaluable resource.

Other reference books include The Best of Science Fiction Television (1987) by John Javna; TV North (2000) by Peter Kenter & Martin Levin; This is Where We Came in (1977) by Martin Knelman; Survival (1972) by Margaret Atwood; The Outer Limits Companion (1986) by David J. Schow; A Choice for Canada, Independence or Colonial Status (1966), and Storm Signals (1975) both by Walter Gordon.

In addition, I should mention two magazines which formed critical resources for science fiction television – Starlog Magazine and Epi-Log Magazine, both of which I collected for years. There are doubtless other magazines and newspapers which escape me.

Regarding online resources, I want to especially mention the Internet Movie Database, which is an invaluable reference. Another key online resource was the Starlost Hub website which provided information on miniatures, models and effects. I recall looking at other Starlost themed web sites in years past with tangible information.

I do want to particularly cite Peter Kenter and his interview with Ben Bova, Bruce Callow and his interview with Gay Rowan, Boris Bohuslawsky and our conversations, Steve Behrends for an update, the Starlost Facebook page, as well as the 70s Television Facebook page.

There are still a number of web pages which contain reviews and commentary. The show is chronicled, sometimes inaccurately, often to no great detail, on various web sites.

I've been interested in the Starlost for years on a casual basis, and like a pack rat, noted mentions and references from different sources over the years, including personal anecdotes, which sadly, I stuck in my memory, but never formally noted. I've made use of this, although it's likely some has led me astray or is speculative – for instance the part about Tau Ceti being a borrowed from a shampoo company.

I did read Ben Bova's 'Starcrossed' novel. Bova also wrote of his experiences in Analog Magazine, but I've never read those editorials/essays.

I caution that these days, most of my library of books and magazines collected over several decades is mainly in boxes and mostly inaccessible. While I've referred from memory to many of these sources, I've not had the opportunity to dig out most of them to review. If my memory of these works has played me false and there are errors, mea culpa.

One reference source I offer with some humility is LEXX Unauthorized, by yours truly, a four book series chronicling the Canadian series LEXX (1996-2001) from Salter Street Films in Halifax, written with the cooperation of many of the persons involved with the show, and which has provided me with insights into the television production process.

Beyond that, I cite such films as Going Down the Road, Paperback Hero, Welcome to Blood City, The Neptune Factor, Shape of Things to Come and Starship Invasions for insight into Canadian film and genre production in the 1970s, and a lifetime of growing up working at a Drive-In, and consequently watching literally thousands of genre movies and cult television from all over the world.

Finally, I wish to acknowledge people whose support and insight have helped me along this journey. This includes Anna Maria Valdron, ex-wife, best friend and muse, Dean Naday, best friend and inspiration, Patrick Lowe, film maker, documentarian and friend, my brother John, my sister Kyla, my late father Andrew who bought a Drive-In and gave me a love of movies, my late mother Mary, my brother John, his son Jared, my sister Kyla, her husband Jody, her children Ryan and Shannon, Mireille Theriault, Angus Kohm and Stefanie Wiens, Ian Ross, David Keck, Steve Lundin, R. Graeme Cameron, Carolyn Gray and Graham Ashmore, as well as Robin Ward, Gay Rowan, Bruce Callow, Peter Kenter all my Kickstarter Contributors, and many many others who inspired me in some way.

Thank you, you have each in your way shaped, inspired and encouraged me on the erratic lifetime journey which lead to this book.

Each one of you, and more, are loved.

Remember that.

THE AUTHOR AND HIS BOOKS

D.G. Valdron grew up working days at the family garage and nights at a Drive-In theatre.

D.G. Valdron born and raised on the shores of Bay Chaleur in northern New Brunswick. Growing up he worked as a projectionist at a Drive-in-Theatre, as an automobile mechanic, a hotel clerk, a carpenter, backhoe operator, ditch digger and an assortment of jobs and vices, all too typical of writers, along the way accumulating University degrees in History and Anthropology, Education and Law. He currently lives in Manitoba, and makes his living in the field of aboriginal law.

From an early period, he developed a fascination with both Canadian culture and more esoteric subjects like B-movies, cult television, speculative fiction and pulp magazines. Eventually, this lead to a fascination with how culture was created, and the details and challenges of the creative process and the technical requirements of physical production, newspapers and magazines, movies and television and how they shaped creative decisions.

Valdron writes almost exclusively in the field of speculative fiction and nonfiction. He has published novels, short stories and essays on horror, fantasy, science fiction and alternate history as well as reviews and essays on genre works and their production.

Descriptions of his most notable books can be found on the following pages.

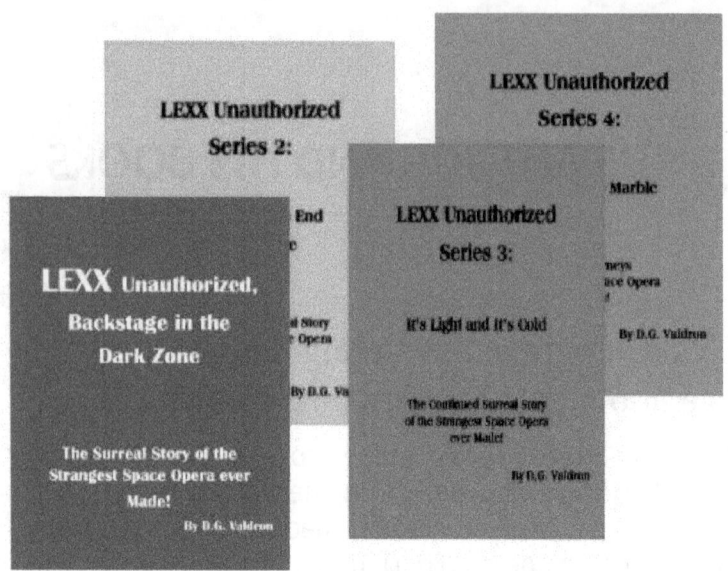

LEXX UNAUTHORIZED

LEXX Unauthorized about the making of a show about a giant space bug that blows up planets, the cowardly security guard who is its captain, and the undead assassin, runaway love slave, and robot head who form its crew.

Originally billed as *'Star Trek's Evil Twin,'* the cultiest of cult Sci-Fi, LEXX's forte was black humor, startling visuals, big ideas, and a sensibility that had more to do with surrealists like Jodorowsky or Bunuel than mainstream science fiction. And, as unconventional as it was onscreen, the story of how it came to be is even more bizarre.

The Pirate Histories!

What's a Pirate's History, you ask? It's the things they don't want you to know about, or that they don't care about, things that are great and marvellous and intriguing... but unapproved. It's a history of secret and forgotten corners of the Whoniverse. The first woman Doctor, the first black Doctor, animations, audios, the stage plays and fan films.

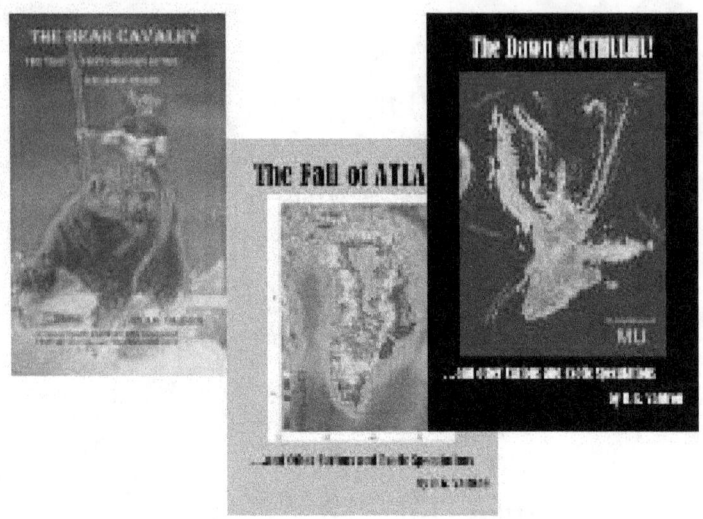

ALTERNATE REALITIES
A Trilogy or Strange New Worlds

The Dawn of Cthulhu - The Secret History of H.P. Lovecraft's Cthulhu Cult; Lost Continents Found – real and legendary; The Monsters of Sesame Street, is a light hearted examination of Muppets as if they were actual animals.

The Fall of Atlantis – Retroverse, An Accidental Cinematic Universe of 50's Sci-Fi movies, Greenland Without the Ice, Rome Crosses the Atlantic, and the Rise and Fall of Atlantis, an ecological catastrophe.

The Bear Cavalry, the True (Not!) History of the Icelandic Bears, an off the wall, short novel about the Viking domestication of bears, their evolution into a medieval cavalry Bonus novelette, The Sharebear Apocalypse.

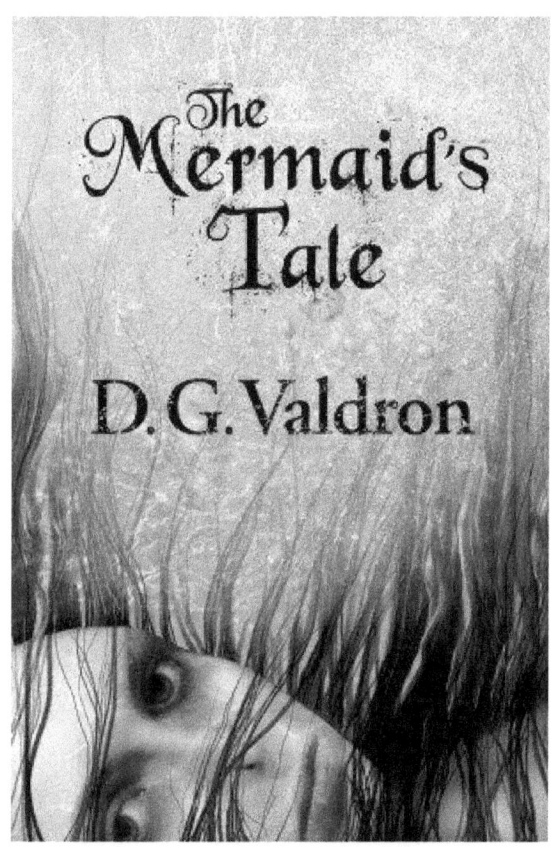

THE MERMAID'S TALE
A Dark Fantasy of Murder and Redemption

There's a City where all the races come together uneasily, descending into civil war.

There's a Mermaid, murdered cruelly her people distraught and crying out for justice.

There's an Orc, the lowest and the worst, her mission: Solve the murder, before it all comes crashing down.

She finds something else... the world's first serial killer.

Drunk Slutty Elf and Other Stories
Drunk Slutty Elf and Zombies
Hilarious Sci-Fi and Fantasy

Two volume of savage, satirical, subversive wicked, funny, frantic science fiction and fantasy. Demented ghost hunters, frustrated aliens, horny giants, drunken elves, sneaky ghosts, wayward barbarians and many more.

AXIS OF ANDES, VOLUME I
NEW WORLD WAR, AXIS OF ANDES II
A History of WWII in South America

Berlin, 1937, Adolph Hitler and his cabinet meet with a strange delegation from Ecuador. The delegates from the small South American nation beg for help, fearing an impending invasion from their rival, Peru. What happens at that meeting sets in motion a chain of events that lights the entire continent on fire. By the time it's done, millions are dead, nations are in ruins, and the map of Latin America will be changed beyond recognition.

HEARTS IN DARKNESS
A Trilogy of Horror Collections

Giant Monsters Sing Sad Songs – The connection between the author of the Necronomicon and a boy in Providence; a girl who meets the last Sasquatch, a poet who shares abandoned Tokyo with a Kaiju, and more...

What Devours Also Hungers – The unkillable killers in masks are recruited into the army, vampires and their hunters, clever monsters, ghosts and more...

There Are No Doors in Dark Places – A childlike cancer that talks to its owner; A single mother drawn into dark magic; A man who turns into a different monster each night; a vampire that twists lives; a pregnant woman finding her body being stolen from her; and many more